This is a work of fiction. Although its form is that of an autobiography, it is not one. People and events have been reconstructed (like most female celebrity bodies) to suit the purpose of the book, which is to pinpoint how and why "the culture" went so wrong. With the exception of public figures, any resemblance to persons living or dead is coincidental. The opinions expressed are those of the character's and should not be confused with the author's…so try not to take it so fucking seriously. Or, as Tate would say, "Don't be such a goddamn snowflake."

What you're about to read is the shocking tale of how Lindsay Lohan stole my life. It's not pretty, but neither are those multiple plastic surgeries of hers (I'm counting the one required for her ring finger reattachment after that boating accident in Turkey, too).

X's & O's,

Tate Carmichael

Table of Malcontents

Preface

I'd be lying if I said I didn't notice the signs. Long ago, in a now fabled period called the 90s. But my undeniable belief that Lindsay Lohan stole my life really reached a crescendo by the time she was starring in the West End production of *Speed-the-Plow*. Come to think of it, Madonna probably thought Lohan was stealing her life, too. After all, *she's* the one who starred in David Mamet's original version in 1988. But Madonna's life is always being stolen. I guess that's neither here nor there... But what is here *and* there is the fact that, if anyone was going to play the role of a more than slightly manipulative and coquettish secretary who uses people for clout—but remains charming while doing it—it should have been me.

So as usual, "Lindz" was totally wrong for the part. What did *she* know of having to get by on looks and the shrewd wielding of them? I mean, not to be rude, but Paris Hilton's ex, Brandon Davis (you don't really need to know who he is), *did* accurately point out that even if she was, shall we say, at least conventionally attractive, she still has a firecrotch that shits freckles. Her "aesthetic" pretty much only worked for her at five when she was doing Calvin Klein ads, which, by the way, I begged my mother to audition me for, but she was too busy securing her daily Klonopin prescription to pay attention to *my* needs and ambitions. My dad, of course, had his own distractions as well—chiefly banging every secretary and intern at the law office he was a partner in. Even so, his antics still paled in comparison to Michael Lohan's. To be honest, I actually wish my dad *was* as shady. Because if you're going to be a piece of shit who gets your daughter a clown for her thirteenth birthday—*thirteenth*, not even third, the only time when it's actually somewhat appropriate or socially acceptable—you might as well be shady, to boot.

But no, my dad, Gary, wasn't a Wall Street trader at twenty, just a Harvard student majoring in business law. How fucking wholesome. And then there was the fact that Dina Lohan had, let's call it, far more of an "edge" than my own mother, Gwen. At least Dina had the gumption to lie about being a Rockette to the media when I think we all know what she really meant when she said she used to be a "dancer." That my parents' names were Gary and Gwen just added to the lameness, the phony baloney storybook nature of my existence without the correlating socialite glamor and acting career to match. Ugh, whatever. Back to how I went to see *Speed-the-Plow* in London. I attended the dreadful event because I had a bone to pick with Lindsay. It just so happened to be one of my many instances of bad luck (*Just My Luck*, if you will) that a totally unhinged stalker would make an attempt on her life the very same night I tried to approach her after the show to have a civilized, adult conversation about how she needed to stop. To just stop with the life-stealing shenanigans. And wouldn't you know it, the guy who pulls a gun out on her manages to flee the scene and slip it into *my* pocket just as he exits stage left. Next thing I know, Lindsay sees *me* with the gun, goes wide-eyed and, suddenly, the tabloid headlines are filled with shit like: "One Mean Girl!: Lindsay Lohan Attacked by Deranged Fan."

First of all, I'm not a fucking *fan*. I'm not some sort of nerd with no life, for Stefano Gabbana's sake. I just needed to tell her that if the stars had aligned a little differently, I could have executed her life a lot better. And, if anything, she should be *thanking* me for making *Chapter 27* all shiny and new again because of my apparent similarities to Mark David Chapman. Need I point out that I'm neither fat nor would I ever spend all my free time reading some book about a teen boy who can't get laid?

So now, here I am, serving out a partial sentence for a crime I didn't commit, feeling much the same way Lindsay must have felt in 2010 when she somehow still had to deal with two drunk driving arrests from 2007 and ended up being slapped with ninety days in jail for failing to attend court-ordered "alcohol education" classes. I'm very precise with dates now that I'm sober, I guess. Filing little pieces of information away every time they let me use the internet. I guess, without access to it on a constant basis, I have a little time to tell you, waiting here in my, yes, very bright, very hideous orange jumpsuit (orange never was, is or will be the new black), how it came to be this way. How my own life was slowly and insidiously ripped right out from beneath me while I thought I was safe in the protective bubble of being blonde, rich and having a face that could be Photoshopped onto just about any other thin girl's for the sake of both solidarity and anonymity (in the Cayman Islands).

So sure, I'll fucking rehash the whole damned ordeal to you. Why the fuck not? I've got nothing else to do without prescription drugs or alcohol to pass the hours. Granted, there is, for no explicable reason, a torn-out magazine picture of Danny DeVito someone left behind in my cell that I masturbate to now and again. That certainly takes some time. Mainly because even DeVito has been "touched" by Lindsay via that unflattering *Mean Girls* reference from Damian. Anyway, here it is. How it all went down. Without the spin, without the social media "rebrandings." Just the *un*varnished, *un*nipped-and-tucked truth.

Chapter 1: Not All Socialites Are Created Equal

*L*et's get one thing straight: not all socialites are created equal. The fact that Lindsay was born in the Bronx should tell you first and foremost that she's of a lesser caliber. Where Paris Hilton was actually born in New York City and even Kim Kardashian was at least born in Los Angeles, Lohan's place of birth says it all. The Bronx. The fucking Bronx. There are no socialites made there. Only "coming up" stories like J. Lo's. That's what people want to hear about nowadays, too. No one cares about the plight of the rich white girl, wants to see her pages unfold in the smeared ink of tabloids that don't even get used for fish and chips like they would in London. And there *is* a plight, believe you me. Not the kind that Kendall Jenner has, which is that she really needs to hire a savvier PR team, the high-caliber sort that knows better than to greenlight a Pepsi commercial involving police and the Black Lives Matter movement. Plus, is Kendall Jenner even technically white? The jury's still out (that's sort of a pun, isn't it? You know, because of Robert Kardashian. Even if he's not her dad).

Lindsay made a good case for that plight for a while: irrepressible self-destruction at its finest—she even finely tuned Winona Ryder's shoplifting game when she took a $2,500 gold necklace from a boutique in Venice Beach back in January of 2011 and then basically claimed, "Oops…it wasn't me." That's been my line for years, trust me. And it was working so well for me even up until 2010, long after Winona blew the lid off every white girl's favorite crime. But Lindsay was the one who *really* ruined it for all of us more discreet socialite shoplifters. Janis Ian said Regina George was a life-ruiner—not true, it was actually Lindsay Lohan all along. But I digress. I'm going to do that a lot in this fucked up little narrative called pre-2016. Yeah, that's right, I still think times before 2016 were just as fucked up, if you can wrap your head around that. Then again, you've probably wrapped your lips around worse knowing the kind of audience I tend to attract. In any case, as I was saying, Lindsay was never supposed to be one of us.

In the beginning, which I count as 1995, when the photo evidence of all true socialites was born, there were only three families, the socialite mafia heavy hitters of Beverly Hills. They were: the Richies (mainly only because Nicole snagged Michael Jackson as her godfather, though as we now know, it wasn't much of a "snag" with that whole confirmation of him being a pedo thing), the Hiltons and the Carmichaels. The Kardashians weren't happening yet, though Kim would like to think so when she inserted herself into our hangout sessions. Anyway, with the 1995 thing as the beginning of all socialite time, I'm referring, of course, to that oh so embarrassing photo of Kim K and Nicole Richie wearing braces at thirteen years old that she felt inclined to post in 2014, "so casually." Yeah right. Kim is always trying so desperately to prove that she's been a long-time staple of "the scene." She'd blow cum bubbles from all the dicks she's sucked for thirty minutes straight to make a point of that. Then again, a part of me can't deny that she's living proof of just how much work it takes to get "free money" from men. Any who, she tried to include a throwback photo of me from 1995 as well, but I wouldn't have it—would never lower myself to that sort of self-mockery.

Tate Carmichael has more dignity than that. Maybe that's why I never achieved my true fame potential—you can't bother with things like dignity when you're trying to become a star. Yet all along the way, no matter how much money my parents made, with no other child to spend it on but me, I never got too big for my own perfectly proportionate head. Lindsay was also an outsider to the socialite world because of her lack of proximity to L.A. The stodgy East Coast types can say that it's the lesser coast all they want, but the world was our playground in that spread-out, sprawling mass that seemed like forever on Melrose and Rodeo. Whatever New York City socialites did, we could do it even bigger, because we had the space. And God knows a socialite is nothing without a pool. I don't count those little wading areas on NYC rooftops as "pools." Maybe they look large when an Olsen twin (each born in L.A., let it be noted—I won't specifically say Sherman Oaks) is in them, but even the most waifish of socialites wants more girth out of her body of water—for the pool float possibilities alone.

So yeah, Lindsay was an outsider, you might say. Or you might not mention it at all as you hardly even thought of her. We didn't even give her the time of day when she landed that *The Parent Trap* schlock in 1998, which, by the way, Natasha Richardson completely carried (may she rest in peace). And that's mainly because Paris had already abandoned us all for the East Coast in 1996, stopping into some, like, Mormon rehab center for "emotionally troubled teens" along the way. But I think that was just an elaborate excuse to hide that she was getting some corrective surgery for her lazy eye. So you see, with all the drama of losing our proverbial Heather Chandler (I won't demote Paris to Regina George), we were a little too busy to consider Lindsay's existence. No one realized she was on *Another World* either, and we skipped school almost every day to smoke weed and watch shitty soap operas like that. I don't even think that, had we been sober, we would have noticed. She was just *that* background to us. To borrow from what I maintain is a better high school movie than *Mean Girls*—*She's All That*—to everyone that mattered, she was vapor. Paris, Kim, Nicole and, of course, I, Tate, were the only quartet that mattered (and I'm being kind to include Kim in the quartet at all) as we would sit on Paris' pristine white sofa that was purchased for something like $10,000 from an interior designer that had done one of their hotels and still somehow managed to remain pristinely white while we all literally drank Kool-Aid (spiked with vodka). Kim would later say she was the Blackest thing we had going for us in our lives—much to the offense of Nicole—but, to be honest, I think it was Paris (racist against Black people though she may be). And when she deserted us, it was like, I hate to say it, we just didn't know how to have fun anymore.

Without our "uniting unicorn," Nicole went back to hanging out with her more ethnically ambiguous friends and Kim and I ceased meeting up altogether because we never really liked each other to begin with. She's a Libra, it's really boring. And, truth be told, my Taurean traits can actually dance circles around her so-called "luxury addictions" any day. If the media ever even gave me the goddamn due I deserve, they would have probably seen that by now. But no, it's Kim's vampire facial this and Kim's Paris (France) robbery that. If Paris wasn't such a sophisticate, she would have paid only the finest Italian hitman (Dr. DiMario, who else?) to kill her the second E! greenlit *Keeping Up With the Kardashians*. Ah, but Lindsay. Lindsay, Lindsay, Lindsay. That's where this story of Paris escaping to New York leads. It was there they became acquainted. As usual, Paris was setting trends, causing paparazzi flashbulbs to ignite in her wake as she strutted briefly on sidewalks before getting into a car with Nicky. At the time, no one ever would have thought to tar and feather her for signing with Donald Trump's modeling agency, T Management (real original, Donnie *boy*—if you've even got the goods down there to prove that you're at least that; no friend of mine ever got close enough to ever confirm for sure). And so, this was what launched her into the thermosphere of "being a socialite" anew—the kind that could be adored by New York City just as much as L.A.

Nicole and I about fucking shit ourselves (and not just because we were on a laxative diet) when she merely "sent us some passes" to attend the L.A. premiere of *Zoolander*, instead of inviting us to New York like she would have done in the past. But, as we later learned, she had made quite a few new friends since ditching her roots (though not the dark ones) for greyer (grayer?, I don't know) skies and starker skylines. Besides Vincent Gallo—ugh, we all knew he served a purpose in her life as the guy that could make her seem "artistically" viable—there was "little" Lindsay. Always lurking in the shadows that her strangely-tinted red hair only casted a further darkness to. Still stuck with making Disney TV movie turds like *Life-Size* and *Get A Clue*, Lindsay was putty in Paris' hands. Almost just the way Kim was, but, admittedly less conniving and guileful about it. Moreover, Lindsay never knew how to use her sexuality to achieve her full potential—least of all the way Kim learned to, and merely by imitating Paris' sex tape video tactic. As usual, old Paris was the innovator: *1 Night in Paris* was released in 2004, *Kim Kardashian, Superstar* was released in 2007. Personally, you couldn't catch *me* with either Rick Salomon or Ray J in any still or moving frame. Even with clothes on.

I think Paris liked this weird naïveté that Lindsay had about her. It was very much a sort of Regina/Cady dynamic before it had been rendered to film. Because Lindsay was non-threatening, a princess, at best, of C-rate Disney movies, Paris finally felt comfortable with adding someone to her New York circle. She certainly started talking to *me* less and less by the time 2002 rolled around. Nicole, on the other hand, well, Nicole would forever be there to stay. The two had been attuned to each other's scent since birth. That's Proustian, you know. And yes, I've read Proust. Or at least had my butler go buy the volume that talks about the madeleines for me at full price from Book Soup. I shouldn't even have to explain myself to you as I'm likely an eleven to your negative one looks and it's honestly a testament to my spirit that I even bother to nurture my intellect when no one in their right mind would ever ask me a question about "literature." Unless maybe, just maybe, they presumed I'm the sort of dickhead who reads Bret Easton Ellis. Read him, no. Star in a screenplay adapted from one of his books, yes. Oh wait, Lindsay stole that from me too.

As I was saying, though, I didn't have the clout I once did with Paris anymore. My parents' fortune had been frittered away, most of it lost to the dot-com crash of the early 00s. And let's just say the car purchases, restaurant outings and trips to exotic locations weren't flowing quite as freely as they used to. Gary had to find a new industry to tap into. His expertise in "consulting" would be viable in whatever fellow rich man he found to invest in his "skills"—the unique ability to home in on a certain facet of a business and turn it into more money. It was just a matter of finding said rich man, which can be hard when you're starting to automatically get boxed out of the inner circle that can help you do so. Whispers around town about how the Carmichael family was going bankrupt didn't much improve my popularity among my former so-called friends either. And when Paris moved back to L.A. to start filming *The Simple Life* (she needed a place to actually crash in between visiting bumfuck nowhere destinations), I was essentially persona non grata. I was already slumming it by going to school at UCLA to major in Theater—really just my way of attempting to break into acting without having to go through the casting couch or simply coasting on my last name without at least having *some* experience with "acting." I'm really just too goddamn noble and pure. That's my fucking problem. It wasn't socially acceptable to go to college until the Olsen twins did it. Yeah, Natalie Portman went to Harvard, but she wasn't a socialite, nor was everyone as on her dick until after she graduated in '03.

It got to the point where I couldn't go anywhere in town without overhearing people talking about me. To avoid the lashing tongues, I started frequenting places I knew no one would ever go to, like the Viper Room. As *The Simple Life* launched Paris further into notoriety, priming her for her peak Paris-ness in 2007, I slipped further into isolation and despair. Why oh *why* couldn't Daddy just get a job? And all the while, Lindsay slithered evermore firmly into Paris' good graces. Even though Lindsay began filming *Mean Girls* in Toronto, the two still found plenty of time to keep in touch or meet up—especially when the shoot took her to, ugh, Jersey (I think I need to take a shower just from typing that noun). Even Nicole foolishly started warming to Lindsay (but she regrets falling into that trap with the wisdom of hindsight). She never turned her back on me though, agreeing to meet me in secret at off-brand places like Red Mango (Pink Berry still hadn't been founded yet, it was, like, the *Dark Ages*) in North Hollywood instead of the one in West Hollywood. She was a kind soul underneath it all, even though many couldn't quite always comprehend her sick sense of humor when she did things like throw a weight-limit Memorial Day barbeque. But really, that was just good business sense. The cost of food—particularly when feeding fatties—is astronomical in this country. Especially egregious when you dine in places like Monte Carlo and St. Tropez. But I'd rather pay more for at least an ambient setting with which to make up for potentially gaining weight. Not that I didn't have myriad pills, purging teas and cocaine to remedy any unforeseen poundage. I'm getting ahead of myself again though—and no, I never did get invited to that barbeque. Basically, all I had going for me then, at the outset of 2003, was that I possessed natural long blonde hair, fake tits that *looked* natural, and Aaron Carter as my undercover boyfriend. Other than that, I was twenty-two with an incomplete degree in Theater.

Looking back, I should have been in constant panic over getting an STD from Aaron. He was younger than me, so I thought I would at least have the benefit of being the more experienced one between us. I definitely was not. And I had even gotten to him a little *before* Hilary Duff. Maybe we all had a hand in turning him bisexual. Then again, I never found it any coincidence that both he and Lindsay dabbled in either of the sexes depending on how it suited them in the moment—and Lindsay with her own *mother*, to boot. No wonder she ended up in Greece, which is, ultimately, the way in which she has perhaps most stolen my life. It was supposed to be me. Living that carefree existence in Europe, surrendering to the night and even opening a fucking nightclub *and* beach house (with what funds, I don't know, but they've got to be from sinister sources). *I* was the one who was supposed to make fading into "obscurity" look amazing.

In any event, it was a very strange time, I don't suppose I need to iterate that to you. Aaron was being warred over by Hilary and Lindsay, for fuck's sake. It was a world that favored blonde-haired, overgrown frat boys for socialite pairings. That much was solidified when *Laguna Beach* started airing on MTV in September of 2004. While most of us crème de la crème ilk were far too attractive for the products of tanning bed/sunless tanner incest that created "men" like Jason Wahler or Stephen Colletti, that was "fine" for commoners like Lauren Conrad and Kristin Cavallari. But let it be known that *we* were the orange ones before these *Laguna Beach*/*Jersey Shore*/Donald Trump twenty-four-hour reality shows. God, there's just no credit for people who blaze the trail, is there? For people who, quite simply, are better.

And yes, Paris was better. No one on the outside ever seemed to fully understand that she literally and metaphorically held the keys to the city. To be on her radar was to be accepted. To be nowhere on it was to be a social pariah—an utter nobody. As Paris slipped away from me entirely, I fell ever further into a pit of darkness, made all the worse when the only job my father could secure was at Goldman Sachs as a *junior* analyst.

My god, the shame. He might as well have stayed unemployed on *that* salary. My mother was more hurt by the slight than any of us. She took it upon herself to head to Palm Springs for "some treatments" during Daddy's "transition." I knew what this meant. She was crawling back to her affair with this older, richer man named, typically, Edward. I only knew about him because I got bored one night and logged into my mother's MacBook (still the same pure shade of cocaine white as when she had just purchased it, or her credit card did). There, I found the slew of email exchanges between them. Briefly, I wondered, could someone as *old* as Edward (he had included a picture of himself by the pool) be so modern in technology use?

Whatever his tech abilities, in no uncertain terms, my mother was making herself open and ready to him, clearly miffed by the disappointments my father had laid upon her like an albatross. She didn't care about us anymore, not now that we weren't contributing to and fortifying her perfect image. And honestly, I couldn't blame her. I was feeling the same way, I just didn't have an older, wealthier man to fall back on for refuge like she did. I was still stuck with Daddy. And really, what are men good for if they can't at least be counted upon for financial aid? Nothing, that's what. Not even giving adequate head, as Aaron Carter was quickly showing me. He'd poke his mouth down there, sure, but never long enough to make anything happen. I was done with him anyway. He bored me long before he started to gravitate toward Hilary. The trouble was, when Lindsay began to "date" him, Aaron was suddenly starting to look all shiny and new again—just like Aaron Samuels looked to Regina George when Cady Heron's attraction to him was revealed.

So sure, while *Extra* and *Access Hollywood* were reporting on the feud between Duff and Lohan, I was the one reaping all the sexual re-wards—he had so much pent-up energy from being stuck with those two tweens, who little knew what to do with a popsicle, let alone the similar shape of a (white man's) penis. And for almost two solid months, it was as though we were in a bubble of bliss. Days were spent fucking and drinking at the Chateau Marmont, while nights we would go to some party in Hollywood where he would inevitably ignore me and pretend to have nothing to do with me. I guess he was ashamed of our age difference—and that I wasn't rich (anymore) or famous the way others in my orbit were. It began to make me feel really self-conscious. No Floridian fuckwad was going to make *me* feel like a nobody ever again—least of all someone as hideous and musically talentless as Aaron. When he left me high and dry on New Year's Eve to go have an orgy somewhere else, I knew it was time to make 2004 different than the fucking nothingness of 2003. So I decided to *do* something with that Theater degree: get an agent, or rather, actually use the agent I had paid and sucked off to *be* my agent.

His name was Teddy Salaman and his last name always made me think of saliva. He was short with thinning hair and he wore only navy suits from Barney's. He was gross—nothing like Ari Gold on *Entourage*. He had only gotten me a few auditions in mid-2003 that turned out to be total washes. Still, I liked him. I wouldn't have fucked him on the reg if I didn't. He wasn't like all the pretentious assholes you found in clubs (for example, at Snatch or Shag.) Plus, he wanted to help me with my career. In just one month, he had already gotten me a national commercial for gum.

The sky was going to be the limit from there, I could feel it. The problem was, I was actually starting to *like* spending time with him. Naturally, he was married, so that sort of put a wrench in the full potential for my desires. And the hotels he would take me to were consistently seedy, mainly the Crowne Plaza by the airport. "No one will find us here," he whispered in my ear as he passed a cheap bottle of champagne over for me to sip from. Didn't even bother with the *politesse* of stemware. God, he was sexy. That hairy chest, that stout body. I couldn't get enough of it. It was a secret shame, a fetish. I kept thinking to myself how Paris and Nicole would never be caught dead with someone this objectively repugnant. And that's when I knew I had strayed too far from them, that I had to crawl up out of the hole I had descended into and claw my way back into their world.

The problem was, of course, that just as I was having this epiphany, I was failing to take into account that it was April 30th—now historically known as: the opening weekend of *Mean Girls*. This was it, the end for me, and I was spending it fucking some two-bit agent who couldn't get me a job beyond the realm of Juicy Fruit; that's right, I was in a Juicy Fruit commercial wearing a white skirt and white polo with, *ugh*, white *tennis shoes*.

It was the number one movie—Lindsay wouldn't have it any other way, that calculated bitch (she perfected the art before Taylor). She was starting to become an actual match for Kim. Jesus, they say Madonna is determined, but Lindsay is the progenitor of the word as we came to know it in the 00s. She knows exactly *what* she's doing, *when* she's doing it. And she knew this was the moment to seize on Paris' jugular of friendship, to prove that she might just be even more of a star than Paris herself. And Paris, dumb bitch that she was, took the bait like a gold digger chasing a hundred-dollar bill at the end of a twenty-four-karat gold chain.

So no, to emphasize once again, not all socialites are created equal: some come from trash and manage to pull themselves up out of the wreckage, while others are born with a silver spoon that gets ripped unwarrantedly from her pristine, blow job-ready mouth. Lindsay was the former, I was the latter.

Chapter 2: Confessions of a Teenage Drama Whore

*L*et me take pause to briefly rewind to the two months before *Mean Girls* came out and the Earth was shattered, before a chasm in the space-time continuum was created because Lindsay became famous and I did not. You see, I was actually supposed to be the one cast in *Confessions of a Teenage Drama Queen*, which, believe it or not, truly was instrumental to the sudden launch of Lindsay's career. For it was the one-two punch of having back-to-back successful Disney movies that made Lindsay a force to be reckoned with, an ultimate Hollywood contender. Without *Confessions of a Teenage Drama Queen*, *Mean Girls* wouldn't have been that impressive. Agents wouldn't have been able to look at Lindsay and say, "She's had two bankable box office hits this year."

And yet, the role might have been mine, because for once, it seemed, Teddy had done something right (in addition to making me cum harder than a rainfall in Niagara). He had miraculously managed to land me a last-minute audition for the part of Lola Steppe. I knew it was beneath me, this hastily cobbled together script and apparent shoestring budget of another requisite Disney movie. But I went along with it, and Teddy made no mention whatsoever that Lindsay was in the running for the part. Though maybe it was better that he didn't as it just would have made me all the more nervous and irritable. It was still 2003 at the time, and Lindsay was coming off riding on Jamie Lee Curtis' (and even Chad Michael Murray's) coattails in *Freaky Friday*. Oof, the way Disney lavished her with film deals—no wonder she couldn't secure a fucking script worth shaking a stick at after she dropped them, thinking she could do better on her own. But isn't that always what happens when you bite the hand that feeds you? Yet even when Lindsay was complacent, Disney still preferred Hilary Duff—everyone did (Aaron Carter, included, clearly). And it was *she* who they offered the part of Lola to first, no audition required.

Needless to say, Hilary has some taste (have you not seen *Younger*?) and said no to the script. In my outsider status of that instant, however, I had no idea of these details and neither did Teddy, bless his out-of-touch, fat heart. So I walked into the audition blindly, not knowing that I was only being used as a prop, a tool to get Lindsay to actually try at acting. I was never even a consideration. Her feud potential with Hilary was more important than choosing the better actress for the part, which, of course, would have been me—for Chrissakes. Fuck, now I'm talking like Carol Kane, who it was my dream to work with at some point, but there went that when I failed to land *Confessions of a Teenage Drama Queen.*

It was probably because of that loss, of being rejected for the part, that I reverted back to Aaron that year, and also to vodka, my constant companion. Who knows what sort of boon starring in *Confessions of a Teenage Drama Queen* might have been to my confidence? Or, more importantly, what sort of detriment it might have been to Lindsay's. I didn't think much about it as 2004 started, knowing full well that the filming was underway in June of '03. I was able to put it out of my mind with vodka and Aaron though, thinking that maybe the moment would never come when it would see the light of day—how could it? Who would understand that kind of kitsch intended for the Disney demographic? And though I wanted to hate it, I couldn't deny its camp sensibilities, its star-making performances—with Megan Fox in the bitch bully role of Carla Santini only adding to the film's historical cachet.

To add insult to injury, the movie charted well, following *50 First Dates* at number two the weekend of its release. In truth, it probably should have been number one to spite Adam Sandler and Drew Barrymore for thinking they could recreate the same magic that existed in *The Wedding Singer.* And yet, how were we all to know that *50 First*

Dates would eventually seem like a masterpiece compared to *Blended*?

The moderate triumph of *Confessions of a Teenage Drama Queen* might have kept Paris at bay. But when *Mean Girls* came out almost immediately after to even greater fanfare, it was game over. There was no way I was going to get her to give me the time of day again unless I, too, got to Lindsay. Crack Lindsay, crack Paris. I know, I know: stop saying "crack." Lindsay was barely eighteen when all this prosperity found her—how could I possibly pretend to relate to her? I was about to turn twenty-four. How was "old" Paris pretending to identify? Then again, she always did rather have the mind of a small child—or maybe raccoon is more like it. So easily distracted by a shiny object. Don't let those articles about her "business acumen" that *VICE* likes to release fool you. The woman's brain is leaden. Maybe the reason she liked Lindsay truly was for her mind. Maybe we had only grown apart because, to be frank, I was smarter, more interesting as a human being. I couldn't talk about the latest Dooney & Bourke crayon hearts bag anymore, least of all when Lindsay had just landed a spokesperson gig for it. God, it was like everything was just dropping into her lap, the way it only should for a socialite. But *I* was the socialite, not her—didn't the universe understand?

I got my answer in the negative even more firmly about a week later when I still hadn't received a message back on MySpace from Nicole about getting together with her and Paris at my house for a small, intimate dinner party with a few not really worth mentioning frat-looking guys I thought I could lure them with. Obviously, even Nicole was running out of compassion for my piteous state. I was being ousted completely, and if something didn't change soon, I thought I might seriously consider pulling a Britney in the "Everytime" video. Appropriately, I was thinking this in my clawfoot bathtub while Mommy was in Palm Springs and Daddy was doing who knows what at Goldman Sachs (probably banging some hapless secretary to prove Mommy wasn't the only one who could "adulter"). Just as I was on the verge of going through with wrist-slitting/drowning, I got a phone call. Lazily reaching for my Razr, I answered the unknown 323 number and gurgled (yes, I'd been drinking), "Hello?"

"Tate, this is Britney."

I sobered up real quick to the sound of that familiar wisp of a voice. What could Britney Spears possibly want with me? How did she get my number? Was this the social resuscitation I had been yearning for (like in the *Sex and the City* episode where Samantha is literally pulled back into the light by someone who looks nothing like Leonardo DiCaprio)? The jolt back into Paris' life I required? Before I could think for too long, I found my words and said, as though she were the oldest friend in the world, "Hi Britney, how are you?"

She tittered on the other end of the line. "Well, I know we don't know each other that well, but Nicole gave me your number. I think we met one night at The Parlour or The Abbey. Fuck, it was definitely somewhere in West Hollywood. And, I don't know, it kinda gets lonely out here on the road. I felt like talking to a familiar voice. Or face. Or, like, whatever applies in this context."

At the time, she was on the *Onyx Hotel Tour* (which I still maintain is her best and most underrated), and I guess she was holed up drunkenly at some luxurious hotel—she'd named the tour as it was because of how often she traveled. Then she confirmed my theory by adding, "I'm in Rotterdam at this hotel right now, and I just wanna talk to someone. I met this guy, you know—he's really cute, sort of a bad boy. And I need to tell someone about it. But no one's been answering the phone. I guess everyone has a life or something."

I didn't take offense at the insinuation that *I* did not. This was Britney fucking Spears, I'd talk to her under any circumstances, even if it was that, evidently, I was the last socialite on Earth available to contact by phone. So I encouraged her to tell me everything, which she gladly did while sipping from baby bottles of overpriced liquor from the hotel.

"His name's Kevin, and he does things to me that no boy has ever been dirty enough to do to me. But you know, like I've been saying for a while now, I'm not that innocent. Kevin's the only one willing to treat me that way, you know, like I'm not...that innocent."

"That's really great, Britney," I said in my highest pitched voice. The thing about attempting to be a socialite is that you have to speak in tones that only dogs—bitches—can hear. "Where is he now?"

"Oh, he's around. We're making a documentary. I don't really know what I'm going to do with it yet."

Looking back, I wish I could have warned her not to turn it into *Britney and Kevin: Chaotic.* Even though that show does get a lot more shade thrown at it than it deserves. To be honest, I'd rather watch *that* than *Laguna Beach* any day of the week. Just as I was about to suggest that she might keep the videos to herself, a crashing sound like that of twenty to thirty plates falling to the floor nearly burst my fragile ear drum (I was going to a lot of shows at The Roxy back then for the groupie allure it gave me). "I think Kevin just got back. Um, I gotta go. But like, would you be wanna meet up during one of my tour dates while I'm in Europe? I can get you tickets obviously. I just, like, really need a gal pal right now who understands what I'm going through. You seem like that person Tate."

Ignoring the part where she used the term "gal pal," I felt like I was actually cumming all over myself. This was my chance. My moment for social resuscitation. To be seen with Britney in Europe would mean that Paris could no longer ignore me. And, frankly, that I owed Nicole Richie my life for arbitrarily giving Britney my number.

I consented to meet Britney in Milan on the 19th. I would arrive a few days early to get some tanning time in Portofino—I didn't want to look totally inauthentically orange, after all. The only problem was, I needed a temporary male escort to keep me company—not someone that would be there with me for my meeting with Britney, but someone that would get me photographed and alert the media a.k.a. Paris to my presence abroad. I knew if I played my cards right, Paris would "just happen" to be in Europe to see me—or admit that she truly did *want* to see me—wherever I ended up. But who to mobilize as a friend to fuck? My list of contacts had dwindled vastly over the past year, and Aaron Carter would definitely not be a suitable choice…but I had recently met this up-and-comer named Orlando Bloom at a party my dad threw back in March of '03 (right around the time I lost my chance at playing Lola Steppe) at our house in his attempt to add "producer" to his endless list of job titles. It's so humiliating when instead of your daddy looking like an "entrepreneur," he just looks desperate for work.

And yet, to my astonishment, the party had turned out to be the social highlight of my year thus far—which was really quite sad and a testament to just how few people my own age I could finagle to surround myself with. Even my mother, usually vehement in her refusal to express any form of emotion lest it leave a wrinkle on her face, couldn't help but smile a few times throughout the night. She was genuinely impressed with all the celebrities my father had managed to wrangle. And here she had thought that the Carmichaels had lost all their power in L.A. But she was pleasantly surprised to find that making the trip up from Palm Springs (looking better than ever as a result of her "treatments" I have to say) was worth it—even though it surely must have cost her a few free expensive dinners from her paramour, Edward (then again, Gwen always said eating regularly was too "bovine" for her tastes).

I almost felt like the rift between them could heal fully, so pleased was Gwen with the shiny-and-newness of Gary, in Aaron Samuels fashion (except that there was no other girl interested in him). It was like he had transformed back into the man she had fallen in love with in the first place. I use the term "in love" loosely, of course, and to mean that she had simply seen that my father was once an attractive man who could probably take care of her.

That's all that was expected of Gwen Racine at the age of twenty-five, when she married Gary. She had been groomed by her own well-to-do family, who had, incidentally, total ownership over the La Brea Tar Pits, to find someone equal in aesthetics and finances. That's why they forced her to go to Pepperdine, where she disappointed them all by not finding anyone in the least resembling James Spader. It was 1983 in Beverly Hills, and my father had been the only man she had ever encountered while driving side-by-side who felt emboldened enough to actually call out to her: "Hey babe-a-licious, wanna get a drink?" The very thought of Gary saying the word "babe-a-licious" was enough to help me persist in my bulimia, but it was also sort of sweet in a gross, make-me-want-to-gouge-my-eyes-out kind of way. It almost gave me hope that even when you love someone just for their looks and money, it can grow into something deeper and more meaningful over time. Or, like, you can at least cheat on the person you're married to and get away with it. I think, largely, however, the only reason she even bothered with an affair was to prove to herself that she was still desirable. She was going to turn forty-six later that year, and it was absolutely killing her. Couldn't say I blamed her. I had trouble even grappling with the notion of turning *twenty-five* in the same month as my Euro Britney Spears jaunt. Like, ew, fucking disgusting. I hadn't even accomplished the one goal I had set out for myself to achieve before then which was to start my own line of perfume—Britney *and* Paris saw fit to take away my dream there, as opposed to Lindsay, who somehow never got on the perfume gravy train. Another clear example of her lack of business acumen, mostly due to being Long Island trash.

Eerily, both of the aforementioned blonde bitches released their first fragrances in '04—Paris was twenty-three, Britney was twenty-two (going on twenty-three in December)—*Paris Hilton* and *Curious*, respectively. So yeah, at least two people in my orbit got to fulfill my *Fantasy* (yes, that's an allusion to Brit's second perfume) for me.

But oh yes, let's talk more about the guest list that managed to get my father a producer's credit on *Love Don't Cost A Thing* starring Nick Cannon and Christina Milian, both of whom were also present at the party, in addition to, just to name a few, Nicolas Cage, Keanu Reeves, Kirsten Dunst and Owen Wilson…whose irregularly-shaped nose I really wanted to feel rubbing up against my pussy as he ate me out. Something I couldn't help but keep envisioning throughout the *fiesta*. Alas, the illicit thoughts of The Nose partaking in so many devious things that could be done to me were interrupted by the sight of Orlando Bloom. I had no idea who he was, merely that I recognized in him an aspiring actor's good looks and eccentricities.

Pirates of the Caribbean: The Curse of the Black Pearl hadn't even been released yet (it was about to be in July, changing Bloom's clout forever)—and people were only interested in it because of Johnny Depp, not Orlando. As I finished a banal conversation with Tatyana Ali about what a dickhead Will Smith is, I found my "in" to introduce myself to this truly beautiful man—he was a lot more beautiful back before his penis had been inserted into Katy Perry. He was alone in a corner with an empty glass of champagne, and I took it upon myself to go up to the bartender and get another glass to bring to him.

"You look empty," I said with dual meaning intended as I handed him the drink.

"That I am," he said in his sexy British accent. I guess Britney and I both have a thing for British accents, she for imitating them, me for letting them cascade through my cochlea.

"What's your name?" I demanded, having never seen *The Lord of the Rings* or *Black Hawk Down* at that point (nor will I at any other). But the second he said, "Um, Orlando Bloom," I felt like a total retard.

"I know, I'm joking."

"Are you?"

I nodded and took a sip of my red wine, which I previously had the good sense to mix with Xanax to help me get through this trying social ordeal.

"Of course, 'lando. Who do you think I am?"

"Oh, I know who *you* are. I've heard *a lot* about you."

The hair I had just waxed off of my arms bristled. "From who?"

"Lindsay."

He didn't need to say anything more. It wouldn't come out until Lohan's pathetic, cry-for-attention "fuck list" got published by *In Touch*, but she somehow managed to not only bone him as he was about to ascend to movie star status, but also during one of his valleys, the time around/after *Elizabethtown*. As my head raced with what possible information Lindsay might have told him about me, my father chose this inopportune time to approach and embarrassingly inquire, "Ah Orlando, have you met my daughter before?"

He smiled. "No Mr. Carmichael, I haven't."

Gary pshawed, "Please Orlando, call me Gary. All my friends do."

I don't think I could have possibly felt more reduced to being five years old than I was in that millisecond until my mother also decided this would be the perfect time to chat.

"Tate, are you going to introduce me to your handsome new friend?"

I grimaced. "I'm sure you know who he is, *Mother.*"

She giggled. "Yes. Orlando. Bloom. Everyone's been talking about you. You're the toast of the town."

Still self-effacing from not having banged anyone famous in the U.S. besides, evidently, Lindsay Lohan, Orlando returned, "Oh, thank you very much, Mrs. Carmichael, but I don't know about all that."

"Orlando, it's *Gwen*," she stated almost angrily. "And of course it's true. A group of friends and I are already planning to have an advance screening of *Pirates* here. We can't wait."

This was news to me. I had no idea my mother was suddenly so interested in keeping abreast of film franchises. Maybe it had to do with her desperate grasp at remaining youthful, "in touch" like the tabloid as her milestone birthday loomed. She was a Cancer, naturally. They of the faux-caring breed (Just. Like. Lindsay). I swear if I ever saw a female Cancer do something caring that wasn't actually somehow intended to make herself look good at the end of the act, I'd keel over from pure shock. Honestly. Really think about it the next time you're dealing with a female Cancer and I know you'll instantly discover just how right I am. Male Cancers, on the other hand, well, that's an entirely different animal, isn't it? If you ever manage to "penetrate" them (emotionally or physically), they quickly turn to mush, like loyal little dogs you can never get rid of. Gary was a Scorpio, which naturally made him my opposite complement on the zodiac wheel, and tended to make me prefer him. Me, a Taurus, whose birthday would miraculously be spent with Britney Spears the following week. Maybe there was a birthday god, after all.

As my mind wandered to thoughts of traipsing through northern Italy with Britney, my socialite standing soon to be revived, I remembered I was in a flashback to 2003, trying to explain to you how I had met Orlando Bloom. Well, what with the relaxing effects of the Xanax and all, I had forgotten all about poor Orlando being stuck talking to both of my parents. When I came to from my reverie, my knee-jerk reaction was to say, "Orlando, why don't I show you the gardens and the pool? They're so lovely this time of night."

He smiled gratefully. "I would very much like to see that, Tate."

And without saying another word to Gary or Gwen, I took Orlando by the hand and guided him away from their leering manner.

Once we got outside, I immediately felt like Cher Horowitz showing Christian Stovitz (noticing the trend in Jewish last names in L.A. yet?) "the grounds" in *Clueless.* Minus the part where Orlando is blatantly gay and I'm just ignoring it. Then again, maybe he is. You would sort of have to be to engage in a relationship with any of the women he has. Except me, of course. Which brings me to how I ended up taking Orlando with me to Portofino. As I edged him against one of the trellises discreetly situated near our gazebo, I cooed, "So, what *have* you heard about me?"

He moved his mouth as close to mine as it could get without actually kissing me.

"You're quite the curious kitty aren't you?"

I shrugged. "No, you don't have to tell me." And just like that, a little reverse psychology worked effortlessly on 'lando.

He whispered in my ear, "She said you're a whore. And you're trying desperately to regain your social standing in this town."

I backed away, genuinely offended by the accusation. How could Lindsay do this to me? Slander my good name in this careless regard? It was bad enough she had taken *Confessions of a Teenage Drama Queen* away from me. Now she had to make me sound like some sort of desperate plebe to imminent Hollywood royalty like Orlando Bloom? No, no this could not stand. Further wielding my expert reverse psychology skills on someone already as dumb and susceptible as Bloomy, I pretended I had no intention of sleeping with him now that he had said such a foul thing.

Backing away, I even employed the tried-and-true crocodile tears method. "That's just not true. I can't believe she would say something so cruel about me." I turned my back to him and started walking inside of the gazebo, where he automatically followed me.

He put his arm on my shoulder and said, "I'm sorry Tate. It was wrong of me to rehash what she said so harshly. I shouldn't have told you at all." His light touch on my bare back (why wear a dress if it isn't going to expose most of your skin?) soon evolved into full-fledged caressing, and when I whipped around to feign being outraged, he pulled my head toward his and kissed me with the sort of vigor I thought he might only be capable of when a thirty-million-dollar paycheck was involved. I continued to play it cool at first, pretending I wasn't going to go through with fucking him full-stop in the gazebo. That made him want me all the more. And when I finally let him have me, even going so far as to lightly place my finger just at the upper part of his crack, I knew I could ask him anything I wanted. Yeah, he was dating Kate Bosworth at the time, but they were always so on and off again. Besides, she wasn't showing enough skin since *Blue Crush* in 2002, so no one really gave much of a fuck about her anymore.

When he orgasmed (I, it goes without saying, did not. You've all seen his penis in *those* vacation photos, it's impossible to work with), I made it a point to get his number and say, "Maybe I'll see you again sometime." That time, whether he liked it or not was going to be now, for my Italian sojourn of '04. When I called him up, he answered right away. "Tate? I haven't seen you since…"

"Yeah, it's been a while. But, um, I'm going to Portofino and wanted to know if you might like to join me."

As he explained that he still had to shoot some scenes in Spain for *Kingdom of Heaven*, but that he could meet me in between, I thought about how what everyone knows but nobody talks about (as Kathryn Merteuil would say) is that all co-stars bang one another. It's just, like, the rules. So I knew he was coming off of a dalliance with Eva Green, a notorious cold fish in the sack, and that he would be all too eager to hole up in a hotel with me. His usual cautiousness being marred by a desire to fuck someone who actually knew how meant that I could absolutely secure multiple paparazzi photos that would not only make Kate Bosworth cry, but also force Paris and Lindsay to acknowledge me.

Strangely, Bloomy's inextricable link (initially through me) to Paris and Lindsay wouldn't rest as, in 2009, he and his next stupid then-girlfriend, Miranda Kerr, were also victims of the Bling Ring. That those trashy Agoura Hills kids couldn't see that I was worth robbing too only adds to the endless list of how I've been wronged as a socialite and by Lindsay Lohan's pervasiveness. Even post-peak…a.k.a. in 2009, when all Lindsay could think to do was design some legwear, the Bling Ring opted to swipe her déclassé garb and jewelry over my high-class fare.

In 2013, when the Sofia Coppola movie came out and, with it, revived interest in the case, all Lindsay could do was cameo as herself in *Scary Movie 5* and, what else, *The Bling Ring*. Speaking of, Sofia Coppola's really quite shit, isn't she? If my dad had directed an iconic masterpiece about the mafia that allowed me to be a nepo baby, I'd be making way better movies than what she turns out. *Marie Antoinette* is solid though. But maybe I only think that because I can relate to the profligate ho it's about.

Chapter 3: Italy Is Where All the Cracked-Out Shit Happens

*I*taly is the country perhaps most accustomed to accommodating "celebrity." Themselves so devoid of any decent cultural icons other than Sophia Loren and Madonna, it's really no wonder they're so keen to please whatever American "star" (even if it is someone like Pamela Anderson) comes to [insert quaint town here]. My arrival with Bloomy was no exception to the rule. From the moment we stepped off my private plane, we were greeted by all manner of obsequious help. And even though Italians have a reputation for being lazy in their work ethic, they really can be so diligent when they know that someone with actual money is involved and can pay them the way most other Italian people can't.

So it was that the concierge of the Hotel Splendido personally greeted us on the tarmac and accompanied us in a discreet black Alfa Romeo he had "chartered" for the occasion. Orlando had been the one to suggest this car, himself getting thoroughly ingratiated in the European culture that was not Britain. Not that Britain can even technically be considered part of Europe anyway. It with its staunch desires to declare itself independent. In many ways, I rather identify, as this is precisely what I've had to do with lesser socialites than I, the ones who try to ignore me because they think I'm too stuck up when, really, I'm just filtering out the riffraff.

But anyway, as we wove through the narrow streets leading to the hotel, I could already tell that my image was going to be splashed in, at least to start with, national news rags like *Grazia*. Bloomy couldn't keep his hands off of me, and by the time we got to the room, he had already managed to remove most of my clothes. He really is surprisingly passionate for an English person. He's *got to* have some Italian blood in him somewhere.

Upon finishing eating me out for roughly an hour, he sighed happily and plopped down at my side. His fervor and attentiveness also didn't really make sense to me because he's a Capricorn, they of the logical, cut-and-dried bent.

"You're very unexpected, do you know that Bloomy?" I couldn't help but say somewhat romantically.

"How do you mean?"

"Oh, I don't know," I returned, choosing to be cryptic for the sake of sustaining the upper hand.

He grinned at me. "I'm going to order room service. Do you want anything? I've worked up quite an appetite tending to you."

"I don't know. Isn't fish the 'thing'?"

He glanced at my vag. "It certainly is." He then dove in for more for another thirty minutes before finally getting around to ordering actual fish. Truth be told, this was getting dangerous. I was starting to *like* Orlando Bloom. And I had far more important things to worry about other than wondering if he might like me equitably and in a way that would last longer than the standard ten months of most "long-term" Hollywood relationships.

My mind racing with thoughts of getting too involved, I knew exactly what I needed to take the edge off: my compulsory dose of Xanax. Not wanting Bloomy to unearth the extent of just how much I needed it (he had met me in the loopy state that it afforded me, after all), I retreated to the bathroom with my toiletry bag to delight in mixing it with some of the Prosecco I had swiped from the jet. Oh yes, this would take the edge off—make me forget all my concerns about having feelings of any kind. And as I wrestled with swallowing another two after popping three, I looked around to notice just how small Italian bathrooms are, even in luxury hotels.

A knock at the main door signaled the arrival of all the crab, mussels and champagne Orlando had ordered. I was starting to feel wonky, and that the consumption of fish of any kind would either make me vomit or have diarrhea or both. But I didn't want 'lando to know about how much of a pillhead I was. I didn't even acknowledge it fully myself until this trip, when I found how important to my well-being it was to mix my Ambien with some cut-up Adderall I snorted for just the right level of (mostly non-) awakeness on the plane. It was so easy when I was in my teens to mix whatever I wanted. But now in my late early twenties, it wasn't so simple to bounce back from putting whatever I wanted in my body.

'Lando called out, "Tate, there's plenty of food out here. Help me eat it, will you?"

I coughed lightly and shouted back, "Yes! Just a minute." I needed air—and fast. I went over to the petite square window and opened it. A part of me wanted to just jump out and take a flight back to L.A. The pressure of getting Paris on my side again was weighing on me. So much was riding on this trip and if everything didn't go exactly my way, I knew there was a strong chance I was going to sink into a deep depression that might actually force me to listen to Coldplay or something.

So I took deep breaths and smelled the salty air, which actually kind of made me feel sicker. It was at that moment that I noticed a hidden photog in the tree branch to my left. Hearing the click of his camera, I felt an endless sense of calm and relief. It was happening. I was becoming worthy of being featured on E!, *Extra* and *Access Hollywood* again (this was still a year before TMZ was founded, mind you). And it was this sound and sight that gave me the strength to go back to the living room and join Bloomy in feasting on the crab and mussels, which

I was only going to yak up later anyway to preserve my figure. When we finished, he somehow produced a cupcake from out of nowhere and said, "Did you think I wasn't going to find out?"

"What is this, a 'Got Milk?' commercial?" I said indignantly. My birthday was May 17th, the following day, but Bloomy was going to have to be back in Spain so he wanted to celebrate now. "I really don't want to celebrate getting older. I'm turning twenty-five, for fuck's sake. It's too ancient to even think about."

He rolled his eyes. "I'm twenty-seven, how do you think *I* feel?"

"It's different for dudes, you know that. And I still wanna be an actress..."

"I had no idea that was your inclination. Why didn't you say so?" he beamed. "Now I know the perfect birthday present to get you."

I took a bite of the cupcake, all chocolate-filled and decadent. "Oh? What's that?"

"A part in my next movie."

Luckily, I had the foresight to say no, even though it could have been me that Nathan Rabin decided to dub the manic pixie dream girl instead of Kirsten Dunst. But I didn't want anyone to think that I had gotten a favor. I wanted to act on my own merits, which, I now know is why I never made it in the business. Couldn't even land something as dismal as *House of Wax* the way Paris did. "That's all right 'lando. I have some things of my own lined up."

"All right, suit yourself. But you're missing out on a great opportunity. Cameron Crowe's directing. And ol' Tommy Cruise is producing."

"Oh god, keep me the fuck away from him. He's literally always looking for a beard. And anyway, Cameron Crowe plateaued in 2000. I won't say peaked, but…plateaued."

"He's a fantastic director though, this is going to be another major comeback."

"If you say so."

"Oh, I do."

It was then I had the epiphany that Bloomy really wanted me to validate his film role choice. Funny how the bigger a star gets, the less secure he becomes. So I offered, "This sounds like it's going to be really great for you, too. Like nothing you've ever done before."

Finally, the smile showed itself again. So did another erection. Stroke the ego, stroke the dick—that's what I've learned as a socialite and a social climber.

We went at it for another two hours before coming up for air again to go to La Terrazza. Turns out, with constant use, Bloomy's penis was more than adequate in getting the job done. And in any case, eating and fucking are the primary activities

Italy is suited for. In truth, it might have been the best birthday—or eve of my birthday—I'd ever had.

As we sat openly on the terrace, I heard the signature sound of the camera clicks again, while Bloomy, conversely, remained totally oblivious. Everything was going according to my will. I couldn't have planned it better if I had actually preordained being born into money. I acted as aloof as Bloomy was to the cameras, ensuring that I turned in just such a way as to showcase my best angles.

When we finished eating our pasta (again, I would be doing a lot of throwing up on this trip), Bloomy looked into my eyes and said, "I don't want to leave tomorrow."

"Then don't," I suggested. "I don't have to be in Milan until the 18th. You could stay another day."

"And you're very determined to meet up with…Britney Spears?"

Was he a little bit denser than your average Englishman or something? Inferring with that tone that I *shouldn't* meet up with the biggest pop star in the world. To confirm my commitment to the cause, I nodded vehemently. "She's doing back-to-back shows so I won't have much opportunity to really powwow with her except after her performance in Milan. I'm not following her ass to Zürich. I fucking hate Zürich."

"Had a bad banking experience there, did you?" he quipped.

I giggled. "No, a bad birthday. My dad took me there for my sixteenth for some stupid business trip I got talked into going on. I just wanted to stay in Beverly Hills with Paris and Nicole."

Orlando guffawed.

"What?" I demanded.

"Why do you like those girls, huh? You're not the same as them."

"Well, yes, Orlando, actually I am. We were all three born—"

"Socialites?"

I started to agree, then stopped. "Not Nicole."

He laughed at me. "Is that all you want to be?"

I took a sip of my wine, continuing to really maximize the pleasant warmness being stirred within me thanks to the latest Xanax. "I told you. I want to be an actress."

"An actress is a working girl socialite, that's all. Don't you want to do something, I don't know, slightly more *meaningful*?"

"Are you suggesting I go to Africa or some shit and do charity work?" The wine was really having its way with me now, making me feel so comfortable and free. "And just what the fuck is it that *you're* doing that's so great? So *meaningful*?"

My voice had raised several octaves and I knew it was going to get me filmed for some Italian report, likely for RAI, as that's, like, the only fucking channel Italians have.

"Don't shout at me, Tate. I'm only expressing concern for you. For your future. You're twenty-five now. You're not allowed to coast on the "I'm a twit of a little girl shtick" anymore, now are you?"

I rose from my chair, throwing my glass of wine in his face as I did so. It put Samantha Jones doing it to Richard Wright to shame (I guess Samantha Jones is sort of my benchmark for all of my reactions and behaviors). I only briefly glimpsed Bloomy's shocked expression before retreating to the hotel room.

I waited what felt like hours for him to come follow me and apologize, but he never did. I later found out he took the jet back to Seville, where he would be a good little ducky and carry out his shooting schedule—and probably shoot some more sperm into Eva Green—that frigid bitch.

***

I had gotten what I wanted. Bloomy and I were all over the news, both European and American. It only took twenty minutes for Britney to call me up gushing about it and forty-five for Paris, who must have had her tail between her legs (and she does have an actual tail) about the admission that I was still relevant to wait that long to do so.

"Tate, sweetpea, I've been so negligent of our friendship lately, haven't I?"

"Oh no, Paris. You're so busy with everything. With your fragrance, *The Simple Life*—all those club appearances." I licked her asshole real good, and by the time we were done chatting it was decided she would meet me in Milan for a much overdue shopping spree on the Corso Vittorio Emanuele the day after Britney's concert.

"I'd love to see Britney too, but I really just can't make it by the 19th. I've got so much going on over here, you have no idea how insane it's been."

"I can't wait to hear all about it, Parry." I reverted to my childhood nickname for her—for an added effect of sentimentality. She would be mine again. There was no way she could free herself from my clutches this time.

And then she said the one word that ruined it all: Lindsay.

"I might bring Lindsay along with me too. Nicole can't come. She had a botched asshole bleaching treatment and now she's just like completely out of commission for the next week."

"I see," I stated, trying to sound neutral.

"Is that a problem? Do you want, like, intimacy time or something?"

"No, no. I'm really looking forward to seeing you *and* Lindsay," I lied.

And with that, I had passed Paris' test. All it took was the loss of the only guy I think I ever might have been able to love. Or am I only saying that because he's the proverbial "one that got away"? Try not to think of the Katy Perry song of the same name. Or of her riding 'lando's wang after he showcased it for all to see in Sardinia in that immortal August of 2016. And now that I think back on it, it was a bastard move for him to go to Italy with *her*. Or maybe it showed he was still slightly sentimental about me since he wouldn't go with her to the mainland—the *real* Italy, if you will. The point is, he betrayed me for a woman who looks like a Muppet. Just another humiliation in a life so chock-full of them, particularly by my socialite's standards. Well, *ex*-socialite at this juncture (and yes, that's my Insta handle, @ex_socialite—look it up…and don't judge the use of an underscore like it's still the glorious Hotmail days).

I checked out of the hotel the following day, deciding that the sooner I got out of Portofino and into the city limits of Milan, the better. I couldn't go there without first popping into Lago di Como for a boat ride though. You know, George Clooney really did ruin that place. It used to be so exclusive. Now it's like every asshole thinks they should go there because it's been "Clooney sanctioned." Like, did everyone forget the guy used to have a mullet and be on *The Facts of Life?* 'Cause that should really strip away all of his credibility no matter how many Oscar-nominated movies he stars in.

Mercifully, he hadn't "fallen in love" with the place in such a way as to totally taint it just yet. And even though I was all "alone" with three bodyguards, I felt really at peace with myself. Sure, Bloomy was probably never going to talk to me again and I had probably caused Kate Bosworth to break up with him for the umpteenth time, but that didn't mean I couldn't travel on my own happily. Part of getting older is finally learning how to be comfortable with yourself, in your own skin, after all. Though I could never imagine being comfortable in the pale, freckled skin that belonged to the likes of Lindsay. The very thought of her imminent arrival with Paris made me shudder. But I had to take the bad with the good. As I said before, crack Lindsay, crack Paris. It worked for Janis Ian and it was going to work for me. Oh Jesus, how I hated myself for being one of the legions looking to *Mean Girls* for plotting inspiration. Why did it have to be such a cultural phenomenon? Maybe no one could really blame Lindsay for not trying after that movie, as she knew she had firmly landed her place in the annals of pop culture history (and anals, too).

Letting the sun wash over me as I stretched out on the boat with some driver named Fabrizio taking the wheel to ensure my relaxation, I suddenly wished it was chic to just bang the help. But no, that was only okay when you were Ben Affleck dating J. Lo. And during this delicate state of my celebrity, I couldn't do anything that might undo the "good faith" created by the paparazzi photos of Orlando and me that were continuing to circulate across the globe as I worked on my tan. If I wasn't persistently on a loop of Xanax-popping, I could have sworn Fabrizio winked at me "knowingly," as though he had seen the headlines. Did he want a taste of my famous socialite pussy too? Probably. I surrendered to giving it to him about eleven minutes later, after we had stopped in the middle of the lake for *pranzo* a.k.a. the paninos he wanted us to eat to fortify our strength. Really, though, his growing eighteen-year-old body (spirit?) as most of the eating was done by him…of me.

I usually tended to hate messing around with younger guys (especially after Aaron Carter), but because Italian men get started so early with their sexual practice, it felt more like I was being pleasured by a twenty-five-year-old than an eighteen-year-old. Sometimes age really ain't nothin' but a number. Except when you're Aaliyah being taken advantage of by R. Kelly or a woman with no money to adequately invest in general facial and Botox upkeep. Then it's a pretty fucking real, tangible number. As I let out a standard sigh of ecstasy when

Fabrizio had finished me off, a phone call from my father interrupted the "festivities." I was really wishing I hadn't set up my Razr to receive international calls and "SMSes" as I foolishly decided to pick it up, some Electra complex-having part of me wanting Daddy to be involved in my post-coital tableau.

"Daddy?"

"Tate, what is the meaning of this *Star* cover? Are you with Orlando Bloom?"

My father read *Star* religiously. It was the most feminine quality about him. And the one that had always gotten me into the most trouble when I was in high school and constantly being featured toward the back at one of those bottom sections of the magazine with Paris and Nicole. Before he knew how to use the internet, *Star* was always the best way for him to keep track of me, and, clearly, it still was.

"I *was* with him in the sense that we visited Portofino together."

For a second, it sounded like he was growling. "That's not all you were doing in those photos, Tate." A pause. "What is this about, huh? You were finally starting to go off the radar a little bit and I thought it meant you had got those party girl ways out of your system. I thought you had matured. That's why I gave you my special credit card to go on the trip to celebrate your birthday.

You didn't tell me you were going with Orlando Bloom."

"What the fuck is this fixation with Orlando Bloom? Why is that the detail you're focusing on? I've come to Italy to celebrate my birth and forget my troubles. *Must* you be such a judgmental downer?"

"Yes Tate, I must. You need to do something with your half Theater degree or I might be forced to cut you off."

"Cut me off? You're barely giving me any money as it is."

He sighed. "It could get a lot worse, Tate. If you don't shape up. When are you coming back to L.A.?"

I glanced over at Fabrizio, who was now massaging my foot.

"I don't know. Maybe I'll stay in Italy forever if things go my way."

"That's enough. I'm booking you a flight for two weeks from now. Be back here then, or don't bother checking your bank account for more money."

With that, he hung up. I don't think I'd ever heard him sound quite so moody. Maybe I needed to nudge Gwen to have sex with him in a way that didn't force me to actually say the words, "Have sex with him." But before I could plot how to get back into Daddy's good graces prior to him seeing me in yet another incriminating series of photos with Paris and Lindsay, Fabrizio felt the

54

need to go in for round two and I just got so distracted with the romance of it all. By now, Orlando was probably the furthest thing from my mind—though I had no doubt he was thinking of me after having to go back to the callous bedroom stylings of Eva Green.

Back at the Grand Hotel Villa Serbelloni, I rinsed myself off in the shower and changed into a replica of the Randi Rahm dress Maria Menounos wore at the Oscars earlier that year (as if *she* fucking deserved to). Except there were even more diamonds on it. I wanted to look my best for the date Fabrizio had asked me to go on that evening. Even though I knew it was ill-advised to be seen in public with him, I couldn't resist the urge to accept. He was just so damned earnest, both in his physical methods and his broken English, telling me sweet nothings like, "Signorina Tate, you so beautiful." Don't ever say socialites are cold-hearted bitches because being spotted with him almost completely cost me my audience with Paris.

As I descended the staircase and predictably took everyone's breath away with my pale lip gloss, understated eye makeup and elegant upswept hair, Fabrizio met me at the bottom with his hand extended. It really did feel like *Beauty and the Beast* (but more like Jean Cocteau's version than the Disney-animated one)...or something. Or maybe like the cotillion I never had. And, by the way, everyone should really thank *Gossip Girl* for teaching commoners about cotillions. It even taught me something since I didn't grow up in a place as formerly stodgy as New York City.

"Signorina Tate, you are…"

He didn't need to finish his sentence for me to know what he was trying to say. I was already well-aware of how breathtaking I looked. And as the flashbulbs went off, I briefly and naively thought to myself, "Maybe it isn't a gamble to be dining with the help tonight. I can still coast on the residual cachet of being seen with Orlando Bloom." I should have had more wisdom than that. Then again, the word "sage" doesn't exist in a socialite's vocabulary unless it's some Santa Barbara-born girl's name.

Fabrizio pulled my chair out for me as we got to our table. In addition to being trained in how to fuck well at an early age, Italian men are also very old school when it comes to chivalry and gender roles. I really fucking love it. It might be what convinces me to settle down one day…for the right Italian. But then I'll have to deal with the inevitable fact that he's going to get a mistress. And, frankly, *I'd* rather be the mistress than the wife. They get all the good trinkets.

As I looked over the menu, it suddenly occurred to me that I had absolutely nothing to say to Fabrizio. Our magic on the boat from before existed purely because of sex. Here in the perfect soft lighting of the hotel restaurant, it was starkly apparent that I couldn't exactly commiserate about fish-mongering, or whatever it was people with a boat background do. So I did what any girl trying to preserve the spark would: I rushed us through dinner (mostly drinks on my end), and got us back up to the hotel room where "that old feeling" could persevere. And oh my, did it, with Fabrizio outpacing 'lando by leaps and bounds with that tongue technique of his—sorry, I don't want to make you jealous as I know your sex life is likely rather prosaic, if you even have one at all. I mean, how great can it be? You're reading a *book*. But hey, don't be envious. It's not like I got to keep my place in the sun after what Lindsay did to me—or like I didn't constantly have to work to sustain it even when I was deemed a "worthy" member of the socialite world.

Any who, after getting caught up in the haze of being sexually satisfied throughout the night, my rude awakening came in the form of a stack of newspapers tossed in the front of my door (remember, 2004 still believed in the value of the tangible printed word). Among the black-and-white ruins was a copy of *The Sun* (a rag I had hoped to avoid in Italy), screaming the headline, "Tate Carmichael Caught Slumming It With Deckhand in Lake Como!" My body temperature went from cold to hot and back to cold again. When my pictures were being taken last night, I must have been completely drunk on the awkwardness of being out of a carnal setting with Fabrizio. Because I was wide-eyed enough to not take into consideration the angles the paparazzi like to employ. The "tilted stage" (oh Taylor, you're not the only one who has suffered) they use to twist and mangle everything— every outing and event—into something it's not.

Standing in the hallway in my Kiki de Montparnasse bustier and thong (side note: I fear the current generation's lack of commitment to foreplay is going to put a real damper on the lingerie business—maybe even decimate it entirely), I was hit with a harsh revelation: I had no self-control. What kind of self-respecting socialite with a legacy of investment bankers to honor would allow herself to stoop so low as to bang the help? The most forbidden sect in the divide between rich people and everyone else. Even someone unemployed (a.k.a. an artist) would be more socially redeeming than simply a "service person." God, it's like my pussy was a dick. It certainly acted like one with all its thoughtless meanderings, ruled solely by "wanting it now" and the sense memory of how amazing it is to have an orgasm.

As I started to glaze over in a sort of fugue state at the sight of the headline touting my whorish-ness and propensity for base men, one of the hotel's pompous guests, a member of the Yeardley family, walked past me in horror as he looked from me to the headline *about* me. The last time I had seen Brian Yeardley, a thirty-four-year-old who had recently advanced from VP to President of his father's Orange County-based oil company, he had his tongue down my throat as I kneed him in the groin and pushed him off me during a routine co-family summer vacation to Montecito. His parents and my parents still remained close since the incident, which was five years ago; and now Gary and Gwen were always demanding why I refused to accompany them on these "retreats" anymore. They weren't upset that I wasn't there, only that I had ruined a potential "merging of assets" for them that they would have whole-heartedly approved of.

But girls like me don't marry guys like Brian. We apparently flit about screwing every pretty little foreigner we see on our travels. Trying to cover myself with the paper to exude a false sense of modesty, I better flashed the headline at Brian just as he passed by me. He side-glanced at me with a smirk on his face, the satisfaction of karmic retribution delighting him to no end. No, even *he* wouldn't try to pursue me now after this smear. I didn't bother trying to speak to him, to explain myself with even the uttering of a nondescript sound. And then, just when I truly didn't think the situation could become more untenable, Fabrizio emerged to caress my shoulder and coo with his uniquely incorrect grammar, "What you doing out here?"

Brian witnessed it all, and would no doubt finish me off among the community of power families that had been built up around the Carmichaels. In many ways, being slandered by someone in this mafioso faction was worse than being tarred and feathered by the tabloids and trashy TV headlines. Because someone *actually* on the inside had far more sway with gossip-wielding than the hearsay of media trolls. I bristled as Fabrizio continued to stroke my shoulder and kiss my neck, totally unaware that each "little kiss" was adding to my social kiss of death. Brushing him off in disgust, I rushed back into the room and started dressing. Slipping into my Paige jeans (Paige Adams-Geller had only sent out samples of her then-new brand to an elite pool of waifish celebutantes) and a silk burgundy tank top with a lace border at the neck, I frantically brushed my hair back and added a black headband for the finishing touch. I would have someone at the hotel send over my personal effects after packing them for me. But right then, I needed to get the fuck away from Lake Como and meet up with Britney, still my only remaining golden ticket to sustaining any kind of status in this world. Who knew that it would take such trash to turn me back into a treasure? No offense to Brit Brit or anything, but Kentwood is a long way from the top of the ladder called Sophistication. And no, reminding me that McComb, Mississippi is her birthplace doesn't really dust off the lowbrow qualities of her "personage" either.

In short, *she* should have been prostrating herself to hang out with *me*, not the other way around. But that's not how everyone else would see it in the wake of my Italian faux pas. Unsweet Christ, why couldn't I have just stuck with Orlando? I had to let my ego get the best of me, make me believe that if Orlando could take a vested interest in me, then I was already back at the top of the food chain anyway. But this wasn't the case. I had built up a false sense of confidence and now it was here to bite me right in my bleached asshole (another thing *I* started doing prior to Lindsay…or Nicole, for that matter) before I could truly bask in the brief after-effects of positive publicity. I had to do extensive damage control and that could very well mean latching onto Britney for multiple tour dates instead of the original one-night stand—so to speak—I was intending on having with her in Milan. I didn't imagine I would be able to tolerate her simpleton vibe too much longer than that.

As I boarded my private jet wearing a Dolce and Gabbana floral-print romper (I really was ahead of my time with the whole romper trend—socialites are, after all, the ultimate adult babies) and oversized purple-tinted lens Fendi sunglasses, I looked back briefly behind me. I wouldn't return to Lake Como for a while. If I wanted to go to a reputable lake for rich people in the near future, it would have to be Lake Zürich (which is actually far enough away from the city of Zürich, a place that, as I said, I hate…and just a stone's throw from Como—should the arbitrary fancy to go there strike me—when you have a jet). Even though I rather despise the coldness (what they call "neutral") of the people in Switzerland. Like, let's just say it would be difficult for me to as easily get one of the members of *that* population to pleasure me with half as much skill and abandon. Is it the weather that makes them so damned frigid or something?

I couldn't think about it—or much of anything else anymore, as I had just popped two Xannies before boarding. When I awoke, it would be to the nearby milieu of Milan, a place that Charles V once remarked of: "My cousin Francis and I are in perfect accord—he wants Milan, and so do I." I had no idea this would be the overall sentiment shared between Paris and me in terms of currying favor with Britney.

*T*he pilot tapped me on the shoulder, at first. I didn't feel it. It was only after about five minutes that he finally started to jostle me in a manner that a socialite should *never* be handled. I took it in stride, shrugging it off as though there was no harm done, but, in truth, I would not be employing this *mongoloid* in any of my dad's private planes again. The gall he had to touch me—*handle me*—like I was any *average* Tate. It's almost like he *wanted* me to give him the whole spiel (pardon the Jewish word, I don't know where that's coming from) about who my family is. So I did.

"Sir, or whatever, it's really nice of you to wake me in that oh so gentle fashion of yours, but maybe I need to refresh your memory about *touching* a Carmichael. My great-great-grandfather established our entire empire on the invention of a fabric that allowed for better protective padding on uniforms during the Mexican Revolution—yeah, that's right, I'm fucking Mexican, but only like one-sixteenth or something so it "doesn't count"—God, I'm sure George W. Bush is probably Mexican too somewhere down the line. We're *all* Mexicans. I'm just saying that, considering my dynasty's backbone was founded on preventing the invasion of the body, you really shouldn't invade *mine* with that egregious method of yours for waking someone up."

He blinked at me in something like awe for a few seconds before I swiped him aside and went about figuring out how the fuck to rendezvous with Britney. In the Towncar that led me away from the airport, I took out my Razr and dialed her hotel room at the Four Seasons (Paris and Lindsay, of course, would be slumming it at the Hilton on Via Luigi Galvani, some dude who pioneered bioelectromagnetics, and I still have no idea what that is, really, after researching it. The thing with me when I'm in Italy is that I always have to look up the people that the streets are named after. It's just an OCD "quirk" with me. It's probably because I would want someone to look up Via Tate Carmichael to find out who I am centuries from now when I'm slightly less well-known…even though I'm aware the likelihood of that is *molto* slim. Everyone knows me. They just don't *know* me.

The phone rang several times before Britney finally conceded to answering it. I could tell from her slur that she had already been at it with the sedatives and the alcohol even more than I was on my brief plane ride. She was a girl who loved her dolls, and rightly so after that first leg injury on the set of the "Sometimes" video. But I was kind of concerned about her ability to perform onstage that night without keeling over. Then again, she must've been used to doing that sort of thing all the time.

"'Lo?"

For a second, I thought she was trying to say "Lilo"—for Lindsay Lohan. Sure, the nickname hadn't taken off at full-speed yet, but it's what crossed my mind when she uttered it. As my obsession with obliterating Lindsay would intensify over the years, I learned there were two meanings from different cultural backgrounds that favored the name Lilo. In Samoan, it meant "curious one" or "generous one." Well sure, she certainly was "curious" about different varieties of celebrity dick, and yeah, even more "generous" when sucking one of them off. But in every other regard pertaining to the adjectives, it definitely did not apply. So I looked to the subsequent meaning of the epithet from the African standpoint: "two-hearted," or "a person who is both good and evil." That seemed more apropos—though any "good" in her got stamped out entirely during the production of *Herbie: Fully Loaded*. Again, I'm getting ahead of myself though— jumping around in this endlessly fucked up timeline.

"'Lo?" Britney drawled again, and I suddenly put it together that she was just saying "hello" from the perspective of her own addled mind.

"Brit? It's Tate. I'm on the way to the hotel now."

Silence.

"Oh…Tate. Um, yeah. Really looking forward to our sleepover. Um, have you heard from Paris?"

Sensing the strangeness in her voice, I lied, "Oh yeah, I just got off the phone with her. She should be at the Hilton in about an hour with Lindsay."

Britney coughed. "That's interesting, because she just told me that Lindsay's not coming."

I froze in terror. There could be nothing favorable about the reason why "La Lohan" (more like La Cokehead) had opted out of the trip at the last minute. And before I could internally speculate as to why for very long, Britney further explained, "She's just a little concerned about negative press right now. And with your whole frolicking with the server situation, she doesn't want her name tied to yours."

I couldn't find any words. Lindsay fucking Lohan, of all people. The girl who would fuck anything with even a nub was judging *me*. That "50 Most Beautiful People" issue of *People* must have really gone to her head. She truly thought she was too hot in both the physical and commodity way to be seen with me. I simply could not bear it.

Britney, sensing my appallment, tried to console, "Look, I get it. I'm with one of my new backup dancers right now. There's something very sexy about a guy who isn't A-list. Except in my case, the backup dancer thing is more socially acceptable because, like, people can understand that you're on the road and you've got to have *someone* to fulfill your needs."

"This is a huge misunderstanding. I'm with Orlando Bloom. That other guy from the tabloids was just somebody I felt sympathetic toward. I wanted to show him the time of his life because he—"

"Stop right there Tate. I'm not drunk enough to go along with these lies. Besides, Paris is still coming. And I'm not going to hold it against you either." That last line was foreshadowing for a *Femme Fatale* single, which I think I directly inspired with this phone conversation.

"Well, what did Paris *say*?"

"She sounded kind of disappointed that her new bestie wasn't going to be here, but you're one of her oldest friends. She's not going to be off-put by some garden-variety scandal."

As she said this, we pulled up to the Four Seasons to the sight of a twenty-large crew of paparazzi. "I just pulled up. I'll knock on your door in a minute."

I hung up the phone, bracing myself for whatever the meaning behind this media barrage would be. For as conceited as I was, I didn't imagine that the Italian *and* American media congregation could have anything to do with me. However, the instant my driver opened the door for me, shouts of, "Tate, Tate! Is it true you're here to get advice from Britney about how to quit dating non-famous people?"

I was so shocked I almost actually lost my poise as I walked toward the entrance in that steely way all socialites are born knowing how to implement when taking any red carpet-esque scenario by storm. I sincerely hadn't the faintest notion that my Lago di Como antics had been examined so closely in Italy and the U.S. Didn't people have other things to worry about? Like Dick Cheney anally raping them in their sleep or something? Fuck, it's certainly a fear *I* stressed out about *all the time* and we had three layers of security gates to protect me, plus a bodyguard stationed in front of my door whenever I was at my usual residence (I know for a fact Dick would never go to any other city in the U.S. apart from L.A. and New York—that thing you saw in D.C. was just an animatronic replica built by the fine folks at Halliburton; yes, I'm aware it would be difficult to differentiate one from the other).

Upon making my distinguished way into the hotel with all the aplomb of Grace Kelly and Audrey Hepburn's lovechild, I approached the front desk with my dignity seemingly intact. I wasn't going to let any sordid questions from the Italian media—themselves apart of a people more sordid than any other on this planet—affect my aura of calm, cool collectedness.

"Hi," I said to the twenty-something female employee at the reception desk. I don't usually take time to describe service people unless they're, like Fabrizio, men that I'm fucking. But it bears noting that this girl had long red hair that looked incongruous because it was pretty clear she was a natural black (there's not an ideal word for black-haired people like there is for brunette ones). My paranoia began to seize me. Had she changed her hair color solely to mirror that of Lindsay's? Was Lindsay the new queen bee—becoming so popular that her aesthetic zeitgeist had even reached Europe, a continent that's notoriously twenty years behind America pop culturally?

"*Signora*, how can I help you?" the little asshole chimed in, ruining my train of thought.

"Okay, first of all, it's *signorina*. And I'm here to see Bambi." That was the code name Britney was going by in this hotel—and yes, she blatantly ripped it off from Anna Scott in *Notting Hill*. She loves Julia you know, even though Julia is a notorious cunt that would sooner bite your head off with those giant chompers than smile at you with them for anything less than twenty-five million dollars (in 2004, that is—who knows what the price tag is now?).

"*Ho capito.*" She leaned in closer as she whispered, "She's in Room 1202." Britney later told me that she always demands Room 1202 even if a hotel doesn't have one because it signifies her date of birth. What a fucking cliché. It's like Lindsay naming her shitty leggings brand, 6126, "in honor of" Marilyn

Monroe—June 1, 1926 was her birthday, you know. And if you don't, you should because that date signifies, like, the inception of sexuality's existence. It wasn't Freud. I could kind of see Marilyn and Freud being a good sexual match for each other though. Just another case of two icons birthed in the wrong time frame in terms of not being permitted to cross paths (a.k.a. genitalia). Anyway, yeah right. Like Marilyn would feel "honored" by anything other than a motherfucking line of custom pill boxes and flasks. Leggings are just insulting.

In the elevator, I encountered an older, silver-haired gentleman who, without delay, sent a certain feeling toward my Agent Provocateur thong. It was, fittingly, right then that my real daddy decided to call me. Reflexively, I answered it with a coquettish, "Hi."

"Tate, where the hell are you right now? I'm this close to coming over to the boot myself to boot you right out of it."

"I'm gonna leave soon, okay? I'm just meeting up with Britney and Paris for a few more days and I'll be right back."

"We need to have a serious conversation about you doing something with your life. You can't be content to just live off the Carmichael money. You could at least pretend to want to start your own business."

"What? Like L.A.M.B. or some shit? No thank you. I'm not a pop star trying to parlay my way into the fashion world with my own clothing line."

"Tate, you don't have to do something *vacuous*. Maybe you want to focus on something of more…substance. Take a page from Lady Di's charity work."

"Ugh. Lady Di *died* horrifically, what does that tell you about doing charity work?"

I could overhear some minion type person in the background giving Daddy a heads up about a meeting in five minutes.

"I have to go. You're lucky this time. But when we speak next, my leniency is going to be completely worn thin. I want to hear you've come up with a plan."

The elevator halted. Neither the silver fox nor I had reached our desired floor. "Okayloveyoubye," I blurted quickly.

The silver fox glanced over at me with a smirk on his face.

"So you're American?" he offered as a lame conversation starter, sporting an accent I couldn't yet discern.

"With Mexican heritage." I like to play the card when it works to my advantage, what can I say? It's what Jews do, too.

"Mm, I see." He looked up at the ceiling of the elevator as it started to rattle and stall. "Well

Miss Mexican-American. It feels like we're stuck here for a moment."

I smiled. "You could just press the call button."

"I *could*…or we might take the time to…get to know one another better."

Considering all that had just happened to me vis-à-vis the condemnation I had received for my sexual decisions, I knew the sensible thing would have been to politely decline his none-too-demure innuendo. Be that as it may, you should know by now that the word "sensible" doesn't really fall into a socialite's vocabulary. So I let him put his hands on my waist and start to kiss me, and well, you can use your own imagination to figure out what happened from there.

Still only guessing that he might be Austrian (an ethnicity Paris and Britney continue to confuse for Australian), he was very thorough in his process, which is why we weren't finished when the elevator abruptly moved to the next floor about fifteen minutes later and the doors opened to the presence of five other guests waiting to board. Even though the silver fox was part of the equation, *I* was the one facing them, the one caught very literally with my panties down right at the moment of truth. And, you know, I'm not liable to waste a sex session, so I finished as the quintet stared on with a mix of confoundment and perverse enchantment. Based on their superannuated demographic (but not the hot kind that the silver fox was a part of), this could have likely been the first encounter they had with the concept of boning in quite a while. I was happy to refresh their memory as I concluded my whining moans and pulled my panties up. In thanks, I winked at the silver fox, whose name and nationality I would tragically never unearth. Some encounters are meant to be that way, I guess. I then walked past the judgmental geriatric mini mob and headed toward Britney's room as originally intended.

***

It took her forever to open the door. And when she did, her disheveled appearance—greasy hair tied back in a high bun, acne on blast and a Juicy Couture tracksuit with a ketchup stain on it (where the fuck did she get *ketchup?*)—made me further question what I was really doing here. I wasn't friends with Britney. I couldn't forge a bond just because we were both celebrities. It's like Madonna said in *Truth or Dare*, "I've found it weird for celebrities to assume a friendship with you because you're a celebrity, too! It can get kind of awkward." And that's when she put her hand in her mouth pantomiming the bulimia gag move in response to Kevin Costner's presence. Even though she said that, like, a really long time ago, it still holds true. On the one hand, only someone who has experienced fame can comprehend just how exhausting it is—all the effort and hours that go into looking this good, even when you're young. On the other, just about any asshole can become famous these days so it's sort of the same game of Russian roulette as it is for commoners when it comes to friendship-forging.

Nonetheless, the so-called "fame bond" is why I thought I could go through with this whole "Operation Britney" thing. But as I entered the room, strewn with clothes both comfort- and costume-oriented, I had to admit to myself that this was a bad idea, and that the only one who could really salvage what was left of this Italian sojourn was Paris. She's the person I went to all this trouble for—the reason why I took a chance on Britney in the first place. If I could just convince her that I was still the same on-brand person as before, and that I had merely been dealt a hand of bad luck these past few news cycles, she would come around again. She would help me ascend back to my rightful place as the third member of the troika that consisted of her and Nicole. Fucking *Nicole*. The two-faced cunt I thought was my friend because she led Britney to me. My alleged chance for social resuscitation. But no. What I would soon discover in early 2005, several months before the book's official release in November, was that she was really just using me as the basis for her main character, Chloe Parker, in her ghostwritten shitshow of a "novel," *The Truth About Diamonds*.

Chloe—again, based on "me"—is a coke-addled Nicole wannabe desperate to secure fame at any cost. Sounds more like Kim, but whatever.

Told from Nicole's perspective, she makes me sound like a goddamn charity case and a complete re re (a term that predates "RiRi," so she really should have known better than to give herself that nickname). Or maybe she was basing me on Carrie, the peripheral friend/hanger-on who will gossip to any tabloid rag or media outlet that will listen about her relationship to up-and-coming reality TV star Chloe. I still can't be sure, but the point is, she was definitely making a dig at me (or my "character," if you must) throughout the entire "novel." If you can really call something that features a series of her glossy photos in the middle of the narrative a bona fide book and not some trashy biography. Thank Tina Fey (I'm assuming she's the only person behind the below-mentioned show that knew who Nicole was) for redeeming her somewhat mildly by getting her a lead role on *Great News*. Which then got cancelled after just two seasons. I suppose *The Simple Life* will have to be Nicole's great TV accomplishment then. Much to her consternation (and hopefully constipation…because it's bad for losing weight).

Even so, *The Truth About Diamonds*, while no masterpiece in the vein of Zsa Zsa Gabor's *How To Catch A Man, How to Keep A Man, How to Get*

Rid of A Man, was at least better than Paris' '04 travesty, *Confessions of an Heiress*, and generated enough buzz to get the barely-there literati of L.A. talking. Some people (like Book Soup workers or whatever) even heralded her as the next Bret Easton Ellis. As if *that* is hard to achieve. Even Lindsay managed to eventually garner such an overused description of someone "edgy" when she starred in *The Canyons*, which Bret "wrote." Don't get me wrong, I love Bret, I even fucked him a few times when he was leaning less toward the gay side and I thought it might help get me in touch with his literary agent, but it's so fucking predictable whenever a Hollywood star comes out with a "post-modern" (or is it post-post-post-post-modern now?) book for critics to compare the work to Bret's. It's like, yeah, we can all write short sentences expressing disaffection. Watch: *I entered Britney's war-torn room. The war seemed to be the one between her manufactured self and what might have been left of her real self.*

There, facile. It's also what most of this narrative sounds like anyway, but I'm sure no one is going to draw parallels between me and Bret Easton Ellis because I never get fucking credit for anything. Back to *The Truth About Diamonds* though. For the first few days, people speculated it *had to be* about Kim Kardashian—who else would Richie make her basis so unfavorably on? Yet as you read through, it not only becomes pretty apparent that she's grafting most of her plot from *Uptown Girls* starring Brittany Murphy (which she freely and ironically name checks as a correlation), but also that she couldn't have possibly been talking about Kim—not if we're going on the waifishness of Chloe alone. The physical description, paired with my recent deluge of headlines centered around accusations of drug use and even prostitution to finagle said drugs (which definitely made Lindsay look angelic in contrast), suddenly turned everyone's attention to me, once again, for all the wrong reasons.

But before I get to how Nicole stabbed me in the back, I have to finish telling you about how Britney did. Beneath that guise of sweetness, let me tell you, there sure is a real cunt rag. As she started to haphazardly clear some items out of the way, a knock at the door interrupted my chance at establishing some kind of social momentum with her. Not even the opportunity to offer myself a drink as the standard greasing agent for what more antiquated people might call "the girl's gift of gab." I had no such gift at the moment, and I would be like an all-ages Hollywood nightclub (utterly undesirable to anyone worthwhile) if I didn't start entertaining Britney and proving my value. Fortune opted to shit on me once again upon revealing that the person at the door was a member of the hotel staff sent to inform Britney that there had been a complaint lodged against someone presumed to be visiting her room. As Britney let the details wash over her—nudity stemmed from dropped panties, etc.—I wondered if maybe I wasn't being *Punk'd*. For real though. *Punk'd* was very much a thing at that time, which is why during an interview Lindsay did with Jay Leno that year, he mockingly asked, "Does everyone just think they're being *Punk'd* now?" Lindsay essentially assented that this was the pervasive celebrity fear of the new millennium (ah, what a quaint phrase, looking back on it) and then tried to make a big deal about how she was friends with "a bunch of people on the show."

In Lindsay speak, this meant she had blown and/or fucked most of the production crew. In her mind, that meant a legitimate and lasting friendship. So yeah, in any case, I really thought it was finally my turn to partake of Ashton's orchestrated faux reality. How else could this terrible onslaught of bad luck be explained? I thought I had paid for my supposed sins by being smeared for my encounter with Fabrizio and subsequently "losing" Lindsay on this trip. The time alone with Paris wasn't worth what it meant to be ostracized by LickHo (that's my work-in-progress play on "Lilo") right now. And with her upcoming hosting gig for the VMAs, even more eyes were going to be on her, which meant a greater accumulation of power.

Resigned to accepting that this wasn't an episode of *Punk'd* at all, I stood there in a state of shock near the desk, which prominently displayed a pen and pad bearing the Four Seasons logo. The tools were beckoning me to write some sort of S.O.S. message (later, I would find out that Rihanna had inexplicably come into possession of the panicked note that read, "S.O.S please someone help me"). I was stock-still as Britney apologized profusely to the glorified hall monitor and promised that no such heinous incident would ever happen again. And, furthermore, that if she found out who it was from her entourage, she would fire them without hesitation. It was this last part of the promise that finally seemed "enough" for the chastising presence to leave.

As Britney closed the door and whipped around to face me, I felt like I could actually hear the chasm forming in the universe. It was a fissure that divided how my socialite life was supposed to go versus all the circumstances that conspired to defile it. Britney didn't say anything to me. She didn't attempt to accuse or condemn, which almost made it even worse than if she had just outrightly called me a whore.

Instead, she went about preparing herself to go to the venue, remarking, "Um, so maybe you wanna connect with Paris, she should be at the Hilton,

like, soon. Just ask for your tickets at the box office.
I got you a special reserved area."

"Thank you *so* much Brit," I said obsequiously,
the false delivery of my pandering even prompting
me to question my sincerity.

She didn't say anything, just put on her
pink sweatpants and an Ed Hardy t-shirt. After she
slipped into her Skechers (she got a lifetime supply
after doing that ad campaign and getting a settlement
from them during their legal battles of '02-'03), she
found it within herself to look at me. It was hard to
know how much my antics had sobered her high,
but it was the least glazed over I'd ever seen her
look. Yet that still didn't stop the muddling of words
as she told me, "Tate, I think you're walking a very
thin line right now. And I walk them all the time—
like literally and metamorphically. So from me to
you, you might wanna go to a Sex and Love Addicts
Amonymous meeting."

It was all I could do to keep my jaw from
dropping. And not just from her mispronunciations.
The impudence of Britney Spears, biggest nympho of
all-time, suggesting that I go to SLAA was surely
Punk'd material. She continued, "I go to meetings
pretty often, and they're super helpful. It's what
gave me the calm and serenity to start really opening
my heart to Kevin."

I wanted to vomit. I truly wanted to stick
my finger down my throat the way Madonna did

in *Truth or Dare* (as referenced before) in response to Kevin Costner saying "neat." It was a worse level of grossness. God, how could she have really let herself sink this low? Was the loss of Justin Timberlake *this* psychologically damaging to her? We had all seen Kevin prowling the clubs of Hollywood at one point or another, back when he was more commonly known as "Meat Pole." And, truth be told, most of us probably gave him the courtesy of rubbing up against us. It's just something every guy gets permission to do in the strange alternate universe of "Clubland." Where the rules of the "real world" don't tend to apply. I hadn't technically "met" Kevin or seen much of him in the club since he started up with Britney. But he was one of those dudes that you had already met long ago as a result of frequenting a particular scene.

Meanwhile, Britney went to the bathroom to do one more line (she, unlike Lindsay, had a true sense of etiquette about where coke should be done). It felt like an eternity before she returned, and when she did, she was wearing pink-tinted Chanel sunglasses which I imagined were on the back of the toilet seat along with some cellulite cream. As though she had never been absent from the room, she continued, "I think you seem like a nice person, but you've got a lot of issues to sort through before I would ever consider trusting you as part of my *inner* circle. You're lucky

Paris still even decided to show up. You two must go way back."

Before I could scream, "Yeah, as far back as Kevin went into your asshole last night," her assistant waltzed in to collect her. "We've gotta get to the car, Miss Brit. The venue is already reporting some sound feedback issues."

Britney rolled her eyes. "I fucking hate coming here. It's so ghetto." She sighed and turned back to me for one final instant—it was the last time I would see her in person before she got strapped to that gurney in '08 and truly understood what it was like to be shunned by the very people that brought you into the spotlight in the first place, that demanded you stand up to the pressures of constantly staying "relevant" (meaning: dance, monkey, dance). It wouldn't be until then that she called upon me as she did in '04. But by that time, I had zero interest in allying myself with her, or her, um, conservator. My ultimate goal has always been to get to Lindsay. To get my life back by destroying hers via the subtle subterfuge that can only come with money and connections.

Left alone in the room for a few minutes, I tried to mentally prepare myself for seeing Paris. I don't think I had gotten any real face time with her since the premiere party for the first season of *The Simple Life*. She had turned her entire backyard into a barn and hired an authentic washboard and banjo duo to play "Green Acres" on a loop for most of the night. In between, they also played their own rendition of 50 Cent's "In Da Club"—at Paris and Nicole's urging. That was right before Paris really did an about-face on me and started veering off toward Lindsay…when she wasn't treating Kim K like her maid. In fact, it was upon Paris' referral that Lindsay started "using" Kim. That's probably how Lindsay and Kim forged such a solid friendship (that is, until Kanye released the "Bound 2" video and Kim officially went A-list, shedding all her ties to the early and mid-00s other than Ye himself—and plastic surgery). Kim was Lindsay's stylist for fuck's sake. Which is definitely the reason why Lindsay always looked like a hybrid of an escaped Amish or Hasidic girl trying to "pass."

I texted Nicole in the car on the way to the Hilton in the vain hope of getting some sense of where Paris' headspace was at. She didn't respond. I guess she thought putting me in touch with Britney was enough of a favor to last me the rest of my life, and I'd gone and fucked up that "courtesy" anyway. Her lack of response wasn't totally a result of me being essentially blacklisted though. I would later find out that Nicole was solidifying her friendship with Lindsay back in L.A.—they were each getting infinity friendship tattoos on their inner thigh. This would be the beginning of a rapport forged entirely on an underlying hatred for Paris and an enduring love of cocaine and bulimia (I still can't believe that a butterfly catching net didn't descend upon them as a means of intervention when they appeared together looking like twigs in ball gowns). Nicole still liked to say she had an "inability to put on weight," but I knew the truth—and the truth was: the coke was making her throw up more than Amy Winehouse during any recording session "break." It was the same for Lindsay.

Without Nicole "Bitchy" to confide in about my apprehensions regarding seeing Paris again in an intimate setting for the first time in almost a year, I turned, once again, to Xanax. My only true and loyal friend (fuck whatever Billie Eilish says…Gen Z is so goddamn lily-livered about drugs anyway). I was starting to require the consumption of five capsules to feel anything and, for this particular meeting, I opted for seven. I've always been a tolerant person in every regard. It's my blessing *and* my curse. And so it was that I embarked to the Hilton slightly intoxicated, to put it lightly. But honestly, it wasn't anything that the troika of Paris, Nicole and Lindsay wouldn't be guilty of themselves all too soon—I forged the path as usual and never got my due, instead maligned for my lifestyle rather than revered and admired for it the way *they* were (and are all the more in the present haze of "noughties nostalgia"). I felt fine though, truly. Like just the right amount of edge had been taken off. Little did I know, the sight of Paris would sober me up real quick.

With her back turned to me and her usual signature tiara placed atop her freshly-combed blonde locks, I could feel a dryness in my mouth like I'd never known. Tinkerbell, her still-alive chihuahua during this renaissance period, scuttled right up to me, dogs having no discrimination or awareness when it comes to one's social standing. I reached out to her and picked her up, hoping that with the canine as armor, Paris would automatically treat me with respect. But respecting others had never been in her nature. And I can't say it had been in mine either, up until I was ostracized by everyone in my class.

She turned around slowly, first revealing her signature permanent stink eye, the squintier one that was lazy. *I will not be the one to speak first, I will not be the one to speak first*, I kept chanting to myself. I immediately broke my own protocol with, "Hey, long time no see," instantly surrendering more power to her.

"I guess it has been, hasn't it?" She reached for her diamond-accented brush and ran it through her hair in a state of absent-minded languor. "I've just been *so* busy, you know? *The Simple Life* is really kicking my ass."

Skipping the pleasantries, I countered, "Well, seems you haven't been too busy to hang out with Lindsay during your 'off' hours."

She stopped brushing her hair. "If you're going to act like a jealous boyfriend while I'm here, I can just get on a plane back to L.A. right now."

That shut me up. Tinkerbell squirmed uncomfortably in my arms, forcing me to let her go. She scurried back to Paris, who picked her up in delight. So far, this was just as awkward as I had expected it to be, and didn't really serve to assuage my concerns that our friendship was irreparably damaged.

At last, Paris showed some sign of humanity by admitting, "I know I've neglected you lately. But that's why I'm here now. I came without Lindsay, didn't I?"

"That's only because *she*, Queen Trashball, thinks *I'm* somehow trashier for banging a member of the help. Some very hot and good-in-bed help, I might add." With her guard faintly down thanks to my bluntness, Paris seemed to soften. The light pink silk tank top she was wearing paired with white boy-short underwear (Cameron Diaz, Nicole's future sister-in-law, had rendered them a "thing" post-*Charlie's Angels*) made her look almost angelic as she said, "Tate, you *are* trash. I'm sorry to have to tell you. And I've always overlooked it because I'm *such* a good friend. But, to be frank, I don't know if

I'm going to be able to anymore. You could really damage my reputation."

"What?!" I squeaked. "How am *I* trash, my family made their fortune off fabric!"

"Exactly. That's so lowbrow. And you don't even have any reality projects in the pipeline. Not even so much as a mall appearance. What are you doing with yourself? You can't expect to leech off of my star forever."

This was absolutely unheard of. I had been trying, everyone knew that, to land the right film role. I wasn't going to take just anything for the sake of remaining in the limelight. Didn't anyone have respect for how careful and selective I was being, or did they just want me to appear in slop like *Zoolander* (in a *cameo* role no less)? No fucking thank you. I had something none of these new-fangled, fame-whoring socialites had: integrity. God, it was like the Astors and the Vanderbilts never happened or something.

"'Damage your reputation'? 'Leech off of your star'? What the *fuck* are you talking about? I think you must have me mistaken for Nicole—they *still* have to introduce her as Lionel Richie's daughter in the opening to *The Simple Life*. Come on. She would be nothing without Lionel *or* you. So how am I suddenly worse? All I've ever done is be a good, loyal friend to your slutbag ass. And, lest you forget, the Carmichaels are worth the same amount of money as the Hiltons."

"Not these days. Everyone laughs at Gary's sad junior analyst job. And his even sadder affairs that scream mid-life crisis. I should probably tell you, even I've fucked him. He's actually pretty good. I might recommend him to Lindsay."

That was the absolute last straw for me. You can say a lot of offensive remarks to me and I can take it, but come for my daddy and I'll fucking kill you. Which is exactly what I set out to do when I took the champagne bottle out of the ice bucket on the table, broke it on the dresser and lunged at Paris with one of the shards in hand. My palm was bleeding and I didn't even notice as I cut her across the cheek—the side with that damned lazy eye. Tinkerbell was barking so loudly throughout that it had alerted one of Paris' security staff, a large Black man who was pretty hot. He came bursting into the room with a gun cocked. I might have known Paris would have a fetishizable bodyguard.

"Drop the bottle now!"

I obeyed, letting it fall out of my hand like Aaron Carter's sweaty palm. The bodyguard regarded me harshly before approaching slowly with the gun still aimed. "Have you calmed down?" he said with condescension. I never understand why men think that asking questions pertaining to a woman's level of calmness is going to ameliorate the mood or situation.

They should really have training courses for that sort of thing when men reach a certain age…like thirteen, when their peak assholery levels start to flourish and then last the rest of their lifetime.

Despite how irritated I was by the bodyguard's question, I returned, "Yes, I'm calm." Though my voice was noticeably shaky with the fear of what might happen next to my already fledgling public esteem. It then occurred to me that maybe I shouldn't mix speed with Xanax, because it definitely felt like the speed was winning out based on this burst of energy that got funneled into trying to kill Paris. How spectacularly I had fucked up my chance at insinuating myself back into the socialite life of glam*or* and adulation.

This much was very well confirmed when Italian authorities (ah what an oxymoron) escorted me out of the Hilton in handcuffs. But hey, I couldn't have asked for more media attention if I had actually paid off every little toad in the press to ensure my name and picture were in the tabloids and on the news 24/7 for the next two weeks.

Upon being summarily "returned" to my father's house—without any charges pressed by Paris—I had to face the ultimate firing squad: Gary. Gwen was, of course, in Palm Springs again with her increasingly crusty-looking lover. I don't know if she believed Edward might bequeath cash or property to her in his will or something, but it's what *I* wanted to believe. Because the thought of her truly enjoying rubbing up against that papery-thin, saggy skin was too much for me to add to the list of things to talk about at my therapist's. Which, by the way, Gary mandated that I go to five days a week instead of my usual three in the wake of my "jealousy-driven episode." That's what everyone was calling it. Jesus, they were all so small-minded. They couldn't see the big picture at all—that my true jealousy was over Lindsay. Paris was a pawn. She's always been a pawn, ask anyone who's climbed over her to get to the top (*cough cough*Kim). I let them all think that it was about Paris though—the better to lure Lindsay into a false sense of security with.

Excuse me, I have to check Firecrotch's Instagram story (from a fake account, obvi) update for a minute before I continue to finish up with 2004... Oh. Madrid. That bitch is just in Madrid, doing nothing, getting paid to eat. This is what she does now. She'll go wherever or promote whatever so long as someone is paying her. Anyway, back in still simpler times (for yes, I had no idea how much I would appreciate 2004 in retrospect), I was lounging out by the pool, drowning my sorrows in Xanax and "skinny bitch" margaritas (I trust my dietician, Anke, implicitly to make me low-cal alcoholic drinks even to this day). I wasn't depressed about the Paris "snafu," but over how the worst was yet to come.

Lindsay was about to host the MTV Movie Awards and everyone in Hollywood seemed to be talking about it just because she had gone on a media blitzkrieg with all the late-night hosts, from Leno to Letterman to O'Brien. She had the audacity to brag about the fact that she learned a hip hop choreography number in honor of *You Got Served* (dance movies were having such a moment back then, not to mention that hardly any music video got released without at least *one* scene of choreography, or the single would be doomed to fail). So there she was, like, playing up this false and *ridiculous* presentation of herself as "actress/singer/dancer." A fucking laugh. At best, her only talent was of the sexual variety, and I'm being generous in saying even that.

So yeah, I was drinking a lot more heavily, okay? I was very stressed and very upset about the state of the general public's taste. I couldn't even coast off the high of seeing myself in *The National Enquirer* anymore because they had moved on to headlines like "Stars With Eating Disorders," "Madonna Breaks Down" (how had I missed *The Re-Invention Tour*, by the way?) and "Sarah Jessica's Fury As Kim Says No More 'Sex.'" Good for her though. *Somebody* had to call out that SJP wasn't exactly an "angel" to work with. If for no other reason than because Matthew occasionally showed up to the set. What a baby-faced toolbag.

But it was hard to focus on commending Kim C.'s bravado when all I could think about was how I was no longer "scandalous" enough to be interesting in my current state of atrophy, and I definitely had no desire to bother with reaching out to Paris to express any form of contriteness whatsoever. Apparently, Daddy felt obliged to do that for me. I wouldn't have even known about it if Nicole wasn't the one to message me the intel on my Sidekick—which, by the way, *I* wasn't tasteless enough to get at the color version launch of it before the X Games. An "event" that *Complex* would, in hindsight, describe accurately and scathingly as "a carousel of B-list celebrities and reality stars, including Lindsay Lohan, Paris Hilton and Wilmer Valderrama, all showing up to claim their own Sidekick." If only people could have the benefit of *foresight* when it matters.

Anyway, my Sidekick was an ultra-custom design with a Lisa Frank-inspired pattern that Lisa herself helped create for me. I even flew to the fucking creepy-ass headquarters in Phoenix to pick it up, fitting in a little bit of spa time in the desert setting for my trouble. Of late, the only people to message me on it were Gary, Gwen, Bloomy (still sniffing around my vag even though I really wasn't interested, in spite of probably needing him more than ever) and my personal trainer, Tracy Anderson (she didn't think she was hot shit back then the way she does now). So even though Nicole's message was super condescending, it was a breath of fresh air: "Hiii, Paris wanted me to tell you that she'll forgive you the day you get more than two minutes of screen time on TV or in a movie. So probably never. xx Nicole."

Gary didn't notice my emotional upheaval at all, instead ignoring my blatant cries for help when I would say things like, "Well, I guess I'll go draw a bath to cut myself in." And while, yeah, I would never cause harm to my pristine body that way, he should have at least pretended to be concerned. A little acting goes a long way on the parenting front. That's why I think I'd make a great one. Meanwhile, I had no maternal shoulder to cry on as Gwen got her proverbial muffin buttered for weeks at a time now. She might as well not even have bothered claiming that B. Hills was where she lived as her full-time residence was with Edward at this point. My dad, ever the denialist, had his own escape from reality to tend to, leaving very minimal time for him to bother with asking how *I* was doing. How being a social leper was affecting *my* ability to live a happy, healthy and normal life.

Like a total loser more repugnant even than that fat girl Emma Gerber in *Mean Girls*, I sat by myself in my room on June 5th to watch Lindsay take the stage at the unquestionable zenith of her popularity. The crowd was eating up everything she said—even the dumbest of jokes (unlike the

way they didn't for Katy Perry at the 2017 VMAs)—
and every move she made. But while I was studying
it, I could only echo Ambular's sentiment as she
seethed, "Hello? Am I the only one who thought it
reeked?" It would be quite some time before the
masses caught up with me in my sane viewpoint of
the Freckled One though. Roughly two more years,
to be semi-exact. In the meantime, the way everyone
sucked on her flaccid dick was making my skin
crawl. I couldn't open up a magazine, listen to the
radio in my hot pink Mini Cooper or go on the
internet without being reminded of her in some
way.

I had to get out of America again when
December rolled around. Lindsay had released that
fucking horror of an album, *Speak*, and every time
I turned on the radio or the TV, "Rumors" seemed
to be playing. And yeah, I bought the thing—or I
had my assistant buy it. I needed to hear for myself
just what the extent of the badness was. The on-
the-noseness of "First" marking the *first* track on it
was made all the more cheeseball by Lindsay
"seductively" insisting, "I wanna come first" as a
not-so-subtle way of referring to her desire to achieve
orgasm before her bedroom companion went limp.
These factors alone quickly affirmed my suspicions
about *Speak*: it needed to shut the fuck up. Yet the
public went apeshit for it. I guess I have to keep
reminding myself that it was the anomalousness of

the era, when anyone pretty or of "it" status could put out a record. Fucking Paris would do the same thing in '06, though I have to say I'd take "Stars Are Blind" over "Rumors" in any scenario. But maybe Jessica Simpson is the one to truly blame for everything. She was the other talentless blonde who got reality TV off the ground (it aired months before *The Simple Life*, it bears noting). Before her, it was just the less accessible kitsch of *The Osbournes*.

I don't know why I tried to pinpoint the source of cultural bad taste anyway. It was Lindsay herself who said, in that damned "Drama Queen (That Girl)" single tailor-made for Radio Disney, "You don't need a high IQ to succeed at what you do." I could've sung it with a lot more conviction had I been cast in *Confessions of a Teenage Drama Queen*, but as you already know, I was not. And honestly, what kind of fucking terrible message is this to send to children, already looking for an easy way out as it is without getting justification from an unqualified-to-give-advice asshole like Lindsay?

Well, I knew just what to do to one-up them all—Paris, Lindsay, Nicole, Kim—the whole talentless quartet. It so happened that Mary-Kate had made a big deal announcement on December 9th about vowing that the Bangladeshi women sewing the tattered rags the duo was peddling back then (The Row ain't sold at Wal-Mart if you catch my drift) would be granted maternity leave. I know, how *fucking generous*, right? Anyway, it was a huge thing to people, and I was going to cash in on the humanitarian angle for myself by personally offering to go to the Bangladesh factory for Mary-Kate and Ashley to meet and greet with the preggo workers reaping the benefits of the new edict. Though, if you ask me, a lot of 'em would ultimately "suddenly" decide to give up their babies for the orphanage once they had enjoyed the luxe life of maternity vacay.

When I talked to Mary-Kate about it—you always have to talk to Mary-Kate, she's the one who understands the value of the Olsen brand more than Ashley's out-of-touch ass—she was completely delighted, and classily chose to not even mention my fallen-from-grace status with Paris and Nicole. She did, surprisingly, however, make mention of Kim K, who she had recently encountered at a record release party for Britney (nothing new, just *Greatest Hits: My Prerogative* featuring that overly Photoshopped into anorexic oblivion album cover). Clearly, I didn't get invited to that after our awkward exchange in Milan and her subsequent skittishness about my predilection for physical violence. She gets very delicate when the threat of a potential loose cannon coming near her enters the equation. Which is a bit hypocritical considering her own mammoth breakdown. But hey, I understand. We all get upset when we have to work hard instead of doing drugs. Pregnancy drove her over the edge too—no matter how much she claims she wanted to be a mom. No fucking pop star wants to be a mom, it's just what they do to anticipate for the time when they're finally day-old bread—which comes faster than Aaron Carter. Just ask Cher about how fast, she's the one relegated to "marvelous mentor" roles alongside people like Christina Aguilera (but to be fair, *Burlesque* was a masterpiece). And so, enter Motherhood, a ruse for the need to do something "more meaningful" with The Hours.

Ah yes, but back to Kim. She puzzlingly made positive mention of me to Mary-Kate. I would need to reach out to Khloé—the most approachable of the trio—about this and figure out the Kardashian angle for such a deliberately slipped compliment. There was no way Kim would "just happen" to say something nice about me without a motive. My guess: she was working on her breakaway (Kelly Clarkson's album had also just come out) from Paris, and somehow wanted to use me as a part of her carefully crafted chessboard maneuver. She was in the thick of "dating" Ray J, and that was elevating her status bit by bit—the sex tape being the culmination of her brand of "status." I couldn't worry about her motivations for speaking highly of me just yet though, I had to go to the doctor to get a slew of preemptive shots for my trip to the unfun part of India, but you best believe I was going to Goa afterward. This socialite doesn't travel all the way to bumfuck nowhere without at least getting one memorable party session in afterward.

At Dr. Montgomery's, who Paris had actually recommended to me a long time ago—when we were in junior high—I was relieved that he didn't bring up my current feud with the House of Hilton. Instead, he kept it super profesh after giving me a complimentary vaginal examination in spite of not being a gynecologist anymore and then writing me a prescription for all the drugs I wanted to take with me on the plane, and for the trip as a whole. He was a little younger than I usually like, somewhere in his late forties—and he miraculously still had all his hair, the perfect shade of jet black. His glowing tan and five o'clock shadow also made me overlook my usual preference for much older men (what, you thought Lana Del Rey had the monopoly before I did? I don't fucking think so), which is why I let him get a little inappropriate during his investigation into my nether regions, not flinching when he let his fingers linger just a little too long on my clitoris.

"So, you're going to India for Mary-Kate and Ashley's fashion line?"

"Yeah, I just wanna help them with this super important cause, you know? And I figure they've got a lot to deal with over here and I'm not especially busy right now, so, why not use my money and clout for something worthwhile?"

"Well, Ms. Carmichael, that's very admirable," he mused as he stared into my left eye with a shining light and held his stethoscope up to my right breast (placed nowhere near the heart, but okay). "I'd like to join you perhaps. It never hurts to have a medical professional on hand when you're traveling somewhere as dodgy as India. I'd be like your on-call doctor…on steroids. What do you say?"

"Um—" Mercifully, my Sidekick beeped at that moment and I glossed over his outrageous proposition by insisting, "I have to check this. It might be Mary-Kate."

How gross and presumptive some (all) men are. Like, what, I'm just gonna bow down to his offer because he's cute and a doctor? Absolutely not. As it turned out, the message was from Orlando, desperate to see me while he was in L.A. for the holidays. Him, I couldn't say no to.

Chapter 6: Goodbye Orlando, Hello Bangladesh

We met at Ivy (I always hated it when people said *the* Ivy). Because it was a place where we would be photographed in a non-obnoxious manner. Orlando was particularly well-dressed in a blue blazer with a shimmery finish, a white button-front shirt, black denim jeans and slip-on black loafers I recognized from the window display at Ermenegildo Zegna on Rodeo Drive. His slicked-back hair looked sexy-sleazy in that distinctly early 00s way I so sorely miss. In contrast to the manifold pieces of Orlando's ensemble, I wore a bright pink spaghetti strap dress that I, admittedly, got from Charlotte Russe during a moment of "slumming it" weakness. I was only at the mall for the purposes of seeing a fellow socialite (I won't throw her under the bus and embarrass her by naming names) do a book signing at the Barnes and Noble at Southcoast Plaza. And well, I got bored. So now here I was sporting an inferior frock, masked only by the genuine diamond tiara I threw on as a finishing touch—Paris isn't the only one who gets to monopolize it as her signature, okay?

Thankfully, Orlando isn't very discerning when it comes to knowing what's quality material and what's not, which was clear when he rose from his chair to caress my back and kiss me on the cheek without uttering anything about my plebeian garment. He waited for me to sit down before he did again as well, which I found rather sweet…almost like he was preparing me for the worst by being so nice.

"I've missed you, Tate. There, I said it. I know it's been months since we saw each other and I should've reached out to you sooner or, fuck, I should've just chased after you in the room that night, but I was upset. You wounded me—literally. You splashed the wine in my face 'just so,' and it really stung my eye, for days after. I think you can even see it in certain scenes. It looks like I'm repulsed by Eva Green. Which I guess I sort of was by the end. Goddamn beautiful women think they can be such cunts and get away with it because they're 'nice to look at.' Utter bollocks."

I arched my eyebrow. "Is that how you see *me?*"

"Of course not. I came all this way to talk to you. Touch you, I hope. I'm supposed to be in Kentucky shooting more scenes for *Elizabethtown* tomorrow, but I told Cameron I needed a week longer."

The waiter, an attractive twenty-something with long brown hair (think Johnny Depp in *21 Jump Street*) came up to our table to take our order. I immediately jumped in with, "I'll just have a flirtini." Stockton smirked at my request. That's what he said his name was later in the men's bathroom (I know, a life before all-gender bathrooms, how archaic!)

that I really and truly accidentally walked into only to stumble upon him at the urinal. He turned his head around and winked at me.

"I know what you're in here for." He zipped up his pants and removed a vial of coke from his pocket. I shrugged. No one I knew was super heavy into coke yet. That would reach its peak from 2006 to 2007. So yeah, once again, I was the "bad girl" who didn't get any "negative but positive" publicity for my antics. This means, of course, that I didn't say no when he gave me a bump of coke. It was so much purer during that time, I can still feel it coursing through me, energizing my very core. In the heat of the moment, I kissed Stockton for his kindness… just as another Ivy patron walked in. I couldn't have possibly recognized him as one of the most important agents at UTA, Matt Rice. Shit, he was a fucking *partner* at the agency, and a really valuable person to make a good impression on—the opposite of what I had just achieved with yet another surrender to ephemeral pleasure. And it just *had to* happen after an audition I thought I had done *really well* (that means performed really well sexually) for. An audition Teddy had gotten me after liaising with another agent at, that's right, UTA.

It was common knowledge that Matt was a notorious gossip queen (all straight men are), and I was certain the news of this incident would spread through the agency faster than Lindsay's rash of freckles every time she went out into the sun. Not to mention whatever actual rash she constantly seemed to require Cortisone cream for (I know for a fact she has a need for it because I saw *several* squeezed-out tubes in her medicine cabinet during the small potatoes era of my sabotage plan, back when I was clandestinely filling her face wash with sunless tanner. I guess you could say I took my inspo for these types of pranks from *The Parent Trap*).

Then there was the even worse problem (at least for any hope of me ever securing someone A-list to be "monogamous" with) of the "little" news item being picked up by the usual gossip rags and TV segments, making 'lando feel like a retrospective cuckold. Before he was made aware of my very public indiscretion, however, I was able to return to the table as though nothing had happened. And even when Stockton (who, by the way, weirdly wasn't actually *from* Stockton) reemerged carrying my much-needed flirtini, I was able to sustain my cool, never letting on that my lips had been pressed against his just minutes earlier. If only people really could see how good my acting is. But no, I'm forever relegated to the cheese of that damned Juicy Fruit commercial (I still have nightmares about the white tennis shoes I had to wear). Stockton, on the other hand, looked visibly wounded by my callous air. Well, it's as Blair Waldorf ripped me off by saying on *Gossip Girl* (I know Stephanie Savage overheard me scream this signature phrase at a party): "You have to be cold to be queen." Except I wasn't. Lindsay was.

But the firmness of the crown on her head was already starting to teeter as *Herbie: Fully Loaded* went into production. Ah, I still smile at what an unfortunate title that was for her lifestyle at that point. What most don't know, and what I'm about to reveal now, is that *I* was the one largely responsible for the sudden shift in her trajectory. Sure, I couldn't have gotten her to go down the self-destructive road she would never turn back from if she wasn't already of that persuasion. And if I hadn't perfectly timed my December trip to Bangladesh to avoid any accusation or trace of culpability, I might have eventually been implicated. That my path would never cross with Lindsay's—up until that night at *Speed-the-Plow*, I had never come face to face with my nemesis—also made my alibi ironclad.

That little cunt might have gotten one last whored-out public appearance in before 2004 was over when she hosted MTV's Iced Out New Year's Eve—the sight of her next to Ja Rule still remains incongruous, but then, they *are* both New York trash—but I would have the first laugh in 2005. Oh wait, I'm still at the table scene at Ivy with Orlando, dealing with the inevitable aftermath of my Stockton cocaine kiss indiscretion. That's what *In Touch* would label the headline: "Cocaine Kiss." Sucking down my flirtini like medicine, I told Orlando, "Look, I don't think this thing between us—whatever it is—well, I just don't think I have time for it right now. My flight to India is literally tonight."

"Why don't I come with you?"

"Because this is a personal mission."

"You mean you want all the media attention for yourself."

I rolled my eyes. Actors are so dramatic. I guess that's why they have to channel all their natural predilections for drama into acting as a career. "Whatever Orlando, if that's what you wanna believe, then that's what you'll believe. I just know that what we had in Portofino was a one-off. You basically treat me like shit and tell me I'm an asshole all the time, and I don't need that. This is an era of female empowerment. Condoleezza Rice is about to be sworn in as Secretary of State, for fuck's sake!"

And as yet another paparazzo's camera clicked and recorded away, getting all the details they would need to spin it however they wanted, I, once again, walked out on Orlando. And it's a decision I never regret, especially every time I think about him with Katy Perry. Oof. It's almost more disgusting than my immortalized white tennis shoes in the Juicy Fruit commercial.

That night, after I kissed Daddy on the mouth goodbye (he was way more supportive of this trip than the Italy one because it was humanitarian), I emotionally prepared myself for all the hideous women I was about to bear witness to in Bangladesh. Usually, all the women I knew tended to be hideous on the inside. And that was fine because at least they weren't an eyesore to look at. When the Towncar dropped me to the tarmac where my private jet was waiting, I almost didn't even feel like taking the Ambien I brought with me, that's how fucking exhausted I was from, like, life. That, and putting my "Operation: Take Down Lindsay" henchmen in place. It consisted of five very specific people, ranging from chefs to personal assistants.

There was Kiki Roberts, Hilary Duff's right-hand woman; Omar Hanteman, one of Nicole Richie's barrage of makeup artists (believe it or not, her eyes look even bulgier without at least two hours of intensive off-setting makeup application); Darcy Renfraux, Paris' personal chef and the head chef at one of Lindsay's favorite restaurants, Koi ("Japanese heaven on North La Cienega" as Nicole would call it); Oriana D'Annuncio, a well-connected nightclub owner primarily well-connected for being Italian (and therefore also easily bribable); and, finally, Wilmer Valderrama himself. He, more than anyone, had the most motive for assisting me in the gradually mounting collective L.A. vendetta against Lindsay that would eventually chase her out, pathetically fleeing to Europe/the

United Arab Emirates as her fortress from our contempt.

Like a lot of girls in my league—of my caliber, we can call it—I'd fucked around with Wilmer when *That '70s Show* was still on. He was, like, as close as you could get to fucking someone ethnic without it being a Black guy. Which was unheard of "back then." Kim was the one who would change that whole game later on with Ray J. Except the stills of her facial expressions from that sex tape really don't make Black dick look all that palatable. Any who, he was already starting to hate Lindsay when they were at their peak relationship moment in 2004, and she was essentially denying their love to people like David Letterman because she wasn't eighteen yet and it would've been "rape" or something in the eyes of the law. Still, how do you think that made Wilmer feel, huh? Constantly being denied the pleasure of having his beloved actually admit that they were together? It was pretty goddamn demoralizing for him, which is why I swooped in one night at a standard private party at The Standard in West Hollywood (don't listen to anyone who says it's The Standard in Hollywood— the West makes all the difference, just as it did in Kim's vagina). By planting his ears with little sound bites like, "God, if you were my boyfriend, I would shout it to the mountaintops—I don't get how she could deny it so effortlessly on TV like that all the time," I quickly got into Wilmer's good graces, followed by his very good sheets. They were, like, the nicest I've ever felt. Crimson silk, as only a true freak would have.

From there, it wasn't too difficult to wrap him firmly around my bony finger. And he confessed plenty to me about Lindsay's numerous weaknesses. For instance, she would never say no to drugs if offered in a social setting. "At first, I thought she really liked them," Wilmer explained. "But when we were alone together, she would never do a line. Then when I delved deeper into the reason why she would never do it when it was just me, she got into this thing about how, her whole life, she's been treated like a child and she doesn't want people to see her that way anymore. She wants to prove how 'adult' she is by doing rails with anyone who offers."

With this information in mind, I put my soldiers in place. Paris was going to have her annual holiday party while I was away. It goes without saying that I wasn't invited. But that was all the better for my purposes. Again, a lack of presence meant blamelessness. So I got Darcy to agree to pay the cater waiters to lace all drinks presented to Lindsay with MDMA. The desired effect, of course, was to prove just how whorish her underlying persona truly was. And the only thing Paris hated more than pennies (I know you read that as penises) was female competition of any kind. That's why Nicole was her bestie for so long until she lost the weight—because she was far dowdier. Thus, with Lindsay on her sluttiest behavior, it was just a matter of time before the Houses Hilton and Lohan came to blows.

Reports from Darcy and Omar, who would spend hours doing Nicole's makeup specifically so that it would start running if she got even remotely sweaty (back then, setting spray wasn't as much of a thing) for that optimal blackened under-eye effect, were trickling in about a week after I had arrived in Bangladesh. But Christ, a week felt like about two years in the "nicest" hotel there, Le Méridien Dhaka. It was barely two hundred dollars a night if that gives you any indication of how "luxe" it was. And even though I'd only been over to the Olsens' factory just once during the week, I had to take three baths a day to cleanse myself of the experience. Poor people really are the scourge of the Earth. Like, what purpose do they serve except to make rich people feel super bad about themselves for no reason? Like, God, sorry I wasn't born under more ill-favored circumstances. How is it my fucking fault?

Anyway, I got the requisite publicity photos it would take to prove I was there and that I semi-cared, therefore that the Olsens semi-cared. Still, I had to serve two weeks in that hell hole to prove that I had *really* invested the appropriate amount of hours in showing gratitude for the work these preggo women were doing. Instead, what I actually did was mainly stay in my hotel room and order rent boys. Though I've got to say, the Indian flavor has never really been for me unless we're talking food—and that's only if I feel like getting it up to engage in bulimia. *That*, let me tell you, is becoming much rarer these days. But I don't want to think about how much older and less resilient my throat has gotten. The one thing I will say for Indian men is that they are very, very tender. I've never been caressed and kissed with such gentility in my life. It's almost like they see a piece of God in women or something. So essentially the opposite of how American men see us.

On my second to last day in BANGladesh, I had developed preferential treatment for one rent boy in particular. His name was Vihaan, and he had skin the color of milk chocolate, with the eyes to match. His long lashes would bat against my cheek and tickle me, which I think was what I liked best about spending the night with him. He had luscious black hair that I loved running my fingers through as well. Best of all, he had an accent that didn't sound too Indian. You know what I mean? Like that accent is usually pretty annoying, but he sounded more British because his mom was. She abandoned him when he was seven years old, but before then, she had shuffled him back and forth between Bangladesh and London, where she was sought after as a high-class call girl—hence the apple not falling far from the tree. She decided to abandon him in Bangladesh when she found a more reliable male cash cow, the kind that could "legitimize" her and take her off the streets by making her his mistress. It was such a glamorous, filled-with-intrigue story that I had to write it down on the hotel's pad of paper in the middle of the night after Vihaan had finished fucking me for about three hours. Maybe I could pitch it to Fox Searchlight or something when I got back.

Then that thought—*going back*—hit me with the full weight of its implications. It suddenly didn't sound so appealing, sending a shiver up my spine. What was the point of returning when no one cared about me enough to photograph me unless it was to smear my character? By now, the "Cocaine Kiss" story was all over the news, and had already prompted my father to call me to express his continued disappointment in my life choices. I claimed to be super sorry and that nothing like that would ever happen again so that he would refill my bank account with another few thousand.

"How else am I supposed to get out of India?" I reasoned. Luckily, he didn't come back at me with some snarky line like, "Fly coach."

That I had this "charity work" still going for me also served to soften the blow, as my father would cling to anything "positive" about me to sustain his high level of denial about my "lack of direction." As I was saying though, I really didn't want to go back to L.A. I was clearly losing my mind (and sense of self) if my preference was for Bangladesh and Vihaan. So instead of confessing the truth to anyone, I called up Mary-Kate and told her there was still more "interfacing" to do at the factory. She was both extremely surprised and pleased by my enthusiasm.

"This is fantastic, Tate. I never would have thought you would take such an interest in the manufacturing side of our clothing line."

"Manufacturing" my ass. A euphemism for sweatshop if ever there was one. Nonetheless, instead of telling her what I really thought of the "manufacturing side" of her business, I simply returned, "It's been so eye-opening, and I feel like I'm really connecting with these women." Not only would my extended stay elevate my stature in the eyes of the Olsens, but it would also give me more time with Vihaan. See? I was doing the foreign guy thing well before Lindsay started shacking up with that Russian devil Egor Tarabasov. And what can I say? There's just something really restorative to the female psyche about good sex.

I remained in Bangladesh through New Year's Day. The last thing I wanted to be reminded of was Lindsay lapping up the spotlight in Times

Square. But at least I had helped to forge the schism between her and Paris at that holiday party. She reportedly flung herself at Nick Carter, who, even though Paris wasn't very interested in him anymore, still fell under the column of: Breaking the Girl Code. The one that stipulates you can never pursue a guy your friend has boned in the past. Even if that friend claims she "so doesn't care." Of course she does.

What's more, Lindsay had already fucked Aaron, and it's just really skeevy when a girl tries to go for an ex's brother. Nick was equally as horrified as everyone else when Lindsay sidled up to him in a corner and spilled most of her champagne on his brand-new Abercrombie & Fitch tee as she attempted to plant a wet kiss on his mouth. The image makes me cringe just thinking about it. Like, I truly could feel the embarrassment on her behalf. And yet, there was still more work to be done—that was one vehement New Year's resolution I had made after toasting Vihaan with some palm wine he had brought for us to celebrate the end of 2004. So far, 2005 was looking to be a *much* better year for me.

While some might have felt that 2005 got off to a slow start (what do people expect though? Only bad things—like Trump's inauguration—happen right away when a new year commences), there was one major event that signaled a shift in Lindsay's tide of fortune. On January 5th, a team of scientists that no one remembers the name of discovered the largest dwarf planet, Eris. Eris, heiress—get it? Ignoring the unpleasant word, "dwarf," that meant this would be the year of the heiress, not the shitty teen queen film star. That we would dwarf the bitch who never should have overshadowed us in the first place. Because we all know it's money, not talent, that makes the world go round. Whether this meant fortunes would improve for me or Paris, I didn't care, just as long as it wasn't Lindsay.

Things were already starting to look brighter when I arrived home to find that Daddy had placed my invitation to the 62nd Annual Golden Globe Awards on my bed. He probably wanted it to be a consolation to make me forget that he wasn't there when I first got back from Bangladesh, only telling me at the last minute that he had gone to New York "on business." I knew this really meant he had found someone of the mistress variety to take on a trip. Gwen was, in the meantime, still languishing in Palm Springs with Edward under that same old guise of "getting treatments." All the better for me though. At my age, I really didn't need my parents around cramping my style.

The awards were to be at the Beverly Hilton as usual. Point one for Paris already. Of all the films nominated, I had seen just two—arguably the saddest, most dramatic ones—*Eternal Sunshine of the Spotless Mind* and *Closer*. And when I say they were sad, I mean in terms of, like, how fucking pathetic people are when they pretend to care about another person, even though it's always actually about them and their precious ego. God, it's so obvious. I should just be a psychiatrist, but that would mean working.

Even if I hadn't seen most of the movies the awards were honoring (who does, really?), I was pretty excited about it. I just knew that the former was going to win for how unique and innovative it was (you know, by Hollywood standards). And as for *Closer*, well, I loved it of course, but I was faintly pained (as I'm sure Britney was too) that Julia Roberts wasn't even acknowledged in the category of Best Actress in a Motion Picture - Drama. She was pushing forty at that point, sure, but did they have to be so ageist against my favorite living legend? And don't even get me started on what a boss she is in *Mystic Pizza*. I watched that movie so much as a child I made my mother take me to Connecticut to experience the film IRL. Needless to say, I fucking hated that town. What a snore. And the pizza, well, I've had better at Mozza on Melrose.

In preparation for the event, I began getting facials twice a week for optimal porelessness and went on the hunt for the perfect dress. I had been leaning toward Rifat Özbek because I felt everyone else would be sporting Prada or Cavalli or McQueen. Also, no one else would dare to do something "ethnically-inspired" what with everyone persisting in being little pussies in the era of Bush. They were all still very wrapped up in the "trashy-chic" look personified by Paris on *The Simple Life*'s first season and Christina Aguilera during any publicity from the "Lady Marmalade"/*Stripped* period. I, on the other hand, would have to march to the beat of my own drum as per usual, setting sartorial trends that people weren't even aware subliminally affected their subsequent decision-making.

At a boutique on Sunset one day, while I was in the thick of narrowing down my final contenders for accessories, I ran into Paris and Nicole for the first time since the Milan incident all the way back in May of the previous year. It was somewhat unexpected in that rumors of Paris and Nicole's falling out were already running rampant well before *The Simple Life*'s final season in 2007, so I was under the impression that they would want to enjoy a sabbatical from one another whenever they were off-camera. Choosing to take the high road for this unplanned confrontation, I stared Paris right in the lazy eye. Rather than look ashamed or afraid, I smiled at them and said, "Well if it isn't the Midwest's favorite duo."

Nicole rolled her eyes as Paris hugged me and kissed me on the cheek. "Oh Tate, your sense of humor never changes." And just like that, her fake nicety felt natural all over again. Nicole, forced to emulate Paris' behavior for the time being (that is, until she allied more intensely with Lindsay and the Kardashians), mimicked the gesture of kissing me on the cheek. I would definitely need to have my facialist come over to decontaminate me after *this* outing.

"Are you prepping for the Golden Globes?" Paris asked, all faux interested, as if she didn't know damn well that everyone in town was getting ready for the Golden Globes. Trying not to look directly at her permanent squint, it was really difficult for me to understand why I would ever seek her approval. She was a glorified stripper, except most strippers wore better shoes than she did. Even so, she remained the primary holder of socialite power, and I had to defer to her.

So instead of mocking her for asking me such a "filler" question, I answered chirpily, "Yeah,

I'm just picking up a few custom pieces to go with my dress."

"Oh? Who's the designer?"

I *tsk*ed at her as I wagged my index finger and said, "Uh uh uh, you know I can't reveal that until the red carpet."

"Come on, Tate. I'm your oldest friend. You can trust me."

What a goddamn delusionoid. Pretending nothing had happened between us at the Milan Hilton. But "in [socialite] world, all fighting had to be sneaky." And, amended *Mean Girls* platitude or not, it was true. So I took the bait from her, working it to my utmost advantage.

"Well, maybe I could show rather than tell. Why don't you come over later?" I glanced over at Nicole and added cursorily, "You too, Nicole."

Paris and Nicole exchanged a brief look, one that must have telepathically communicated their accord since Paris responded with, "Sure. Do you mind if we bring Kim? She can carry our garment bags."

Without skipping a beat, I demanded, "What about Lindsay?"

Paris and Nicole eyed each other once again. Paris then shook her head. Nicole spoke for both of them by explaining, "I don't think so. She's been acting super weird lately. And by that I mean you can't put drugs of any kind out in front of her without them disappearing."

I suppressed the massive grin I wanted to allow to spread across my face. Playing it ever so cool (again, a testament to how I was born to be the actress that Lindsay never could be), I replied glibly, "That's a shame."

At that moment, the salesgirl, a teen-looking waif with a generic face and a floral-print romper, scampered over to us to present me with the jewelry and headbands I had selected (I could always return what I didn't want, I reasoned when I noticed how massive the pile looked in her twiggish arms). "Here you go Miss Carmichael!" she needlessly shouted. Noticing Paris and Nicole for the first time, she gushed, "Oh my God, you two are so funny on *The Simple Life*. I still watch it even though all my friends say I should give up and start watching *Medium*."

Nicole appeared as though she was about to turn green, while Paris merely seemed constipated in her irritation. Then again, she always looks a bit constipated. "Um, gee, that's really nice of you," Paris said in return. "Do you want, like, an autograph or something?"

The shopgirl beamed and (again) shouted, "Sure!"

Nicole sneered, somehow knowing what sort of "personalized message" was to come. Paris encouraged, "Got a piece of paper? Maybe the receipt roll from the register?"

The girl perked up at the suggestion. "Yeah, one sec."

She came bounding back like a Saint Bernard with the suggested receipt roll and a blue ballpoint pen in hand. "Here!"

Paris simpered, taking the materials from the unsuspecting youth and writing something that would undoubtedly either haunt the girl for the rest of her life or propel her to do something amazing with her future. The note read:

Dear Shopgirl Who Will Never Amount to Anything Other Than Having a Movie Named After Her,

You're even more generic than Claire Danes.
Love, Paris

She handed the paper and pen back to her and added, "You won't know what *Shopgirl* is until October, but I can promise the comparison is spot-on." She then turned back to me and said, "We'll see you at your place later. 7:30?"

I nodded. "Yeah, see you then."

The girl, noticeably pallid from this entire ordeal, asked me feebly, "Are you paying with cash or card?"

"Card."

***

Driving home in my Cadillac DeVille (I was such a bad bitch for driving it for most of that year), I reflected on how cunty Paris was. The one time I ever sided with Lindsay, in fact, was in 2006, when she got caught by TMZ on camera saying the bald-faced truth: "Paris is a cunt."

The thing was, I never remembered her being quite *such* an asshole. Something had changed her in the past year. Maybe it was the twenty-four-hour surveillance of being on reality TV that was taking a toll on her patience. Or maybe it was that she could somehow sniff in the air the sea change that was to come with the ascendance of Kim. At the same time, it could have just been that all the fame and the money had finally gone to her very small head, now made big by unadulterated ego.

The detriments of getting everything you want all the time can weaken your perception of reality, therefore make you vulnerable to your enemies. And I was definitely fast becoming an enemy. For Paris was to be my pawn in crippling Lindsay to the point of total disuse. I was going to turn her filmography into the laughingstock of Hollywood if it was the last thing I did. And being that she had already signed on for *Herbie: Fully Loaded*, most of what I needed to happen next would take care of itself. Rumors were already spreading rampantly that she was out of control—and Wilmer was only fanning the fire(crotch). In the interim, though, I would need to savor my Golden Globes moment of glory. Feeling once again like Cher in *Clueless*, I began setting the mood of my house the second I got back from Sunset. Paris and Nicole hadn't been over in a goddamn minute, and I needed to play up the interior decor's opulence as much as possible.

To do this, I asked our housekeeper, Juanjo, to clean up a bit. My mother was the one who insisted on hiring him, even though, truth be told, I really feel a female could have gotten the job done better. It was Gwen's contrived way of appearing progressive for hiring a man to do a woman's job. That, and she occasionally fucked Juanjo because he was pretty hot, and also only thirty-three—real young, by standards for men.

Juanjo spent about an hour "sprucing things up," as he called it with a faint lisp. But when I went through the main room (where we would be conducting our "affairs") to give it a once-over, it appeared as though he had done jack shit. That's what you get when your mother employs a glorified rent boy as the head of your housekeeping staff. Fearing for Paris and Nicole's imminent brutal assessment of the state of our house, I decided that desperate times called for desperate measures— which is why I turned to my next-door neighbor, Val Kilmer, to ask for use of his cleaning lady the way you might ask for a cup of sugar in the old days or whatever.

Val and I had a brief dalliance back when I was sixteen and he was still coming off the high of *Batman Forever*. He hadn't yet made that shitty movie about being a blind guy desperate to be loved by any woman who could overlook his defect, *At First Sight*. I never let him fuck me, though it wasn't for a lack of him trying. I did let him do some extensive sucking on my tits at one of his parties before my dad walked in on us and banned me from ever going over there again. But that was before I turned eighteen. He couldn't stop me from going over there now.

When Val opened the door (he was really humble that way, never letting his servants do these tasks for him), the look on his face mirrored the kind you might see on an unsuspecting bachelor when they wheel out a birthday cake and a stripper pops out.

"Tate?"

"Yep, it's me. In the flesh," I winked.

"What are you doing here?"

I shrugged. "Need a favor, of course."

He motioned for me to come inside. I obeyed.

Not much had changed at old Val's. Oops, maybe calling him old at that point was wrong. He was, at the time, just forty-six. And Clooney still gets away with being labeled as hopelessly eligible (even if he is married to that uppity know-it-all, Amal), so why shouldn't Val? So what if he's "beefed up" of late (and also can't talk, which is maybe some kind of misdirected karma for playing a blind guy in *At First Sight*). It didn't take long for him to lead me through the overly mahogany corridor that spilled out into his living room, bedecked with the heads of a lot of animals that he didn't kill. It was the aesthetic of someone trying to come across as way butcher than they actually were.

"Do you want a drink or something?" he asked in earnest.

"Not really, Val. I don't wanna make a whole 'thing' of this. I just need to borrow your cleaning woman—I'll pay you for it."

Crushed by my lack of interest in sticking around (so he could *stick* it in), he pouted. "Lupe is *very* busy today. I don't know if I can spare her..." His eyes perked up. "Unless..."

I knew what was coming. "Unless what?"

"You give me a blow job."

I ran my hand through my hair, thinking I might as well just call somebody out of the phone book (that's right, the phone book) or something. You know, rather than once again prostrating (there's a reason that word sounds like "prostituting") myself to a white male celebrity. Except, that wouldn't be "in my nature." Plus, a blow job actually takes me way less time than using the telephone the way *I* do it. Seriously, I can make a guy explode in under thirty seconds with my technique. So I consented to the "deal," instructing him to unzip and sit down on his taupe leather couch and relax.

True to form, it only took him about twenty seconds to splooge, after which I wiped my mouth with the back of my arm only to find that a debonair reporter (working for what I can only assume was some rag called *Outdated and Irrelevant Magazine*) had shown up to interview Val about his role in Shane Black's *Kiss Kiss Bang Bang*.

"Mr. Kilmer…is this a bad time?"

Val zipped up his pants and exhaled. "Not at all. It's the best possible time." The description of this introduction would, naturally, find its way into the opening paragraph of the piece, which, yes, called me out by name… Well, I might have had a hand in that. I didn't want to prevent Jonathan (that was the journalist's name) from finding success in his field, so I allowed it.

True to his word, Val "gave" me Lupe for a few hours. The both of us couldn't get out of Val's atrociously-decorated abode fast enough. It seemed Lupe was more comfortable in my environment as I got her to clean my house so well that day (it was almost as though she felt I had given *her* a BJ by proxy) that Paris asked me if she could hire whoever our housekeeper was. But my recommendations, along with my name, would once again be associated with "whore" in the months leading up to the release of Val's film in October.

After exiting from the house that always seemed to find me walked in on doing something sexually illicit, I was able to put on the perfect casual-cool, "I'm just lounging around" outfit. This turned out to be a white Juicy Couture tracksuit with the waist cut extra inappropriately low and the hoodie pulled up over my recently blown-out hair. I added some Uggs for good measure and then plopped down on my bed to wait for the trio of skanks to arrive. Lupe came up about two hours later to tell me she was done and that she thought she saw a pink convertible pull up in the driveway.

No doubt about it: Paris was back on my premises. As I peered out my window, I could see that she had also decided to bring that damned chihuahua, Tinkerbell (who, yes, I did ultimately have to kill). And, true to what they had promised me at the boutique on Sunset, Kim was carrying their garment bags. She really did look like such a different person back then—partially because she was so much more concerned with being the one to please than the one to *be* pleased.

Flouncing into the entryway through the door that Lupe, in her incompetence, had left ajar as though she had been coming over every day for the past year, Paris exclaimed, "Bitch, where are you?"

I took my time about descending the stairs. The last thing I wanted was for them to think I was eager. They made me wait this long, I could make them wait a little longer to see my angelic-looking ass in that sick tracksuit.

When I got downstairs, they were vacantly thumbing through magazines, with Nicole particularly interested in a Diane Lane interview from *InStyle*. "Like, how does she never age? Seriously. I want to look like her now and I'm a bajillion years younger." It was true, somehow Diane Lane could do whatever she wanted as a result of always looking exactly the same, especially after *Under the Tuscan Sun* came out. And even though she mistakenly chose to follow that up with the terrible one-two punch of *Fierce People* and *Must Love Dogs* at the start of '05, she was bangable nonetheless. That's all that matters in Hollywood, in case you haven't figured it out by now.

Kim certainly had, working her way up in the world after styling for Brandy and thereby ingratiating her way into the heart (or rather, bedroom) of her brother, Ray J. It really is a marvel still when I look back on it, the way Kim managed to crawl out from under Paris' oppressive clutches. That sort of thing just doesn't happen in this town, so in that regard, I respect Kim for really pulling herself up by the bootstraps (bra straps?) to become what she is today: the queen bee whore reigning over them all. Making everyone who stepped on her along the way to her ascension to the throne feel utterly stupid for treating her as they did. Back in January of 2005 though, she remained very much Paris' throw pillow.

Nicole finally looked up from her magazine long enough to notice me and declare, "Well, it's about fucking time."

I smiled. "I could say the same to you."

Paris smirked as she twirled her hair and cradled Tinkerbell in one arm. "Are you ready to show us your *look*?"

I quipped, "I'll show you mine if you show me yours." And with that cliché, we returned to being "besties"—at least for the month of January. It was too soon to say if we could sustain this almost *Crossroads*-like near-slumber party we were having. Knowing these bitches, my guess was already a *fuck no*. But I was enjoying it while it lasted.

The hours spent changing in and out of different permutations of our Golden Globe costumes were ones of pure, non-catty joy. Except for the times when Paris and Nicole blatantly snickered at how bad Kim looked in the white girl outfits they pointedly selected for her. The dumb cunts really had no foresight about how much the tide would turn against the skinny bitch physique in the impending years.

By the time we were done with our full-scale fashion show, it was almost 11:30, prime "going out" time in clubland. It was Nicole who demanded that we show our faces at Hyde, a nightclub I look back on as being insanely cramped and cheesy. But then, I guess the point was for everyone to be as cramped as possible so that the creepy DJ could watch scantily-clad girls rub up against each other and conveniently hide his erection behind the partition of the booth.

Somewhere in the back of my mind, I intuited that going out with the three of them would be a bad idea, that it would somehow result in a tragedy of the humiliating variety. I just didn't know that said tragedy would, once again, befall *me*. Even so, you ignore intuition when you suddenly feel like you're back on the inside again.

***

Hyde was packed to the gills, and it was when I saw DJ AM spinning behind the booth that I realized why Nicole was so gung-ho about going there. Paris looked a little "heart-eyed" herself, but she wouldn't bang Goldstein until one of her especial low points: 2007. It only took about ten minutes for Nicole to sidle up to Adam at the booth and start flailing and writhing about so that her sorry excuse for tits bombarded him at every angle. It wasn't exactly a graceful move, but it was highly effective. I looked over at Paris, who had found a rando to ally herself with, and then Kim, who pretended not to see me when I glanced over at her. Fucking cunt rag. In my strapless, shimmering pale-blue bodycon, I tried my best to move through the crowd in matching stilettos. It was not a prosperous endeavor, as I tripped right into the arms of the sleaziest possible person, Joel Madden. Everyone knew he had been dating Hilary Duff—whatever "dating" means when you have to keep it a secret because she's underage, Wilmer and Lindsay-style. I, however, was not privy to this info as of yet, thanks to being on the outs with everyone for so long and then being literally on the outs of L.A. by going to Bangladesh. So when he took me in his arms to escort me off the dance floor, I pushed aside all the terrible Good Charlotte songs I could hear in my head when I looked at him. I took it as a rare act of chivalry. And that's why I let him lead me even farther off the dance floor into the bathroom. Always the fucking bathroom with me, it's my kryptonite of tableaus.

Before I knew what was happening, we were going at it in one of the stalls—like in that Chemical Brothers video, you know the one. If you don't, I probably wouldn't hang out with you. Not that I would anyway, because I make the stories and you just read about them. In any event, Kim was the one to basically pry open the stall to make sure it was me in there so she could take a picture and video of the whole event. She was always a social media whore, even back when no one was watching what she did. Which is exactly why she had to get people to watch what *I* was doing instead. Clout-securing comes in all forms, after all. Even zaftig ones that narc on you for having a bit of fun in the *toilette*.

Joel appeared more concerned than I was upon turning around in mid-orgasm to see Kim angling her phone at us. In a very unsexy, high-pitched squeak, he screamed, "Kim, what the fuck? Put the phone down!"

"It's too late, I already have all the collateral I need," she smiled. "I'm sure Hilary would be very interested in seeing your cinematic debut."

I arched my brow. "Hilary?"

"Yes silly. Everyone knows she and Joel are an item right now. Well, everyone who doesn't have to read the tabloids to find out *real* information," she added for an extra malicious effect. She was already starting to act above her place; it was as though she'd given her social climbing a shot of steroids and was hulked out on a bender that required exterminating anyone in the circle she saw as being potentially weak enough to oust. Admittedly, that was definitely me. *I* had somehow become more oustable than *Kim*. Kim who we always made fun of as kids for eating ethnic food like how they make fun of Nia Vardalos in that opening scene of *My Big Fat Greek Wedding*. The thought that she had more power than I did made me briefly ignore Joel as he disengaged his dick from my hole, pulled his pants up and continued to obsequiously beg Kim for mercy, promising that he would do anything just so long as that photo and video combination never saw the light of day. This whole time I was focusing on Lindsay, maybe I should have been worrying about Kim. Then again, no. That was always Paris' battle. One she had blatantly and sorely lost (see: "I created Kim Kardashian. Her whole family owes me life." Not exactly a classy statement, but classy statements are not Paris' signature). In the sex-stained stall of that bathroom, I witnessed the germinal formation of a monster…but I still had my own nemesis to deal with.

"Kim, just tell me what you want and I'll give it to you."

"*Any*thing?"

"Anything that I'm capable of making happen," Joel specified.

Kim simpered. "I'd love to go on a shopping excursion with Hilary this week. Maybe you can arrange that."

Joel nodded vehemently. "Yes, yes. Of course. She'd love to." He eyed her pleadingly. "So if I set it up, you'll never show anyone…the video?"

Kim shrugged. "Not now. I'm going to 'store it away' though. At least until you and Hilary break up. I like knowing that you *know* I have it."

Even though it was a bitch thing for Kim to say out loud, the demise of Joel and Hilary was easily predictable, and paved the way for Nicole to swoop in as she so often does when she sees an available piece of trash, ideally sporting bad tattoos. This was, indeed, the primary foundation of her friendship with Paris, fast dwindling perhaps precisely *because* Nicole was about to take a more staid, domestic route (even counting her infamous swimming-in-a-ball-gown appearance with a coked-out Lindsay in '07).

In my state of shock/having a revelation, I still hadn't put my underwear back on (unlike Britney and others, I chose to wear them because I'm not a dirty ho, but a clean one). I was just sitting pathetically on the toilet as though waiting for Kim to commute my sentence. Joel looked back at me and said, "Uh, sorry Tate. I, uh, gotta get outta here." And with that, he practically sprinted out of the bathroom and the club. I didn't see him again until Nicole's wedding, where he accordingly avoided me at all costs. Kim, true to her word, never leaked the evidence to anyone, thus sparing me from Nicole's potentially permanent damnation in addition to Hilary's.

Kim stood over me wielding her phone like a baseball bat. "I almost want to help you, you look so sad on the toilet like that. But I'm here to help one person get ahead, and that's me. If you continue to stand in my way, I will make your life hell."

Not ready to surrender to the Armenian wig, I suddenly found my balls again, stood up and informed her, "You better listen up real good Ms. *Ass*dashian. You're a fucking fraud. A phony baloney. No one is ever going to be convinced of your bona fide socialite status. Your dad was a *lawyer* whose only "meaningful" accomplishment in life was dating Priscilla Presley for a minute. I guess that's where you get your gift for the social climb. For fuck's sake, the man was only worth thirty million dollars when he died. That's how much the Carmichaels have spent on a vacation. On redecorating. So for *you* to tell *me* that you plan to 'make my life hell' if I 'get in your way' is obscene. *You're* the only one in anyone's way. And that's also mainly because you're a fat whore and even your faux dark skin can't slim down your true appearance."

Kim was authentically stunned. She must have really believed that I would bow down to her because she was willing to lash out at me the way she never could at Paris. No one ever seemed to know who the fuck they were tangoing with when it came to me. And, truth be told (and on a vague side note), Paris might have been over-embellishing a hair when she took full responsibility for Kim's ascension. If we really want to blame someone, it should be Beyoncé, whose body shape was taking over in the wake of that kinda shitty debut solo album. Come on, you know you only liked "Crazy in Love" and "Baby Boy." And that's because of the male vocals contributing. She wasn't so much of a "feminist" back then. Not that she really is now, so much as a capitalizing businesswoman who knows which writers and poets to use in her work to appear "socially aware."

Kim continued to stand there like a statue until I literally pushed her out of the way, spit in her face and left. Back out on the dance floor, Paris was happy to see me. Mainly because Nicole was still essentially boning DJ AM in the booth and Paris had lost the guy she was dancing with before. "Come dance with me, whore!" she urged out of desperation. And I did. Our bumping and grinding against each other to "Rumors" by, well, Lindsay Lohan, was timed perfectly to Kim's reentry into the main room. Making sure she saw me, I started to kiss Paris and the crowd went wild. Miffed by the lack of attention being focused on her, Kim slipped out. I don't think she ever has forgotten that moment, because she's never tried to fuck with me since.

After that night, it felt like Lindsay was a ghost of problems past as Paris and I returned to our inseparable former glory. By the time the Golden Globes rolled around, we had already promised to be one another's dates. Back in the day, they weren't so fucking uptight about who they let in, and we were "permitted" to go to both the show and the after-parties, including Madonna's, the mack daddy of them all. We were graceful and elegant with our discreet (as Kathryn Merteuil) coke use in M's hallowed home—truly emblematic representations of what it is to be a socialite. Liliane Bettencourt would have been proud if she wasn't so busy piling the makeup on her face all the time and swindling money into Swiss bank accounts. I guess, what I'm saying is: it wasn't like that Golden Globes in 2013 when Lindsay embarrassed herself for the umpteenth (or whatever suggests even more of an infinity number than umpteenth) time by tweeting all about the ceremony even though no one asked her to. Her unwanted "takes" ended up incurring the wrath of Jennifer Lawrence, unquestionably an *actual* talent in the acting business…even if she did lower her cachet by falling prey to the chode that is Darren Aronofsky for a brief period.

Being, as stated, an *actual* talent familiar with cinema history, J. Law quoted a movie everyone should know verbatim, *The First Wives Club*, in her acceptance speech for Best Actress in a Motion Picture – Musical or Comedy (for *Silver Linings Playbook*, which is a bit cringe now). The reference, "I beat Meryl," got dolts like Lindsay up in arms because she apparently isn't versed enough in "old movies" to be an actress. Which, I guess, is why she isn't.

For the most part, though, Lindsay remained suspiciously quiet in the early months of the year, perhaps actually working on that shitty car movie or maybe just basking in the post-fame glow of *Mean Girls* and *Speak* for as long as she could. Sadly, she's made the mistake of continuing to do so even in 2019. It really is as they said after her Coachella antics in 2014 (a.k.a. relapsing on her whole sobriety kick while the *Lindsay* docuseries was being shown on OWN): "Lindsay's in denial and telling everyone that she's fine." It's a defense mechanism she was probably forced to implement from a very young age as a result of having a shithead father and a whore mother, but one that went into high-gear around the time she started having to block out just how catastrophic her filmography was getting. *Herbie: Fully Loaded* signaled that time. It was hard to know which boy might also be distracting her that year—could've been Robbie Williams or Colin Farrell or Ashton Kutcher (to make Wilmer jealous, obvi). So much is speculative with her because, well, she lies. The same way she lied to ingratiate herself with The Plastics in film is what she also did in real life. But Paris' warm, fuzzy feelings toward most of the people she once thought closest to her were starting to wane.

With Lindsay super distracted by different dickholes and Paris not yet preoccupied with Stavros Niarchos because he was still banging Mary-Kate on the reg before he prompted her to take a leave of absence from NYU to "pursue personal interests" (a.k.a. go to rehab for her eating disorder), this meant the friendship between us was fortifying, mainly because, well, she didn't have many other options. That's why we jet-setted to Berlin together on February 8th to make it in time for the Berlin International Film Festival. Dressed in our chicest cold-weather attire, Paris and I were the talk of the event, with many producers approaching us to ask if we would be interested in being the subject of a documentary.

Paris wasn't as excited about the prospect as I was, more concerned at this point with getting her fucking "music career" off the ground. She hadn't yet admitted that trying to make it happen was going to result in a huge insult to the music industry, and that its lack of sales is what would ultimately lead her down the path of "DJing." Which she can lie about all she wants and claim she was "compelled" to do it because she requested a song one night in Miami and got denied, inciting her to always be the one to call the musical shots thenceforward. No, no. Total crock of shit. It was simply that she could never recover from dropping a lyric like, "My heart beats like a drum…when I hear you cum." Yeah, that's something she actually said on "Heartbeat." I just saved you the emotional trauma of listening.

So Paris, content with her stint on *The Simple Life* and not yet ready to admit that Nicole was never going to come back to it now that she had found her own fame and boyfriend, rather fucked up my chances of making my way onto the silver screen as I had always dreamed. I'm still not counting my cameo as a young phone sex operator in Spike Lee's *Girl 6*. Even though it was pretty memorable and I put Lolita to shame on the irresistible-to-pedophiles front. I think she also more than vaguely wanted to keep me down at heel. That was her whole thing with friends: always keep them as lackeys. One supposes that's why she's lost so many over the years—and why they've all become so much more relevant and successful than she is.

Caught up in the reverie of being her number two bitch again, I couldn't fully see what she was doing to me. So I went along with how she directed the itinerary in Berlin, basking in the glow of the flashbulbs as I never had before. And even though the headline, "Amerikanische Sozialisten Erobern Berlin," was on the derogatory side—we weren't social*ists*, we were social*ites*—it didn't matter. We knew the Germans were lapping it up and, most importantly, that Lindsay was the furthest thought from anyone's mind.

While we were on a European roll (unlike the year before), we swooped in at the BAFTAs to catch a glimpse of Leo D (because Paris wanted to take a crack at his D). He won that year for *The Aviator*. To tell you the truth, I couldn't sit through the damn thing, walking in and out of our private screening room and only actually enjoying the scene of Leo as Howard Hughes pissing in all those cups. Afterward, we went to The Punchbowl, where Guy Ritchie and Madonna were throwing a private party at which I foolishly hit it off with Rhys Ifans. You know, that gross guy who played Spike in *Notting Hill*? Well, in truth, he's just my type: greasy, sleazy, pale and packin' that stringy-ass hair.

It occurred to me that we might hit it off in the back of my mind, from the moment I saw him knocking back pints and chain-smoking in the corner. And yes, just as it did for Britney, *Notting Hill* had always held a special place in my heart. It was the last great rom-com before things started getting unbearably icky and technology-based (e.g., *In Time*—that's right, I paid attention to Justin Timberlake even after *FutureSex/LoveSounds*). Thus, to be with Rhys would be like living out my own fantasy of being Julia Roberts as Anna Scott…or I guess it's more like being Emma Chambers as Honey Thacker. Since she's the one who attracted him with those bugged-out eyes. British women really did get dealt a bad genetic hand from their stocky, "well-built" forebears. Thank god or whoever Daddy didn't fall for a British woman, like in *The Parent Trap*. I could have turned out looking even more of a fright than Lindsay does now with her latest plastic surgery incarnation. Who does she really think she's fooling besides herself?

As I moved over to Rhys like I was being pulled by some magnetic force—as though I were attached to an invisible pulley from the ceiling just leading me straight to him—Paris got in the way. In her usual annoying drunk fashion, she jumped in front of me and threw her arms up in the air the same way you're picturing it in that famous image of her wearing the "Stop Being Poor" t-shirt (that really said "Stop Being Desperate" but, either way, it was a dig at poors). She cawed as she bragged, "I think Leo might take me back to his hotel tonight."

I nodded and smiled, hoping that she would get the fuck out of my way. But Paris wasn't done dangling her accomplishment at me.

"Aren't you happy for me? Or are you, like, jealous or something? Is that why you have that look on your face?"

"I'm smiling, what are you talking about?"

"Your mouth is smiling, but your eyes are frowning," Paris accused, pointing her index finger a little too close to my face.

"No, I think it's great, I just…have to do something right now…" I started to trail off, my tongue practically dangling from my mouth as I salivated at the sight of Rhys lighting up another cigarette. Without waiting for Paris to say another inane word, I made a beeline for the end of the bar, not bothering with something so British as tact.

"Hi Rhys."

He squinted at me. "Er, hi."

"Do you know who I am?" I asked shyly, not wanting to assume someone as perpetually blacked-out as Rhys would bother with keeping tabs on American celebutantes like myself. Wait, what am I saying? Lindsay was the celebutante. I was the *debut*ante, trying to make my debut into the society of Rhys' bedroom. Or wherever it was he might have slept. He seemed too rugged to own anything that might resemble a "luxury apartment." Not really something that exists in London, no matter how much money you have (and not even if you're Rihanna).

He gave me another squint and shrugged. "I reckon I do. Why?"

In an expression of bold forwardness, I touched his arm. "I just want to tell you that I think you're the greatest British actor that's ever lived."

He blinked at me and burst out laughing. It was an endless stream of laughter that others were starting to notice, so it was completely embarrassing to me. I tried to laugh along with him as though I was in on the joke too, but I couldn't keep up the pretense for more than thirty seconds. His cacophonous cackling finally attracted the attention of Guy Ritchie himself, who, desperate to break away from Madonna any chance he got, sauntered over to demand, "What's so bloody funny then?" Rhys finally collected himself long enough to make eye contact with Guy and explain, "Nothing, this young lass just said the funniest thing I think I might have ever heard."

Guy arched his brow. "Well, what was it then?"

Rhys teetered toward a dangerous burst of laughter before reining it back in and repeating what I had said to Guy. Guy looked from me to Rhys and back at me again and then joined in on the raucous sniggering.

Guy chimed in, "No, not Michael Cain, not Peter O'Toole—Rhys Ifans is the greatest British actor that's ever lived." He chortled once more before informing Rhys, "Don't you see mate? She wants to shag you."

Apart from the headlines about me banging Fabrizio last year, this had been by far the most mortifying thing that had ever happened to me, and I could suddenly comprehend why Madonna would eventually end up divorcing Guy's crass ass. Then again, I might owe him a share of debt—for if he hadn't been so blunt, Rhys probably never would have picked up on my very overt hints, and I would never have gotten to fulfill a long-time fucking fantasy. Even if it did, as usual, somehow cost me my social standing once more. I swear, it's like the socialite universe forces you to put a chastity belt on if you want to sustain your clout, but at the same time, who you fuck can send your status to the next level as much as it can destroy it.

Out of the corner of my eye, I could feel Paris watching me, her damned lazy eye burning a hole into my cheek. Well, I wasn't going to let her judgment and enviousness prevent my dream just because Leo didn't want to take her back to his hotel in the end (likely deeming her too "old"). With Rhys fully in the loop about what was going to transpire, he linked me by the arm and escorted me out of the bar, where he promptly hailed a minicab and took me back to his flat in, to my aghast felicity, Notting Hill.

"*You* can afford to live here?"

"No need to get cheeky, love," he snarled as he grabbed me by the hand and led me to the door. "I make a decent living, don't I? So *yeah*, I can afford to live here."

I could tell already it was going to be a hate fuck. Maybe I was to serve his purpose of taking out all the rage he had ever felt on every pretty girl who had rejected him—especially the American ones. Who could say? I didn't really care. I just needed that pale, thin, uncut dick inside of me.

He took me on a safari of orgasms throughout the night, turning me on all sides like a rotisserie blow-up doll. It was everything I dreamed it could be and more. And it didn't stop with how he treated me (roughly) during the night. He also woke up before I did to make me a full English breakfast, a concept that, in the past, I had always refused to fuck with because I'm not one for gaining five pounds in a sitting unless I'm super hungover and it's for In-n-Out. But for Rhys, there is (or was) nothing I wouldn't put in my mouth. And I still often feel that way even to this very day. Wish Rhys could say the same.

While he snorted a line of cocaine and then sipped from his tea, I indulged in the bacon portion of the plate. "You like it then, do you?"

I nodded. "Yes Rhys. It's delicious." I could hear myself sounding like a Stepford Wife, but didn't care.

"Do you like it enough to stay here a bit longer?"

I mulled over his proposition. To stay in London longer meant that I would miss going to the Grammys with Paris, and that she might invite someone else to replace me. Someone who could, again, usurp my current position as her right-hand woman. But to leave meant that I might never get this kind of romantic chance with Rhys again. And if you haven't learned anything about me by now—even the extent of my loathing for Lindsay—it's that I am *always*, but *always*—first and foremost—a sucker for romance. So I stayed. Without question.

When I called Paris at the London Hilton on Park Lane from Rhys' rotary phone downstairs, her reaction to my announcement was even worse than I could have anticipated. "What the fuck Tate? We're supposed to walk the red carpet together, like, tonight. The jet leaves in an hour. How the fuck could you do this to me? What the fuck kind of friend are you—you know what? Don't answer that. You're exactly the kind of friend Lindsay warned me about. You're just a leech. Using me for my global influence. I hope you're, like, really happy with your choice because that Reese guy is gonna toss you out on your bony ass in less than a week. And I'm not going to be there to comfort you about it. No, I'm going to be rubbing up against some way more attractive guys at Hyde with Lindsay."

Before I could offer any defense, she slammed the phone down. So that was it. My one fluke chance at "reintegrating" was squandered because I was like a little girl chasing butterflies. If the butterflies were actually just *one* butterfly representing Rhys' caterpillar dick (I mean that in the sense that it writhed around inside me in an innovatively and somehow ethereally pleasurable manner).

Not wanting to think too heavily about the opportunity I had just lost, I returned to Rhys' bedroom to distract myself. He was doing another line and turned to offer me some. "Wanna little bump?" he asked sweetly. Now I could understand how Kate Moss and Amy Winehouse had fallen so deeply down the rabbit hole: it seemed all British men were drug addicts. I indulged in his offering and then proceeded to do so for the next few months, ignoring the appearances Paris and Lindsay were making in public together. The reports of the orgy they had with Adam Levine after the Grammys wouldn't die out, rendering anything that happened to me—like getting caught shooting up heroin at Turnmills—totally un-newsworthy somehow. It was like I could literally do anything I wanted and it wasn't going to get a bit of notice 1) because I was in Europe and American consumers of media could really give two shits about what goes on there and 2) Lindsay and Paris were simply too "hot" to be toppled in the headlines.

Orgy rumors aside, they were at every new club together, further spurring the rumors that Nicole had somehow done Paris dirty. But it wouldn't be half as dirty as Lindsay fucking Stavros Niarchos before the corpse of Paris' relationship with him was cold. Then again, it might have been karma for

Paris stealing him away from Mary-Kate in the first place. Bottom line is, Greek guys are assholes and women shouldn't fight over them anyway. They're like lesser versions of Italians with not as enjoyable food (say what you want about the Greeks coming first, but the Romans perfected every rudimentary thing they "established").

Paris couldn't be forewarned of Lindsay's inevitable betrayal, however—apparently needing to learn the hard way for herself. She certainly did enjoy licking that metaphorical (and maybe even literal) pussy of Lindsay's even more than Kim seemed to enjoy licking Paris'—but, as you know by now, beneath every metaphorical pussy lick is a lashing tongue. This was a fact made evident by their next majorly publicized appearance together: 50 Cent's album release party for *The Massacre*. Afterward, 50 Cent was spotted with Paris and Lindsay at Club LAX—the same club that would, only later that year, be dubbed by Paris as attracting solely "D-list celebrities." She had a point, I suppose, as Mischa Barton and Nicole were frequently seen there together toward the end of 2005. Paris, as we know, is notorious for calling the kettle black—but rarely known for hanging out with Black people. Which is why her cameo with 50 was particularly momentous. Except, since I was the only one who knew Paris with such a profound depth, only *I* could see what her purpose was in deliberately being his hanger-on that night. And that was to keep up with Kim, already setting a new precedent for "white" girls being with Black guys. If there was one thing Paris abhorred, it was when someone else established a trend that she didn't. To her, it signified the ultimate loss of power. Indeed, she was very much starting to lose some of her once ironclad dominance.

For the time being, however, she continued to delude herself into believing that if she inauthentically latched onto someone (Black) like 50, her "prestige" could persist in reigning supreme. Lindsay was foolish enough not to spot the very clear signs of the shift toward Kim that were afoot, which is why she only hastily glommed on after it was too late to be deemed genuine. That's why every photo you see of Lindsay with any of the Kardashians is extremely cringeworthy, with neither party at all emotionally invested in the other.

After March, reports of Paris and Lindsay seemed to go dormant for a while, or at least from my side of the pond, where all anyone could talk about was *Doctor Who* being revived as a new series for the BBC. Yes, I had managed to somewhat prove Paris wrong by keeping Rhys' interest, but that was only as a result of all the drugs I was furnishing him with. Using all of Daddy's allowance, I funneled whatever he wanted up his nose and into his veins. I knew, of course, that this was why he "loved" me so. But I didn't care. It was just nice to be loved (however disingenuously) by my fantasy man. Plus, Rhys promised he would get me an audition for Guy Ritchie's next project, the script for which he was still working on (Rhys told me it might take a minute for Guy to be at the auditioning phase as he was already highly dissatisfied with initial opinions of *Revolver*). I couldn't miss out on that opportunity, now could I? So I kept staying. Hoping to reinvent myself as a more powerful socialite in London with the likes of Kate Moss and Amy Winehouse at my side. Or me at theirs, I guess. After all, it was their domain, not mine.

Surprisingly, hanging out with Kate at that time was more hardcore than doing so with Amy. Kate, after all, was in her Pete Doherty phase—arguably far more damaging than Amy's fledgling Blake Fielder-Civil period at that point. Because at least Blake was spurring Amy creatively—for her, a lot of 2005 was spent experiencing the inspiration for 2006's *Back to Black*. An album she would never be able to replicate, not even bothering to release a third in her lifetime. Then again, she did release every feeling and emotion at its utmost intensity on that record, so who can blame her for not wanting to do it again? It takes a lot to feel anything. Except, well, sheer contempt.

That's what Kate and I were feeling one pre-dawn in May at the Metro Club (when the

Blow Up night had taken over), which most people I knew just called Blow because that's all that you went there for. We were both rolling our asses off when Boy George, notorious skulker that he is, sauntered into the club in that goddamn purple fedora of his. Kate immediately shot me a look that said, "Oh Christ, not *this* asshole." And he really is one. The undiluted archetype of a cunty gay who still wants to use you to climb the social ladder. He always tried to do just that with Kate, who wasn't inclined to give two fucks about pretending to be friendly toward him, which is probably why he was so obsessed with her.

She leaned in to shout in my ear, "I'm going to the bathroom, then let's go to Pete's!" I nodded in reply. Boy approached me just as Kate made her escape for a nasal pick-me-up.

"Tate, you're looking...fuller."

Like Kate said: *this* asshole. Except I would dare put the whole phrase in italics: *this asshole*. Already fed up with his cuntery, I retorted, "And you're just looking fatter. What's new? Sung at any bar mitzvahs lately?" Bar mitzvahs being the height of pop star irrelevancy.

Boy gibed, "Darling, you know there's no Jewish people other than Amy in the U.K."

I shrugged. "Maybe she'll have a crack baby and perpetuate the species."

Boy sneered. "You're ever the anti-Semite. And the optimist, considering…"

"Considering what?"

He eyed me cautiously, feigning that he wouldn't *actually* tell me. It only took him about half a second to break, announcing, "Well love, word on the street is that Rhys has got himself a brand-new supplier…sexually."

I clammed up, not wanting to show anything resembling an emotional reaction. Instead, I steeled my facial expression and returned coolly, as though I wasn't dying inside at all (better than outside though— I much prefer rotting without any external detection of it), "Why shouldn't he? Rhys isn't my husband."

Boy, disappointed by my reaction, cocked his head incredulously and remarked, "That's a very *evolved* perspective, innit?"

"It's nothing the Brits haven't been doing undercover for years. Just look at Prince Charles. And I mean, honestly, just because you people hate the French doesn't mean you're not exactly like them."

Kate returned from the bathroom looking ever so chipper as she pulled me by the arm and said, "Come on love, let's get the fuck out of this D-list cesspool."

Boy appeared both pleasured and pained by the dig. He's a classic sadomasochist.

In the car on the way to Pete's, Kate glanced over at me and asked, "What's the matter love? You look almost sallow."

Right as she said "sallow," I threw up all over her lap. It wasn't ideal. The last thing I needed was to upset my London "high society" meal ticket, too. That's just what I did though, as, evidently, Kate's leather skirt was custom-made by Karl Lagerfeld himself. According to her, "He actually put his hands on the fabric. He never does that."

I offered the consolation, "But Karl loves you, he can make you another one."

"No Tate. He can't. Because I can never tell him this happened or he won't love me anymore." She placed her hands in a sort of Jesus/martyr pose (envision what you will with that) as she fought against the urge to wipe the barf off of herself while contending with the unavoidable knowledge that to touch another human's puke is disgusting.

Being that I was carrying a microscopic YSL bag, I couldn't exactly offer her anything from it to clean with so that she might avert touching what amounted to my insides with her bare, bony hand. All I could offer instead was a pitiful, "Kate, I'm so sorry."

She refused to look at me. "You know what? It's my fault. My fault for thinking you could handle your drug intake." She then muttered. "Lindsay and Paris would be able to handle it."

"*Excuse me?*" I practically shrieked.

"Nothing, nothing."

I felt like I might burst into tears from Kate's accusation of inadequacy.

"Kate, you know, Boy just told me some really upsetting information in there and that's why I—"

"Are you serious? Are you telling me you let some lie peddled to you by *Boy* bloody *George* is what's got you ruining my custom Lagerfeld?"

Sheepishly, I returned, "Well, I think it might be true."

"What did that little prat say?"

I sniffled. "He told me everyone knows Rhys has been seeing someone behind my back."

She scoffed. "Darling, did you really need Boy George to tell you that? I thought it was fairly obvious."

I instantly felt like the biggest joke of all time. How could I have been so *naïve* (being bicontinental, I feel obliged to put an umlaut over the "i"). Me, now *firmly* in my mid-twenties, somehow able to believe that a sleazoid guy—a *British* sleazoid guy, no less—would remain faithful.

Kate, perhaps sensing the epiphany washing over me all at once, turned sympathetic and swiftly gave me an embrace that ended up getting my own vomit on my silk slip dress (I've always maintained that you can never go wrong perpetually dressing like the third member of Romy and Michele's duo). I didn't care though. That Kate was showing me this modicum of affection meant that I could ignore the odious Paris and Lindsay comment she had made.

Vis-à-vis those two tits, although Paris was still spotted regularly at every worthwhile club in Hollywood, Lindsay had been rather off the radar of late. But June was when she started to noticeably reemerge, making an appearance on *TRL* to commence talking up *Herbie* (an impossible feat for most to do with a straight face), which got a primo June 22nd release date. Her real agenda, however, was to inform Damien Fahey (that's right, I know other VJ names besides Carson Daly and Jesse Camp—yes, I'm once again dating myself with these references, but fuck you, you'll be old one day too, you self-righteous plebe with nothing but youth and anonymity going for you) that her next album was going to sound like Keane and The Streets and Gorillaz. Is that what *A Little More Personal (RAW)* sounded like to you? Probably not. Because you probably have ears that, like, have a functioning cochlea. P.S. how awkward for Damien to have to interview her with Justin Long and ask about their kiss "in the movie," considering that Damien, too, had banged Lindsay back in '04. Another telltale sign that she would fuck anything, even in the prime of her celebrity, to prove her so-called "Hollywood prowess."

I had to watch her lap up the attention with her new blonde hair color (it was enough to make me want to go black à la Ashlee Simpson), *still* coasting on the fucking high of *Mean Girls*. But oh what a rude awakening she was in for as, in addition to *Herbie* being a total embarrassment on a critical level, she was also obsessed with talking about the "trauma" of her car accident (the one that got CA's then-governor, Arnold Schwarzenegger—never forget Californians love "celebrity" governors, as Reagan also proved—to pass a law entailing higher penalty fees for any paparazzo that caused physical harm to a celeb during the pursuit of their precious photo). Rehashing the same stock story to every late-night talk show host about how she was "innocently" turning the corner at 3rd and Sweetzer (as though expecting the Midwesterners who watch that late-night shit to know what intersection she's talking about) when it happened, Lohan really had that damsel in distress act down, just like Tai Frasier.

This "3rd and Sweetzer" debacle would become but a continuation in a chain of seemingly endless car accidents—said "accidents" mirroring the trainwreck that was fast becoming Lindsay's personal and professional life. She had already caused a head-on collision in Studio City back in August of '04 (she really did feel especially untouchable that year). One that she would get sued for, though, granted, no celebrity could ever get sued for a car accident as mercilessly as Brandy in 2006.

Another thing she kept parroting on these talk shows was about the change in the signature hue of her tresses. Even if she was touting that she had gone blonde for her role in "a Robert Altman film" co-starring Meryl, I could see the cracks in her veneer. Ones that could instantly be spotted via an alteration in appearance. Especially hair color. She didn't give a fuck about acting anymore, and maybe she never did. All she was concerned with was being linked to "it" boys and partying. The vapid twit. All right, fine, so maybe I can't say that my interests were (or are) all that much different, but had *I* been given the luxury of an acting career built on the backs of innocent tweens' and teens' poor taste, I wouldn't have squandered it as she has. Ugh, but then again, is opening a nightclub in Greece really squandering it? Honestly, I can't begrudge her for that. I can only begrudge her for doing something that I wasn't able to. Yet.

While Lindsay was showing the extent of how much her acting career had been a fluke, my summer went by in a haze of drug use (though I do remember very distinctly being backstage at Live 8 and shooting up with Peaches Geldof—RIP). Another night whiled away with Kate at Pete's flat or Amy at some dive in Camden. Another morning spent sauntering in relative shame back to Rhys' in Notting Hill, by this time having decided to dispense with the pretense of being exclusive with me altogether. I wasn't going to stand for it any longer. I had wasted enough of my time in the fuckhole that is the United Kingdom.

It's an island for assholes and missing links if you ask me, the same way Australia is. Even though the Brits would like to think they're somehow better than their "cousins." They're fucking not. Might be worse actually, with their false sense of superiority.

As the blitzkrieg for *Herbie: Fully Loaded* began to calm down (box office revenue always usurped negative reviews, so she still remained "bankable" as a star in spite of the objective badness), my anxiety disproportionately escalated. My return flight was scheduled for October 5th. And I tried to suppress my jealousy of Lindsay's effortless success as the private jet descended upon L.A. L.A. who (I choose to use "who" as she *is* a living, breathing prostitute) I had abandoned for so long just to let a thin-dicked fuckboy enter me upon occasion. Well, I wouldn't be leaving her again anytime soon. I shouldn't have been so hasty to believe in the endurance of my enchantment with Europe, a continent that consistently managed to fuck me over, both with men and with headlines.

But it's not as though Los Angeles was embracing me with anything akin to "open arms" either. For I couldn't have predicted that, as I landed, everyone in Beverly Hills would be buzzing about Lindsay's latest accident. This time she was blaming it on a van that crossed her path near Robertson Boulevard, but I think everyone knew that Lindsay is basically just a shitty driver, even when she's sober.

It's the curse of being from New York, where driving isn't a congenital part of the culture. Bottom line though: my grand entrance was, once again, somehow upstaged by something Lindsay did. The collisions she found herself in after 2005, however, would be far worse in terms of pervasive and negative coverage as, soon enough, there was nowhere she or anyone else of her "caliber" could go without being hounded by the cameras of TMZ, roughly a month away from launching on November 8th.

But before then, there was Halloween to worry about; it would be the holiday I would use to establish my grand reinstatement into "Hollywood society." With the 31st approaching, it bore repeating Cady Heron's adage: it's the "one night a year when girls can dress like a total slut and no other girls can say anything about it." And I wasn't about to rein in my *looque* (read: look) by any means.

Everyone was going to be at the Halloween Mansion Party hosted by, for some reason, Haylie Duff. In spite of being utterly ignored during my London stint, I somehow managed to receive an invite. The Carmichael name remained of value, and I think certain people wanted to see how I would interact with Paris, Nicole and Kim after all the drama that had been going on. Yet one person who would not be there, to my shock, was Lindsay. No, she suspiciously chose to skip the L.A. festivities in favor of dressing like a slutty firefighter on the streets of New York. Not really much of a stretch, if you ask this always Halloween-ready body. But me, I was going all fucking out by dressing as the eponymous lead in *Corpse Bride* (to my chagrin, people were still obsessed enough with *Mean Girls* to ask me if I was supposed to be Cady Heron as an "ex-wife").

I feel like I was the only one who truly appreciated this movie when it was first released, as I've consistently associated marriage with death. Probably because I'd watched my parents' attempt at monogamy drag on long enough to be perpetually aware of the "revelation" that two people together forever is just a construct financed by Harvey Weinstein...or at least formerly financed by him. That being said, it didn't mean I wasn't going to need a headline-making date to play the role of Victor to my Emily.

So as I let one of my favorite pedicurists, Ming Ho Chin, give me an intensive foot rub in the comfort of my own bedroom, I shuffled through the contacts in my Nokia N70 (Paris told me I should get the LG Chocolate, but she might have actually been on crack cocaine when she made the recommendation. I always knew smartphones were the way to go—Paris just really didn't have any foresight in the technological [or boning] regard). *Who to bring, who to bring?* I mused to myself. It was suddenly starting to feel as though there were no single, young, attractive *and* rich men left in L.A. Surely, I couldn't go alone though. It would just scream *pathetic*. Then it hit me like a tab of ecstasy in Ibiza: Jake Gyllenhaal. He was still sort of on the rebound after things ended with Kirsten (who Orlando was getting his fair share of right now in the embarrassing wake of *Elizabethtown*), but that could, as usual, work to my advantage. He was getting a lot of praise not just for *Brokeback Mountain*, which I had already seen a screener of and masturbated to, but the hat-trick of the back-to-back critically acclaimed films that were *Brokeback Mountain*, *Proof* and *Jarhead*. In short, he was really making Kirsten look like a has-been.

When I recovered from my Brazilian (also done at home by my prized waxist, Anelle P. Robe), I called him up and explained my interest in doing a coordinated *Corpse Bride* costume for the Halloween Mansion Party. Even though we had only met a few times at various premieres, he treated me as though we'd known each other for ages, and instantly agreed to my vision. Meaning I was going to blur everyone else's vision with my unforgettable *rentrée* into The Scene.

***

In anticipation of Jake's arrival at my house on the night of the party, I had our new maid, Rosa, answer the door. Because I always adhered to the Cher Horowitz method for driving boys wild—which was, of course, to make them wait longer than they needed to. When enough time had passed (a.k.a. twenty minutes), I descended the stairs fully bedecked in the tattered ruins of a wedding dress and veil, my skin channeling the same hue of blue as the Corpse Bride herself. I could tell by the elated look on Jake's face that it was going to be a night to remember.

I suppose that's why I let my enthusiasm get the better of me when I told him he could come up to my room while I put the "finishing touches" on my lipstick (I like to be very precise, okay? There's no sense doing anything if it's not done right—unless, of course, you're Lindsay). The only finishing touches, in the end, were on my *other* set of lips, which, as mentioned, I had just gotten waxed, making my vag more sensitive to Jake's particularly sharp thrusts. Like most white men, especially actors, Jake had, at best, a medium penis and, at worst, a small one. But I've always been good at working with minimal tools—isn't that how rich people get rich after all? (I mean apart from generationally-inherited wealth)—so I finagled an orgasm, no problem. And even though I knew it was against the code of sustaining a man's interest throughout the night to allow him entry right away, I also knew it was nothing Paris, Lindsay or Nicole hadn't done before, and they still seemed to be "A-list" trash. Maybe I had erred in not taking a page from Kim though, who clearly didn't give it up quite so easily unless she could get something bankably concrete out of it (like a sex tape or Kanye). This is what I was starting to think when we arrived at the party and Jake almost immediately ignored me in favor of other Hollywood debris. Including Paris herself, who had opted for the lack of subtlety exemplified by a Playboy Bunny costume. I knew I couldn't have expected much else from her though—her total absence of originality was as "sheer" as the line of perfume she had released that year.

The pain of being discarded so quickly by Jake hurt. It was like being Miranda at a porn party in the "Escape From New York" episode of *Sex and the City*, when Carrie said, "I can't believe how open and 'Hi, have sex' this place [a.k.a. L.A.] is. In New York, sex is so bottom shelf, paper bag." Miranda couldn't have concurred more when she provided her own little corroborating story, agreeing, "Exactly. It's all hidden, like me… Last night I talked to this cute guy. We were having a great time. Then a woman in a tight dress walked by, with big breasts, just boom, here they are. He totally went for it… The thing is I wanted to have sex too but it was hidden in my witty banter and my little looks. She just put it out there, sex, and she got the guy."

For once, I wasn't having a Samantha Jones experience. Instead, that's exactly what Paris was having with Jake, who was clearly in uber (in my day you could say "uber" without thinking: misogyny and sexual harassment hiding behind a rideshare app) rebound mode. Worst of all, the more I scoured the area for any decent people to converse with (read: do drugs with), the more I had to admit that this party was strictly B-list.

Case in point, Joel was there with Hilary. He still hadn't moved on to Nicole yet, who he transitioned to real quickly after things ended with Hil in November of '06. I don't even know what Hilary was supposed to be, but Joel was doing the douchebag *Phantom of the Opera* thing. She just sort of gothed it up like a little asshole to coordinate with her man of the moment. She was so predictable like that, catering to whoever she was with. Of course, that's why she always got the nice girl rep— but really, is there anything "nice" about having no personality of your fucking own? Sure, maybe in Hollywood. But if you're an ordinary rich person instead of an "actress," you don't have to play by the rules of those "in charge." Because money is far more powerful than fame. That's why socialites run this town: we've got money *and* fame (because of the money). No aspiring ingenue is any match for *that* combination. Try as they fucking might. That's why none of us ever had to "let" Harvey rape our ass.

So if you're still wondering how Lindsay hasn't managed to sustain her star power from the mammoth boost she got in the early 00s the way Paris has (because yes, she treats DJing like a career since she can afford to), it's because of all that gauche credit card debt. Rich people don't have credit card debt. They just don't. The way happy people don't kill their husbands. Further, she really oughtn't to have defended Donald *or* Harvey—she could at least have half the brain to intuit that "feminism" isn't a "trend" that's going to fade away anytime soon. I mean, if she really wanted any chance at remaining relevant.

As I settled for doing a bump with Mike Tyson in the bathroom (at least *his* penis wasn't going to be small), I thought about my next move for the new year. Acting clearly wasn't working unless I got Daddy to produce a movie that I could star in, but then it wouldn't be on my own merits, and I just wasn't comfortable with that the way Paris was, is and will always be. And then it hit me more heavily than my coke high: record an album. If Aaron Carter, Ashlee Simpson and Willa Ford could record music, why couldn't I? For that matter, if Lindsay could, then there was no reason I should be boxed out from a hit single either.

So that night, when I returned home alone, I went into the recording studio we conveniently had at our basement level and started letting it all pour out of me: the rage, the angst, the feelings of jealousy and inadequacy. With the help of the coke, I recorded through the early hours of the morning, finishing the rough cuts for what I had planned to call *Social Light* around ten a.m. It was that day, however, that Lindsay "just happened" to begin her sudden media onslaught with regard to promoting *her* album. It was as though she could sense my every attempt at eclipsing her spotlight. I was so distraught by the sight of her face on TV discussing the "complexity" of the record—Jesus fucking Christ, any asshole can talk about how her father fucked her up (including Jesus Christ)—that I didn't even bother to pick up my cell phone when Paris called, presumably to apologize for taking Jake home with her like the little sloppy seconds slore she never took issue with being.

Then again, Lindsay didn't mind being sloppy seconds to Paris when looking back at the Stavros phenomenon. It was every bitch for herself in those days though, so I can't say I really blame either of them for their ruthless and cutthroat methods. At the time, however, I did. I believed them to be the fugliest slut frenemies around. And, as usual, the only person I could trust was Nicole, who I decided to confide in first about my new album, which I brought over to her house for her to listen to in the hope that she could talk Lionel into producing.

I didn't want to be totally tasteless in my approach though, as I knew that Nicole was a more guarded person than people suspected her of being because of the constant favors she was asked by the type of aspiring musicians who should mostly just be grateful if they managed to secure a gig at the Silverlake Lounge. That's why I went to her house with the pretext of wanting to bring her a new batch of edibles my hot drug dealer had just baked for me. Nicole could never say no to any form of weed during this period, a true testament to her California nature. Her real last name was Escovedo for fuck's sake—there was nothing more Californian than someone who was of Mexican blood. She never got credit for that, instead being written off as a stock white girl thanks to her constant association with Paris. But I, I could see the real her. That's why we had our undercover rapport, one that would have made Paris despise me even more than she not-so-secretly did.

Yet Fortune was soon about to turn Paris' scorn toward Lindsay anew in the looming wake of the Stavros revelation. This forcing her, as usual, to turn to *me* (hopefully, you can hear "I Turn To You" by Xtina playing in your head right now). Because Paris was *quite* over her alliance with Nicole by this point as well, and Kim was nothing more than someone to clean out her closet—not a girl you could actually gossip with. That day, Nicole was the girl *I* could gossip with as we got turnt off our asses on rainbow sprinkle cookies that loosened her up enough to listen to the album I recorded the previous night on her JVC CD player. To remind, burning CDs was the height of 00s "mixtape" culture, and this was my auditory love letter to the world if Nicole would just say she'd have her dad listen to it and then automatically talk it up to all the right people.

But when we had reached the last track on the disc, Nicole assessed, "I don't think it's got any place in the charts right now, Tate. I think you show a lot of promise, but ultimately, it's just another frothy, unwanted pop ditty that any white girl with the funds or the ability to suck dick could, er, put out."

My friendly take on Nicole would change about a year from this episode, when Paris came out with *Paris* and I was aurally assaulted with the fact that Nicole had "helped" her write some of the songs by directly ripping off lyrics from mine, *especially* for "Stars Are Blind" (we all know Lady Gaga was lying when she fake gushed to Paris, "I always thought 'Stars Are Blind' was one of the greatest records ever." Shut the fuck up, Upper West Side slag). Just goes to show, you can't trust anyone except yourself in the hellmouth that is L.A. Except I never seemed to remember my own advice about erring on the side of caution with regard to placing confidence in people, whether fellow socialites or ordinary famous people. This phobia I already had because of the constant confirmation of imminent betrayal was made all the worse with the founding of one little three-letter company: TMZ (an abbreviation for Thirty-Mile Zone, if you want to be, like, a dweeb about it and understand that it refers to the geography of H'wood's "studio zone").

It was unleashed on, as I said, November 8th, and, in addition to Lindsay releasing her sophomore album, it was the most awful thing that happened to me that year. The first story they broke? The one that took them right out of "Like A Virgin" territory and into full-fledged whore? One of Paris' car accidents (Lindsay wasn't the only one who couldn't drive for shit, sober or otherwise). And who was in the car with her but me, Stavros (driving, that little asshole), Kimberly Stewart and Talan Torriero (I don't blame you if you don't know who the last two people are either). News of the scandal broke almost the minute it happened, and I had already risked yet another recent threat of being cut off by Daddy for my antics. The blatancy with which white girls—especially socialites—could get away with things was now on full blast for all to see. That's right, before TMZ, the LAPD didn't even have to pretend like they cared about punishing us.

But motherfucking Harvey Levin had to go and obliterate not just our glamor and the hush-hush nature of being elite, but also our privilege. If not for TMZ, who knows if Lindsay would have had to endure those endless court dates (even though the bitch deserved all that and more) as a consequence of her well-documented inability to drive without drugs?

When Daddy sent our driver to come get me after the news broke on the internet, I didn't feel pride for my sins the way Paris, Lindsay and Britney always seemed to, but rather, a genuine sense of loss, as though being a socialite would never again feel or come across as *dazzling*. The myth of celebrity had been debunked once more. It was *Confidential* magazine all over again (the rag that revealed the dirt in the 50s when no one else would—not even Hedda "Gets No Head" Hopper— e.g., "Why Joe DiMaggio Is Striking Out with Marilyn Monroe!").

As my stoic chauffeur pulled up to the house, I had an unshakeable sense of dread for what was in store for me in the coming years. Would I have to live my life in a bubble in order to preserve my carefully curated image? The answer was, of course, a resounding yes. And this is also why I could never transcend Lindsay: she was willing to show off her trainwreck ways in a manner that I simply could not. It was where her true talent lay (or is it lied? I really should have finished college). She still kept trying to prove that she was talented via other avenues though—like when she released that turd of a second album, *A Little More Personal (RAW)*—as if *RAW* in parentheses makes it so much "harder." God, I have more edge and grit in my pinky toe than she does in her silicone-packed body.

Despite this, I still watched her damned appearance on *TRL* and *Ellen* to promote it. Even bought the fucking thing on vinyl (Daddy made it a point to instill within me an appreciation for records long before Urban Outfitters ever did). For the album cover, Lindsay paraded her particular dumbness/predilection for white girl clichés by also including a red (communist much?) Chinese symbol projected onto her back. A symbol that I've never bothered to look up to unearth its true meaning, but I'm guessing it's not super profound. In the face of all its off-putting qualities, I wanted to give it a chance, really I did, as I handed the CD to my driver à la Madonna to Ali G in the "Music" video. I even admitted once out loud to Paris that I liked "Rumors." Or "Rumours" as the karaoke DJs would make us spell it whenever we were in London years after its "hit" status and wanted to make fun of Lindsay.

It goes without saying (but I still will) that the album was a complete dumpster fire. Yet the only one who seemed to grasp the full depth of just how bad this "music" was appeared to be Whitney Strub, some nobody who wrote for PopMatters. She said it best in remarking, "Its first track and lead single, 'Confessions of a Broken Heart (Daughter to Father),' immediately commences with a line about 'wait[ing] for the postman to bring me a letter,' which suggests songwriters dipping into the well of cliché without worrying about freshness. The world might not need another version of Britney Spears' 'E-Mail My Heart' [so not true, by the way], but good lord, that song came out in 1999. Perhaps a text message might arrive faster than snail-mail in late 2005, should Lohan's song-persona deign to enter the twenty-first century. From its insipid beginning, the song goes on to strive for the bombastic balladry of Celine Dion, which it fails to achieve on the basis of its maudlin lyrics (in which our singer wears her father's polo sweaters and bleats out questions such as 'did u ever love me,' as the lyric sheet has it) and Lohan's extremely limited, practically tinny voice." I couldn't have said it better myself. But it didn't matter what Lindsay put out (while constantly putting out) at this point. She was still a commodity by "virtue" of being tabloid fodder for TMZ.

The hypocrisy I had always known her to possess reached a crescendo in the new year. In her smug cunt way (that took hold immediately after *Mean Girls*), she had declared to Billy Bush (pre-being more famous for a certain "locker room conversation" with Trump), "You'll never see me in a nude scene." This was roughly around the same time she said she would never be in *Playboy* to Jay Leno. Obviously, she's a fucking hypocrite since, by 2012, she had gotten desperate enough to have done both. But in January of 2006, she was still attempting to play the "virgin" coquette. That's why MTV's Jennifer Vineyard (is that a real name?) would write of the *Vanity Fair* pictures she "so generously" posed for—like she wasn't lapping up the publicity—"Lohan has since regained some of the weight, which she shows off by posing nude in the…photo spread." With such a "spread," she had officially dipped her toe into the *Playboy* pool (figuratively and literally) by stripping down for a magazine. Telling herself it was "tasteful" because, what, it's *Vanity Fair*? Get real.

Re: Vineyard's quote, first of all, thank god we no longer live in a time where journalists feel the need to be PC about a celebrity's drug habits ("regained some of the weight" being the most tiptoeing description of all-time). Luckily, that all went the way of the dodo when Vanessa Grigoriadis wrote an article called "The Tragedy of Britney Spears" for publication as the cover story two years later in *Rolling Stone*'s February 2008 issue. In said article, there are no bones made about Britney's "habitual, frequent and continuous" drug habits. God, I still enjoy having parties themed around close readings of some of those more brutal sections, like, "She is not America's sweetheart. She is an inbred swamp thing who chain-smokes, doesn't do her nails, tells reporters to 'eat it, snort it, lick it, fuck it' and screams at people who want pictures for their little sisters." Or, better still, "She's the perfect celebrity for America in decline: like President Bush, she just doesn't give a fuck, but at least we won't have to clean up after her mess for the rest of our lives." The sheer ferocity of the "reportage," paired with the naivety of not foresee-ing Trump coming along and being so much worse than Bush could ever be, makes me practically, like, cry every time. Yes, Grigoriadis set the bar for a new form of high art in trash talking, but she also really missed the mark on writing with something of a premonitory steez. Oh dear, I've spiraled off topic again. There's just so many people to casually criticize, you know?

As I was saying, Lindsay Lohan: hypocrite extraordinaire. Trying to poison the well of her "veneration" wasn't working for me anymore as it had during my Bangladesh stint. This much was confirmed at the book party for Nicole's clearly ghostwritten "novel," *The Truth About Diamonds*. For everyone soon realized by thumbing through its not-very-glossy pages that nowhere in the book is Lindsay "alluded to" (better known as: shaded). In short, she was not a "diamond" (Nicole's cornball word for "true friends"—like diamonds, they're "bright, beautiful, valuable and *always* in style." Lindsay embodying none of those traits). Even though Nicole felt free to lambast *my* "personage" in it, I guarantee you I'm the only one of her friends who read that shite from cover to cover. To think there are real writing geniuses out there who can't get book deals because of people like her. Anyway, Nicole was an unequivocal pussy, if you ask me. Writing this damn faux autobiography under the guise of acting as "Chloe's" guardian angel friend or whatever in it. But one thing she did get right was the description of the L.A. club scene in that epoch: "The nightclubs of L.A. are like soap operas… There's always some bizarre drama that plays out every single night, and everyone in the cast—I mean, *everyone*—is great looking, stoned and/or drunk."

But *The Truth About Diamonds* would be nothing compared to the real-life bizarre drama that was about to play out with even more bombast in the coming months. Because 2006 is the year I pinpoint as the definitive beginning of the end for Lindsay, who, in this regard, still stole my life because it took me but a few bad choices to fall from grace, while it's literally been over ten years since getting on Paris' bad side and the release of *Just My Luck* proving her flagrant inadequacies and she's only just *now* being truly ostracized. This perhaps best revealed by the girl (old bag?) not even getting cast in a sequel to *Life-Size 2* with Tyra Banks. That's pretty fucking huge pariah status. Then again, her inability to be cast in the same role could simply be because Black women look forever young and white women do not (even with a steady diet of La Mer and plastic surgery…ooo, *La Mer and Plastic Surgery.* Another potential autobiography title when I reach my fifties and am on the moon or wherever with all the other rich people). Plus, casting *ethnique* actresses like Francia Raisa is just too chic to pass up right now.

The point is, the number of chances Lindsay has been given as a non-socialite is unquestionably outrageous (as Britney would say). Not to mention an unprecedented anomaly that has many more pages in this book (soon to be screenplay) to fill. 'Cause I've got nowhere to be and it's apparent that you don't either.

<u>Chapter 9: Stars Are Blind, And So Is
Public Taste</u>

As I think I've iterated in various manners throughout my tale of woe thus far, my whole problem in life is that I'm too intelligent *and* attractive to be designed for mass consumption in the way that Paris and Lindsay were (or are, to those still living hopelessly in the past and refusing to accept the present—that includes a certain account called @popculturediedin2009). There was no irony to their shtick until after they'd both become has-beens. Nicole and Kim were the ones who played the long game well, parlaying their *The Simple Life* personae (don't forget that Kim appeared on that show too in her glorified assistant incarnation) into something that has and will continue to feed their family for generations to come (who could have predicted that House of Harlow and a sex tape would be so profitable?).

And then there was me, still on the outside looking in. After the self-esteem gut punch of Jake going home with Paris on Halloween and Lindsay's second album not sinking her career completely, I needed some time to reflect on where everything had gone wrong. Even though I usually like to be in L.A. for awards season, I didn't want to see Jake at the Golden Globes, and obviously he was going to be there because everyone was sucking his and Heath's dick hard over *Brokeback Mountain* (no pun intended or whatever). At least Jake didn't get nominated though—all the accolades went to Heath, as though Hollywood could somehow sniff out that he was going to die soon enough. Philip Seymour Hoffman winning what should have been Heath's Golden Globe for Best Performance in a Motion Picture - Drama just accents that the industry was only lightly flirting with showing what is now unequivocal reverence for all things homo and beyond ("beyond" meaning trans—though Felicity Huffman also won Best Performance in a Motion Picture - Drama that year for her retroactively offensive role in *Transamerica*).

In 2006 though, Hollywood was still in bed with the conservatism of the Bush years, which, in contrast to "the Donald," somehow kept them in check rather than making them more rebellious. I guess, at the bare minimum, the Academy would kowtow to "progress" by giving Three 6 Mafia the award for Best Original Song. Incidentally, the image of members of the Academy (including my father) listening to "It's Hard Out Here for a Pimp" was one of a few that helped me smile during the first hour after I had to go to prison for my Lindsay "attack."

What I'm trying to say about the awards hoopla in '06 is: I didn't want to be around for any of that bullshit. So I set off for Istanbul (again, I was doing everything before Lindsay did it). It just sounded like the best place for me at that time. Except I hadn't taken into account that my trip would transpire right as John Paul II's would-be assassin, Mehmet Ali Ağca, was being released from prison. There was a lot of tension in the air as Ağca insisted he was "only" a mercenary in the attempt on the Pope's life (sort of like Lee Harvey Oswald with Kennedy).

In contrast to some twit of the Lindsay variety, I took a truly vested interest in the affairs of the country I was making my temporary home away from home. I didn't realize that I myself would become part of the scandal by requesting a meeting with Ağca in my hotel room—the Four Seasons at the Bosphorus, not that fuckery one at Sultanahmet. It honestly didn't cross my mind that I might be attracted to him, really. You're probably being super judgmental right now and just assuming that I fuck anything that walks, as our modern poet, Eminem, once said (fucked him too, by the way—and during the physical peak of his "Stan" days).

In all honesty, I just wanted to talk to him about his situation—and the political situation at large in Turkey, which was small potatoes at that juncture compared to how things are now. How was I to know that when he came in escorted by two security guards that I would melt over his silver fox aesthetic? It makes a lot of sense that he was a member of the Grey Wolves. If you weren't a Lindsay or Kim fan, you would probably know how funny that play on phrases (phraseology?) is. It's like Enid said in my favorite movie of all-time (because, again, I have some taste), *Ghost World*, "God, everyone's too stupid!"

The second that Ağca barked for the guards to leave us, I knew where this was going to end up. I'm putty in the hands of any potential father figure. In that sense, I could always empathize with Lindsay's wretched taste in men (which would shine just as bright in '06 when she started dating Harry Morton, the heir to the Hard Rock Cafe "empire"— Lindsay just loves heirs). At first, he did make the attempt to explain how the whole Pope assassination attempt thing was only a colossal misunderstanding. He likened himself to being the Lee Harvey Oswald of Turkey (did I call it or did I call it?), just one big government pawn. I pointed out that Lee wasn't so lucky to have sustained his life, to which Ağca dreamily returned, "I often wish I hadn't come out with mine."

It was super sexy, so when I reached my hand out to comfortingly stroke his leg, I didn't mind when he responded with an all-out face sucking. I love when men take the initiative in a non-rapey way, it really is increasingly rare. By the time we were through with one another in the hotel room, rumors of our tryst had already traveled throughout the land, and people were tarnishing my name more than they ever did with Lindsay's when she started speaking with that fake accent. Jesus (Muhammad?), and here I thought that a Muslim country would revere a man who tried to kill the ultimate emblem of Catholicism.

The stigma against me after I was found out for my Ağca dalliance got so bad that I had to flee to a remote island on Greece—one that I can't even name check because it's *that* exclusive for amnesty. But what people don't seem to realize is that island existence is actually a waking nightmare in any season that isn't summer, so I basically just felt like I was a prisoner confined the way British people relegated to ancient Australia must have back in the day. On the other hand, though, it gave me a lot of time to tackle some creative ideas that I hadn't yet felt centered enough to pursue. I even started writing a little bit of this back then, somehow intuiting that I would eventually need to set the record straight about my side of the story. Most importantly though, I continued working on my album, the one that Nicole discouraged me against, and that she would ultimately steal primary aspects from to feed to Paris. Ugh. The Paris Lackey Syndrome was so real. I never thought anyone I knew would crawl out from under it. And then Lindsay, of all people, started to.

The timeline of the Paris/Lindsay feud is debated by many, particularly those who automatically like to trace it to the instant Paris giggled rather than stepped in to defend the accusation of "firecrotch" by her "boyfriend" (a loose term, to be sure) of the moment, Brandon Davis. By the way, a few words about Brandon: like Stavros, we all had our turn with him. Where Paris made the mistake was in actually getting it in her head that she would have any sort of exclusive hold on the beast. It's like Mr. Pussy in *Sex and the City* (yes, I make a lot of *Sex and the City* references, I'm a heteronormative white woman), "You don't fall in love with Mr. Pussy. You enjoy him and then set him free," with Carrie adding in her annoying voiceover fashion, "To Samantha, Charlotte had committed the ultimate sin. She was bogarting Mr. Pussy."

And that's what Paris had attempted in her dealings with both Brandon and Stavros, each one obviously making his rounds through various Hollywood starlet trash before finally getting to Lindsay (though Brandon would never admit to it). That Lindsay actually *responded* to Stavros' advances (while of course probably making some of her own because ho is life) was what irritated Paris most of all. Because more than inferring she no longer had a hold over Stavros, it meant she no longer had a hold over Lindsay.

That's why the feud really begins in May, when Lindsay was first reported to be making out with Stavros all over Manhattan, including at Butter and Bungalow 8 (not to bring up *Sex and the City* again, but these places are also notable for being now-defunct hot spots referred to in…*Sex and the*

City). When Paris confronted her about it at Hyde the same month, Lindsay fought back verbally in a manner that Paris had never experienced. So it was this—not the double whammy nosedive of back-to-back film choices consisting of *Herbie: Fully Loaded* and *Just My Luck*—behavior that spelled Lindsay's fall from the spotlight's grace. Then again, *Just My Luck* (co-penned by *SATC* writer Amy B. Harris, because it always goes back to *SATC*) didn't help matters upon its release on May 12th.

Even though Chris Pine (and his clay-molded body) was in it to theoretically bolster the attractive qualities of the movie to the female audience, he was still too new to the game to be a bankable matinee idol (the poor sap only had *The Princess Diaries 2: Royal Engagement* as a primary highlight on his embryonic resume). And based on plot alone, which for some reason heavily revolved around close-ups of dog shit, there was no way *Just My Luck* was going to thrive, not even to an audience as tasteless as the one that would have usually flocked to a Lindsay or Lindsay-like (read: Amanda Bynes—more on her later—or Hilary Duff) movie. Paired with the long-simmering Paris beef that had now boiled over, I could tell that Lindsay was due to take a tumble. Which is precisely why I timed my return from Greece for June, just weeks after Brandon went off on his TMZ-captured tirade.

What's more, I needed to be present for Paris' upcoming album release party—being that I still had no idea that she and Nicole had done me dirty with regard to swiping my lyrical and sonic content. And yeah, maybe you're thinking, "How hard can it be to write something like 'Screwed'? Of course it's not going to be a stretch to 'steal' banal lyrics." But that's where you're wrong. Vapidity is a skill that not just anyone knows how to wield correctly. I would have done it better than Paris, because at least I would have understatedly imbued my work with meaning. Like the true artist I am. With Paris, it was all scum disguised as effervescence. That's why she's so well-suited to those foam parties in Ibiza. In any event, I made my usual cameo at Gary's (I had taken to calling him Gary rather than Daddy as there was nothing paternal about him, least of all when considering how our relationship had become un-deniably sexual of late) to change into a worthwhile ensemble for what Paris was unoriginally calling "Paris at The Beverly Hilton." I didn't even see the house as Gwen's anymore. She had practically moved to Palm Springs at this point—but that's not a subject Gary would dare broach when I asked him when she was coming back.

For the occasion, I put on a custom-made black sequined dress from The Row—Mary-Kate and Ashley had expressly requested that I be one of the "models," so to speak, to help them advertise their new label. When I saw the designs they were toying with at the outset, I really didn't think it would last. Then, that was foolish of me, as there's no business venture an Olsen can't sustain, salvage or repurpose. They've been turning shit into gold since *Full House*. That was before your time so maybe you have no idea what I'm talking about without Googling it. That's the true test of age, you know. If you have to Google something that you're too young or too old to have experienced for yourself.

I arrived fashionably late to the fête. I didn't want everyone to notice right away that I didn't have a piece of arm candy, which was sort of a first for me. Me, Tate? With no date? It was unheard of. I had always known the value and power of showing up in a couple. It's what the people want. I suppose my greatest flaw is that, through it all, I've remained a people pleaser. Honestly, I don't know why I bother. Look what happened to Gretchen when she kept trying to lick Regina's asshole: cast aside for the social status reaper to take away. No, no. If I've learned one thing throughout this whole ordeal called coveting Lindsay Lohan even at her lowest points, it's that you can only try to please yourself. Because the second you don't get the reaction you want from others after all you've done for them, you're going to be disappointed.

That's how I felt about Paris and Nicole that night. The Kardashians were there too, but the reality show was still a year away so no one cared. They were all focused on Paris, who was in top form. And there were plenty of available C-list snacks for her to choose from. Even Nick Carter was there. Not invited because Paris had forgiven him for cheating on her with Ashlee Simpson (he clearly has a type), but because she wanted to dangle it in Ashlee's face. She also wanted to fully let the cat out of the bag in terms of kiboshing rumors that Ashlee had written "Boyfriend" about Lindsay accusing her of somehow stealing Wilmer Valderrama (as if anyone would want to fight over that) by directing the song's content back to herself. This marked yet another public slight toward Lindsay, whose only attempt at legitimacy in 2006 was starring in Robert Altman's worst movie, *A Prairie Home Companion*. Like anyone was gonna be into that shit unless they were already built-in nerds about the radio show. Even Meryl Streep and Lily Tomlin couldn't make it palatable to the mainstream. And if Lindsay was about anything at all, it was the mainstream.

Though the rest of us had made it through the summer relatively unscathed, Lindsay couldn't shake the stink of her box office bomb. *Just My Luck* was possibly the most uncouth foil to Woody Allen's *Match Point* there could be (funnily, Lindsay never finagled her way into one of that molester's movies while still in her prime). And what's worse, Amy B. Harris lowered her talents to the level of the project.

Here she had been one of the top women I would have loved to work with on a film apart from Patty Jenkins (*Monster* obviously changed my life). And now, she had sullied her reputation. Centered on the premise that a little luck can change your life, the concept was all too eerie in terms of being a precursor to Lindsay's fate in the coming years. For as you already know, 2007-2008 was a rocky period for every celebutante who had her place in the sun in the earlier part of the aughts. Ugh, I hate that word. It really is pretentious as all get-out. The type of term people who didn't live through it like to use. They can never know. Never understand what a moment in time it was (yet for some masochistic reason, I'm still trying to break it down for you daft motherfuckers).

That Lindsay would also get dumped by someone as lame-o as Harry Morton in September only added to her increasing spiral. It didn't help matters that his rejection of her was caught on film, and that the reason he cited for ditching her was simply that being with her was too dramatic. In a way, I almost—repeat: *almost*—felt sorry for her. Mainly because she should have been the one to get styled with the "A Little Bit Dramatic" tee in *Mean Girls*. But, alas, Regina George always wins.

Sipping my (pain just like) champagne in the corner while ruminating upon this fact, Paris had, as per usual, started dancing on a tabletop. Nicole was watching from afar with Benji, who was still pretending to carry on with Hilary, even though he would break up with her in November. It seemed, in fact, that everyone *except* Hilary already knew that Benji was cheating with Nicole. And though the fallout between Paris and Nicole had already occurred, they remained beholden to one another because of *The* goddamn *Simple Life*, condemned to run through the following year—again, 2007 really signaled the beginning of the end for us all. That is, white hoes.

Nicole was still trying to play nice (which, I reckon, was the reason she had funneled my musical ideas to Paris), but Paris wasn't having it, acting every bit the cunt she can be to both Nicole and Kim throughout the party. Lindsay, who didn't get invited, was also maligned at various moments, with Paris quipping to Kim, "I'm going to go into *serious* acting next. Like Lindsay in *Just My Luck*." Kim's reaction to every insult about anyone, of course, was to titter or blink. She was like a wind-up doll made expressly for Paris. And Paris did like all her puppets custom. That's why I was surprised she was so chatty with *me* that night. We'd had our fair share of drama, and I'd forgiven her for the Jake Gyllenhaal thing by now, but things were still feeling tense to me these past few months.

So when she sidled up to me to start telling me about the trip to Ibiza she had just gotten back from with Kim and DJ Caroline D'Amore, who Paris would expressly never tack on the DJ title to in spite of Caroline being in the game for way longer, I felt ill at ease. Caroline was, indeed, the person who had assisted Paris navigate the Ibiza club scene when she was nothing but an unformed and unopinionated zygote on all matters Ibiza. She was even artless enough to think Pacha was the end all, be all at that time. Without Caroline, Paris would probably still be stuck in Eivissa Town rather than gradually making her way to Amnesia. I knew all of this as Paris rehashed the highlights of their trip together, and how it came at the perfect time for her to put the final mixing touches on *Paris*. She then proceeded to tell me that I absolutely *had to* come next summer, and how she would *just love it* if I could be the one to round out the trio with her and Kim this time, instead of Caroline.

I suddenly started to reappreciate that gift she had for making you the center of her universe. Because when she did, it truly was magical. But when she didn't, well, then you were relegated to whatever scraps of work and publicity you could get the way Lindsay was (no one was drawn to *Bobby* because of her minor part in it, for example, and she even resorted to a cameo in *The Holiday*, a long way from being the star of a Nancy Meyers film like she was in *The Parent Trap*).

As the night wore on, Paris got increasingly confessional with me, taking me up to her suite at one point to dish about how gross Brandon Davis is, and how she had the sneaking suspicion that he had been intimate with Nicky. It would make sense, Nicky was always jealous of Paris' congenital ability to bask in the limelight when she "couldn't" (it was still the biggest mistake of her life to pass up the chance to co-star with Paris on *The Simple Life*. Then again, she probably wouldn't have landed a legitimately aristocratic husband with that kind of reality TV smear on her record). Nicky also coveted Paris' predilection for being wild. The only wild thing she ever really did was in 2004. Copping Britney Spears' move with a shotgun wedding just eight months after she married childhood friend Jason Alexander, Nicky did the same thing with her own childhood friend (yes, socialites have endless reserves of male friends), Todd Meister.

No one really cared or wrote about it, as Britney's Vegas wedding was far more interesting because of how trashy it was. What's more, Britney annulled (or rather, Larry Rudolph annulled) her nuptials in just fifty-five hours to Nicky's three months, making for greater tabloid fodder. Britney's lust for love only persisted in July of the same year when she announced her engagement to K-Fed. And this contrast in impromptu weddings is exactly what differentiates a pop star and/or actress (read: Britney and Lindsay) from a bona fide socialite.

While no one else believed Paris about her intuition regarding Brandon and Nicky, I certainly did. That's why I couldn't fault her for setting her sights on Travis Barker as a distraction well after the Blink-182 peak had passed. But that was always Paris' type. If it wasn't a Greek heir, it was a musician in a shitty faux punk band (that includes, most overtly, Deryck Whibley). She hadn't quite gotten Travis pinned down because he was still trying to make it work with his wife, Shanna Moakler. Apparently, that only left *me* as the most viable option for a hookup that evening because, one minute we were talking about how shitty Blink-182 was, and the next she was sticking her tongue down my throat and slipping her hand down the front of my dress to finger my nipple. Like Amanda Seyfried (who knew her career would outshine Lindsay's *and* Rachel's?) as Needy in *Jennifer's Body*, I couldn't help but let it happen. There was just something so enchanting about her. And I do tend to think that her lulling lazy eye was a part of it.

More than the MDMA we had both ingested downstairs (how could she *not* have molly-laced punch at a listening party for an album like *Paris*?), it was the long-standing emotional connection between us that led to what we later confessed to one another to be the most intense orgasms of our life. But the second I made Paris cum with the deft movements of my tongue, she had a complete anti-lesbian freakout that would have made any number of "closeted" celebrity lesbians (*cough cough*Cynthia Nixon) balk in disappointment. So there I was, practically drenched in socialite discharge, as Paris suddenly exclaimed that she didn't like me "like that" while also snapping a picture of me in my state of undress. Later, I realized she had taken it as some form of collateral that she wouldn't even bother to blackmail me with, instead just sending it right over to Perez Hilton with the caption: "Guess who got caught sneaking out of Aaron Carter's house this morning?"

Of all the people to accuse me of banging, that was the lowest blow. It wasn't just that Aaron hadn't been relevant in five years, but that the only thing people had been discussing about him of late was the rumor that he was HIV-positive. There was calculation in Paris' decision to select him as the purported source of my discharge-sprayed face: she knew it would make me untouchable by proxy. Once again, I was betrayed by the very person I thought was my best friend. Lured like a middling insect to a spider's web. But goddammit, I knew *I* was the spider. And not a bitch black widow of a spider but a benevolent, self-sacrificing Charlotte one. That's my burden in life. Being too sodding nice for this world. Sorry, a side effect of being a socialite is incorporating British slang into your vocabulary to prove how well-traveled you are. And there I am apologizing for no reason to you.

And there was no reason to apologize to Paris either, who had, once again, made me *persona non grata* along with Lindsay. Speaking of that freckled misogynist-lover, the only thing that seemed to cause a break in the scandal from my Aaron Carter rumor—which Aaron, being the perpetually starved for attention asshole that he is, did nothing to negate—was Lohan's latest car crash in November. By that time, she had moved on to a new temporary boo, Calum Best. He being a—well, there is no word for a male socialite, though there really ought to be. If I was going to coin one, it would have to be "*hommeriche*" because it's French. That way, poor people wouldn't be able to pronounce it. Really always a great way to weed out who you should and shouldn't be talking to. If their accent is terrible, walk the other way immediately because they've probably never 1) gone to an appropriate private/boarding school that would vigilantly teach the correct pronunciations and/or 2) they've never been to Europe.

As I was saying, Calum is an *hommeriche*, the son of British soccer god, George Best. Think of him as, like, the grandfather to David Beckham. By the look of things, however, Lindsay was having trouble keeping up with Calum. There's just something about British boys that make them immune to mass drug intakes (see: Pete Doherty, Blake Fielder-Civil).

194

It can be the downfall of many a girl attempting a "relationship" with one.

I don't even really know what Lindsay was doing in London at that time. If she had some sort of "project," I certainly wasn't aware. She took some bullshit hosting gig for the World Music Awards, the really creepy edition where Chris Brown did a tribute to Michael Jackson so he could accept one of those, like, achievement "honors" and then sing "We Are the World" with some kids who were Blacker than Michael Jackson ever wanted to be. Anyway, I think Lindsay was just trying to get away from Los Angeles for a while, sort of surrendering what little patch of the throne she had left to Paris, Nicole and Kim. Even though Paris ended up showing herself in London anyway, unable to miss a red-carpet opportunity of any kind—oh, that and she thought she was genuinely a musician herself because of that fucking album she put out. And while Lindsay whored up her aesthetic more than usual to secure a taste of Calum, *I* wasn't even a consideration in her mind as we still had yet to cross paths (though I'm sure several of the same dicks had crossed our *vaginal* paths).

It was likely because of having to deal with yet another car crash in London (while driving away from Kabaret Prophecy with Calum) that she decided to come back to L.A. even faster than she had left it. Perhaps solely to fulfill the destiny of being part of the historic "peace conference" that was to take place on November 27th, barely a couple weeks after the accident in LDN. The date, of course, refers to the now infamous photo session of the trifecta that included Britney, Paris and Lindsay driving chaotically away from paparazzi. The ensuing images of the trio led to one of the *New York Post*'s greatest headlines of all time: "Bimbo Summit." And oh, *quelle surprise*, no one felt compelled to tell Nicole or me about the little gathering that included a jaunt to Guy's (it's a club, in case you're too young and addicted to screens to comprehend that people used to dance, like, just to do it…not because there was potential to go "viral"—unless you were caught with Joel Madden by Kim in one of the bathroom stalls).

Then again, Paris was being very transparent about her motives in wanting to include Lindsay in the trio, immediately making her tell the TMZ-centric paparazzi that she never got violent with her. Because the night before, in yet another L.A. parking lot, Lindsay approached the cameras of her own volition to tell them, "Paris Hilton—and I'm saying this on tape—she hit me last night, for no reason apparently. At my friend's house and I didn't know she'd be there, and she hit me. She hit me with a drink and poured it all over me and it hurts and it's not okay. And I'm sorry for everyone that thinks I'm crazy. I'm not. I'm just trying to act."

She then "dropped the mic" by flashing a peace sign before she slithered all Jafar-like back into her hotel, getting off on her own performance for the paps. That bitch don't even need to *try* to act in life—artifice just comes naturally for the purpose of her self-delusion. But she does need to try harder to in any future TV movie she might finagle. Any TV movie that surely has to be better than yet another "last attempt" at a "comeback" like *Among the Shadows*. Not to be confused with the flawless mockumentary that is *What We Do in the Shadows*...god, how have I never fucked Jemaine Clement? I really need to get that New Zealand stamp on my sexual passport.

Paris, never one to allow bad press of the non-sexual variety to stand, used her minx-like powers to persuade Lindsay to come out the following evening for a bit of damage control (much later, she would claim Lindsay "wasn't invited"). Yes, only Paris during this era of her power's apex could have gotten a vulnerable (especially in the wake of two horrendous movies) Lindsay to publicly tell the paparazzi that her prior adamant declaration was utterly false. To build upon the "angelic Paris" persona, it was almost as though she deliberately chose Britney to join her that night so that she could liquor her up and act like a self-sacrificing nursemaid as she guided Brit Brit into the Benz while ushering away the press, chastising, "Guys, don't be perverts!"

as they tried to get a glimpse of the underwearless pop star's vajayjay (an 00s vocab word if ever there was one—which we can thank Shonda Rhimes for inventing because of the stodgy Broadcast Standards and Practices people reining in use of the actual word, "vagina," on an '06 episode of *Grey's Anatomy*).

Paris didn't have to try that hard to come across as "caretaker" though, because Britney was really commencing her senile person phase, that's for sure. No panties and a glazed-over look were just the beginning. Unsatisfied without a blurred-out crotch shot to offer *Us Weekly* or *People* (or even *Life & Style* or *Star*), one of the vultures asked, "So Paris, did you hit Lindsay?" Timed with suspicious perfection, suddenly Lindsay emerged, though she was nowhere to be found before. Paris then insisted, "No. Ask her, she's right there. Lindsay! Tell them the truth."

As though parroting a rehearsed statement, Lindsay vaguely slurred, "Paris never hit me, she's my friend. Everyone lies about everything. She's a nice person, please leave us alone." The paparazzo kept probing the issue, inquiring, "So you're friends?" More vehement than before, Lindsay concludes, "Yes. She never did that, she's a good girl. She's a nice person. I've known her since I was fifteen. Please stop trying to make us hate each other."

The lady doth protest too much, constantly repeating "Paris is my friend" like a mantra that she wants so badly to be true. She even tried to make herself believe it the second after getting caught calling Paris a cunt on camera on November 9th and then, once again, vowing, "Paris is my friend." This desire to turn the repetitive chant into a reality mirrors Franny Glass' want for The Jesus Prayer to become an unconscious mantra so natural it's like a second heartbeat. In both women's cases, it was not to be so.

As for me, I was putting the finishing touches on my own record, and was determined to release it in February of '07, a notoriously slow month with regard to new music coming out. Meaning I might actually attract enough interest in spite of being an "unknown." If all went accordingly, I wanted to tour around small venues in L.A., you know, the Wiltern, the El Rey, those types of places. What I'm trying to say is, I was distancing myself from the Paris and Lindsay drama as much as possible, finding it all very drab and played out at this point. Maybe Lindsay was of the same mindset as she once more got left in the dust by Paris, who was content to select Kim as the lead member of her entourage to go to Sydney over the course of six days running over the New Year. I guess they paid her half a million (which really is like a penny to Paris, so I don't know the true motive behind her decision to travel so fucking far to "work") to promote some typically shitty Australian beer brand.

By now, Kim had officially graduated to being called Paris' "stylist," though I, personally, wouldn't have wanted to take credit for that no matter how non-famous I was and in need of clawing my way to the top by any degrading means necessary. 'Cause Paris had some real shitty fashions back in the day, namely her low-riding pants that shamelessly showed her crack. I still shudder at the image.

With the Australian "paparazzi" (I, of course, use that term for lack of a better one) lapping up Paris' presence—not so much Kim's—they were kind enough to pay intermittent attention to who Paris' "companion" was by adding captions like, "Daughter of former O. J. Simpson lawyer Robert Kardashian." God, how I relished this period of Kim's "fame." But '07 was to commence the ultimate sea change in shifting powers and alliances.

Chapter 10: I Know Who Killed Me (& My Reputation)

As you probably know (because I don't imagine you're reading this unless you're just as nostalgic for a simpler, more scandal-ridden epoch), 2007 was an extremely trying year for us all. And even though Lindsay was doing her best to ignore the very real fact that her fame cachet was plummeting (/turning into full-tilt infamy), one could tell by the initial days of her January that she was in retreat mode. Hence, going to Miami for a few days before then taking another little trip…to the hospital. For an "appendectomy."

By January 17th, she was already checking into her first publicized tour of rehab. At Wonderland. Promises would come later. Seriously, what the fuck is with the condescension of these rehab names? Clearly, they have no bearing on what happens once you get out, as Lindsay was "released" and partying barely two weeks after her mid-February relinquishment with that trashball, Steve Aoki. She persisted in enjoying her partying through most of March on both sides of the country, with rumors likely started by her own damn mouth that she had allowed entrance into her vag by Jude Law, James Blunt (remember him?), Stavros (always goddamn Stavros) and Ryan Phillippe (everyone knew he was off limits as he had literally *just* separated from Reese, and everyone also knows you don't go against America's sweetheart, whoever she may be at the moment).

She was still intermittently juggling Calum Best through it all (the British fuckboys are even more irresistible than the American ones), but by the July 4th party that found her still attempting to sport her ankle monitoring bracelet like a must-have beach accessory, he didn't seem all too interested in her. And it didn't even have anything to do with Paris also being in attendance. She, too, was starting to fall from "grace" (if that's what we want to call it), what with Ryan Seacrest securing a reality TV series for Kim and her family that would premiere on E! in October. Timing-wise, it was a major fame pendulum shift, as *The Simple Life* would be ending in August on the same network. In terms of a seismic shift being afoot with regard to celebrity, this was, I would say, the most palpable indication.

Yet another car crash on July 23rd secured that much in Lindsay's case. I got on my computer that morning with a piping hot cup of coffee to read all the gossip: lurid headlines of a hundred-mile-an-hour car chase on the Pacific Coast Highway. Which occurred, most embarrassingly of all, after her personal assistant had walked out on her during a party because she was so heinous to work for that even the perk of being able to rub up against B-list celebs and have access to all the coke and alcohol she wanted wasn't worth being this has-been's lapdog.

Woooooo. My contempt sometimes capsizes even me with its waves. Apologies. Let me continue. I was so taken with the extent of Lindsay's humiliation that I wanted more. I wanted her to really process just how *over* she was. More *over* than the song, "Over," that she wrote about Wilmer. That's why I called up the assistant mentioned in all the articles. For "safety" purposes, I'll refer to her as "Laura."

I asked Laura if she was in search of new work. I was her tenth offer that morning, she told me, but I eventually cajoled her with the right price and the promise of "light work." I had to get more intel about Lindsay. Figure out what her greatest, most foolproof weaknesses were and then exploit them to a point that would end her career for good.

Without her presence in Hollywood, Paris would be all mine again. I knew she hated Nicole and Kim now, and was just looking for a viable reason to come back to our friendship on a more permanent basis. Tactically, I would have to do something to elevate her new, yet waning obsession with DJing. Because, as much as she tried to insist she "could not have been happier with the crowd's reaction" in São Paulo after doing a set for some bullshit J. Lo/Kelly Clarkson show, I could tell she felt inferior about her foray into "that world." And J. Lo and Kelly Clarkson didn't even matter then, so I guess maybe Paris just used them to dip her toe in the water and see what she was capable of. And who was the one there front and center to take it all in and pander to her delusions? Moi, of course. Ugh, how quickly our friends forget about their true and constant allies. But before I catered further to "DJ Paris," I would need to gain Laura's trust so that she could slowly reveal the necessary tidbits to ensure Lindsay would never get over her addiction.

By August 5th, she was already heading to the Cirque Lodge—this is most definitely not to be confused with Le Cirque in New York. No, this rehab center is in Sundance, Utah. Not just a place where celebrities go to watch their shitty indie movies, but also a place of "healing." I don't really know what sort of healing Lindsay did there, other than maybe healing her vag a little more on a few randos' dicks. Because, surely, it must have been the steady orgasms that incited her to release the very "zen" statement: "It is clear to me that my life has become completely unmanageable because I am addicted to alcohol and drugs. Recently, I relapsed and did things for which I am ashamed. I broke the law, and today I took responsibility by pleading guilty to the charges in my case. No matter what I said when I was under the influence on the day I was arrested, I am not blaming anyone else for my conduct other than myself. I thank God I did not injure others. I easily could have. I very much want to be healthy and gain control of my life and career and have asked for medical help in doing so. I am taking these steps to improve my life. Luckily, I am not alone in my daily struggle and I know that people like me have succeeded. Maybe with time it will become easier. I hope so."

How touchingly "heartfelt." Anyway, it was one steady dick(head) in particular, Riley Giles, who kept Lindsay busy throughout her stint. And by the time she was out—for the third fucking time that year—the two were a full-on item. That is, until he inevitably betrayed her for the money furnished by *News of the World* for his "story." Something to the usual effect of: "she's a slut," which he chose to elaborate on by detailing the highlights of their sexcapades ("She has a great body. Her backside is fantastic, perfect, all plump and round"—um, sure). and Lindsay's nymphomaniacal tendencies ("We once did it four times in a row straight. That was crazy. Lindsay was insatiable. She'd demand sex again and again. We'd go at it for hours. She'd have worn out most guys"). I could believe that. Except no one's a bigger nympho than I am. So do I need to stress again how Lindsay Lohan stole my life? Even the nymphomania brand. It was as though she took one look at my existence and said (to quote 50 Cent's illustrious "rhyme"): "If you be a nympho/I be a nympho." Fine then. I would be an assistant poacher.

***

Laura brought me my usual round of all the essentials—*Us Weekly*, *In Touch*, *Life & Style OK!*, *Hello!*, *Entertainment Weekly* and even *People* (which I always thought took itself way too seriously)—one afternoon in late September. She got used to me pretty quickly, and I relished her willingness of late to rehash that night to me, the one that made me hire her. She even corroborated one of Lindsay's passengers' stories, insisting that she screamed, "I can't get in trouble. I'm a celebrity. I can do whatever the fuck I want!" Laura rolled her eyes and said, "I totally believe it. It's completely in character."

I also pored over residual reports about what might have caused Britney's extremely embarrassing performance of "Gimme More" at the VMAs on September 9th, during which she hobbled around in a vacant body and manner (both inspired by the bovine). But like I said, I wouldn't see her again until '08; we'd lost all contact since my Italian sojourn back during '04. And though I didn't want to admit it, some part of me felt as though Lindsay's absence from the VMA ceremony in Vegas (the tableau really foreshadowed Britney's *Britney: Piece of Me* k-hole) was, in part, why Brit was so disinterested. She probably genuinely thought Lindsay was her friend after that overly photographed November night in '06—she was jejune that way, until she started to get wise to con artists ("Womanizer" is the crystallization of her finally realizing that to have faith in people is to allow yourself to go insane).

And yet, ironically, Britney did a friendship solid for Lindsay that cringeworthy evening at The Palms (MTV was still riding high off making it a thing after *The Real World* season there). Because if this performance proved anything, it was that perhaps Britney's sole purpose in '07 was to take some of the media heat off of Lindsay. Jesus, she had Rihanna, Chris Brown and *Kid Rock* snickering in the audience over her flaccidity. That's pretty damned humiliating, and therefore understandable that the tabloid-centric media would still be having a field day with it these few weeks later. To make the whole spectacle even more disgracing, Justin Timberlake won pretty much every award that night, including "Quadruple Threat of the Year." This ephemeral "honor" being one of the more random and arbitrary attempts on MTV's part to stay "on-trend," catering to the notion that you had to be "multifaceted" to be famous (which we can all plainly see is not true). And, no, they don't even have the bullshit award anymore because no one poses a "threat" of any kind to multiple industries except maybe Rihanna (Beyoncé's too busy tending to her litter, and so is Kim and all her fellow familial breeders, for that matter).

So yeah, it was pretty goddamn humbling for Britney to go from the most bangable girl in America after that '00 sheer skinsuit performance of "Oops!... I Did It Again" to this hot mess of a heifer barely propped up by all the drugs she was on in front of an ex who had already publicly shamed her. And Lindsay couldn't even show her freckled ass face in support because of...*rehab*? It was a true testament to just what kind of "friend" she was—or rather, was not.

My thoughts were interrupted by the sound of Avril Lavigne's shitty song, "Girlfriend," from her shitty album that came out in April, *The Best Damn Thing*, playing somewhere inside my house. I didn't remember turning on the TV or my iPod dock at any point, so it was kind of freaking me out. I demanded, "Laura, can you go check to see where that fucking turd of a song is coming from? For Edie Sedgwick's sake, I'd rather listen to 'Boyfriend' by Ashlee Simpson."

Laura nodded at me acquiescently, though it looked as though she might be having flashbacks to working for Lindsay as a result of my barking tone. I didn't care, the last thing I needed was some intruder infecting my home with bad music, let alone actually deigning to steal something I could easily replace—I'd prefer the courtesy of a thief who had finer taste than that. While I waited for Laura to figure out if we were going to be murdered to the tune of "Boyfriend" (the type of soundtracked scene you would find in a Bret Easton Ellis novel), I stared at myself for what felt like hours in the nearby full-length mirror. I twirled my hair, pulled my skirt down lower. Pushed my cleavage together to help visualize the answer to whether or not I should get a(nother) tit job. Then I accessorized what I was wearing with my custom Versace sunglasses (they had tiny hearts made of diamonds at the side of the pink-tone lenses) and slightly pulled down my pink and white striped crop top. Having forgotten about Laura, I could see her approaching (read: stealing my spotlight in the mirror's reflection) all of the sudden…with Kim behind her. Miss "K" had a devious aura about her that sent a shiver up my very thin spine.

I whipped around and snapped, "Kim, have you ever heard of a motherfucking doorbell?"

She tittered. "Oh Tate. Your brash manner is part of why you'll never be as famous as the rest of us."

I wanted to wring her then barely-there neck. This upcoming reality show she had managed to secure for herself thanks to allowing that now vintage Ray J sex tape to leak was already going to her overly spray-tanned head (listen, even "Armenians" aren't that "tan" without a bit of extra aid). I still maintain she was biding her time to have it see the light of day, knowing full well that 2003—when the tape was first made—would never be her moment so long as the blonde white girl physique reigned supreme. No, she intuited the correct era to allow it into the collective consciousness. Obama was soon to be president, after all, and there can be no denying that Michelle helped to make curves just as palatable as Kim did.

"What the fuck do you want, ho?" I pressed.

"I'll be super candid with you, bitch. I want to hire Laura."

Laura suddenly looked like an innocent little pig being vied over for her slaughter potential. And I wasn't about to lose my meat. Even though I'm a vegetarian. Sometimes… You get the metaphor.

"Why? What's in it for you? She's barely competent."

Laura guffawed at my insult.

Kim countered, "Then you won't mind me taking her off your hands and paying her double whatever your pittance is."

Laura perked up at this, overtly ready to abandon my ship in favor of getting into a yacht with Kim.

"Oh wow. So you're full of silicone *and* shit. What do you want her so badly for?"

Kim claimed, "Don't you get it? She's only the hottest commodity in town since Lindsay's latest vehicular incident."

"That was months ago. I don't believe you."

Kim rolled her eyes, almost losing one of her glued-on fake eyelashes in the process (she hadn't yet started to go to the salon for actual lash extensions). "Fine. Nothing gets past *you*." Kim sighed and admitted, "She just happens to be the only one in possession of evidence I can use to topple Paris, once and for all."

I glanced over at Laura for some indication of recognition in her face over what it was Kim could be talking about. And yes, there was definitely a flicker.

"She was *Lindsay's* assistant. And *you* were Paris'—who would know better than you how to take her down?"

Kim cleared her throat in irritation. "First of all, I was her *stylist*. There's a very big difference. I wasn't fucking picking up her prescriptions or washing her fucking stupid chihuahua."

"Don't you dare talk about Tinkerbell that way!" I shouted reflexively (though, yes, as I said, her death would be at my own hand).

Kim sighed. "Your loyalty to her is pathetic, and it will in no way reward you when things come to blows. Or when Lindsay starts doing blow again."

"Isn't she already?"

"No, fuckwit. Do you ever actually read any of the magazines you make Laura pick up?"

"Yes, I was just about to finish them."

She waved her hand dismissively at me, all the while with Laura watching us as though regarding a tennis match. "It doesn't matter. Lindsay is working on some new stupid movie. Another attempt at being 'credible' as an 'indie' actress." With that, she handed me *In Touch* and turned to a page with an item about how Lindsay was back to work on a project called *Dare to Love Me* (a semi-bold title for someone as unlovable as she) and was taking tango lessons for the part. I didn't really see how that was much different or more impressive than the pole dancing lessons she had decided to take for *I Know Who Killed Me*. And, obviously, critics weren't that taken with her "commitment to the craft" either.

I thrust the magazine back at Kim. "What does this have to do with Paris?"

Kim remained glib. "Lindsay holds the key to ruining Paris. She always has. It was never Nicole, and it was never me."

"And never me?"

Kim scoffed. "Honey, you barely even register on our social Richter scale."

Before I knew what I was doing, a half-empty highball glass I had filled with my kale and apple smoothie was being heaved in Kim's direction. Like the image of her that would become immortalized on computer desktops with files replacing her tears, she began sobbing and hyperventilating as the glass flew past her nose. It was a surprise to me that it didn't actually make contact seeing as how she still hadn't gotten the reduction. It was huge. But somehow still flat enough to evade colliding with the trajectory of the glass' landing.

Placing her hands on her pointy face protectively, she blubbered, "I can't *believe* you would actually try to commit violence against me." She turned to Laura and added, "You saw that. You can testify that she's a dangerous person. And to be honest, you probably shouldn't even be working for her for your own safety, Laura."

Laura was frozen, likely torn between the comfortableness of familiar bitchery and the fear of losing out on more money. Kim went in for the kill. "Laura, I really think you should just come work for me. It will be a *much healthier* environment."

The damaged assistant made somehow more valuable than the Hope Diamond in the wake of Lindsay's car chase took a deep breath. As though coming to terms with a decision she had already made long ago, Laura declared, "I don't want to work for either of you. I hate this town, and I hate whatever this 'industry' is supposed to be. I'm moving back to Pasadena where nothing happens and no one cares."

I couldn't argue with her there. Pasadena was so boring that no one would ever deign to set the backdrop of a movie there after *Rumor Has It...* with Jennifer Aniston came out. I smiled, vaguely taking a sense of pride in Laura's defiance, like I somehow had a hand in helping her discover her voice, or whatever.

"That's the best choice you could've made. And I want to commend you for not falling prey to 'celebrity.'" I said that last word with audible quotes around it in mockery of Kim.

"Oh shut the fuck up. You don't respect anyone. Least of all yourself," Kim chortled as she eyed my white wedges, white Juicy Couture skirt and aforementioned pink and white striped crop top.

I laughed. "What? You wanna style me now? Make me look as 'good' as you did Paris?"

Kim shook her head. "You *wish* I would style you. Should've taken the opportunity when you had the chance."

"You mean when you were still social climbing?" Laura took this second in our escalating verbal sparring to excuse herself silently from the premises. Sometimes I do still wonder whatever happened to her. Because I could've sworn I saw her in a YouPorn video I was watching years later with my boyfriend (at least for a hot second before Selena Gomez started writing all her songs about him, luring him back in like the manipulative cunt she is), Justin Bieber. Before I soon had to make him my ex-boyfriend due to how unsatisfying he was when it came to having any savvy in how to physically pleasure. The whole reason we were even watching a YouPorn video was under the guise of "being sexy," but I kind of just hoped he might pick up a thing or two from watching. In retrospect, he was probably intimidated by how much more know-how I possessed than he did in the bedroom. Forever a scared little boy that would've preferred a eunuch to a real woman (peppered with some silicone here and there) like me. Enter Hailey Baldwin. Who was suspiciously quick to shed that last name in favor of Justin's.

What's more, I tend to agree with Stefano Gabbana's assessment of Gomez: "è proprio brutta." If you don't speak Italian, I don't know what you're doing as my audience. 'Lando didn't seem to think she was so *brutta* though, when that fucking cad posed with her in a photo for "charity" in the spring of 2014. Sure, Seth Rogen was in the picture with them as well, automatically rendering everything sexless. But then there was that picture of them together outside of *The Chelsea Handler Show* soon after. Christ, it's like 'lando gets an erection from being surrounded by obnoxious and untalented women. Just like the rest of this goddamn tasteless society I've been relegated to.

Meanwhile, Kim seemed to be considering her options in continuing to engage with me. I felt she knew that I would never let her have the last word, that I would always one-up her with my vitriol. And it was then that she concluded, "You know what? As usual, talking with you has been a total waste of my time and vocal cord strength. I'm going home."

"Yeah, better not miss any potential camera opportunity. You might get overshadowed by your cow of a sister."

Kim gave me a wannabe Paris-inspired stink eye as she responded, "First of all, which cow of a sister, and second, let's not be petty with weight comments, shall we? Pretty soon you're going to wish you were as 'fat' as my sister, any of them. Because our body types are about to take over the world. If you had any vision or foresight, you'd get on the right side of things. But you have fun over there in Irrelevancy Land with Paris and Lindsay."

The cold manner in which she stated this actually caused me to take pause and think about a world in which Paris wasn't the queen bee. Lindsay was already very much in Janis Ian territory with the way she was digging her own grave straight out of Hollywood and into Dubai or wherever the fuck else someone would pay her to make an appearance (usually a random and out-of-touch foreign billionaire a.k.a. whoever actually thought financing *Among the Shadows* was a worthwhile "artistic" investment, or that making her the spokesperson for lawyer.com over, say, Kim was pertinent to anything other than the art of the non sequitur).

Watching Kim waddle out of my room, I had a brief vision of watching the best days of the 00s also walking out of there with her. Soon after she had "popped in," I found out that Gary Hamilton, the producer of the project that Kim made mention of, *Dare to Love Me*, couldn't afford to insure Lindsay for the "film," though he claimed it was for "other budgetary reasons."

Everyone knew the truth though: Lindsay was more trouble—therefore more money—than she was worth. And as we went into 2008, her tango lessons were about to go down the drain (unless she happened to remember any of the moves from J. Lo in *Shall We Dance?*). Not only that, but I think we could all see that Lindsay was going to do what she did best when her career continued to perpetually spiral toward a rock bottom that she still—*still*—has yet to reach: engage in a bit of personal controversy.

<u>**Chapter 11: A C(unt) Change**</u>

I never could quite figure out what piece of intel Kim wanted from Laura. But, suffice it to say, Paris was in peak of her powers mode as we entered 2008—regardless of her so-called divagation from the spotlight. Or maybe it only *seemed* like she was in peak of her powers mode since the year began with Britney getting strapped to a gurney and taken to Cedars Sinai for an "evaluation." Christ, it was only January 3rd of this thing called 2008 and Hollywood was already creaming itself over the first major drama of the season.

I can never understand why poseurs sell those mugs and t-shirts that say, "If Britney Can Survive 2007, You Can Survive Today" or "I Feel Like 2007 Britney." Sure, she shaved her head that year, which I'm barely mentioning because it's so overwrought at this point and I was, like, out of town when it happened so it's not as though I have a personal story to tell about it. But it was *2008* when she felt all the aftershocks. For fuck's sake, sole custody of her kids was given to *Kevin Federline* the day after her hospitalization. How would that make *you* feel? To be deemed more of a trainwreck than K-Fed? For K-Fed to be construed as a more "fit" (though he's real fat now) parent. It would be utterly decimating. And I don't even have a maternal bone in my body to fully empathize with Brit's kids being ripped from her like that.

So here we have America's most simultaneously "virginal" and "slutty" pop star sacrificially offered to the altar called "knocking a celebrity off her pedestal after enough time at the top" and the once formerly revered queen of all teen movies in total shambles from the get-go of 2008. It should have made me feel like the happiest girl in the world. But all I felt was the usual hollowness inside from throwing up everything I ate. With two early 00s icons pummeled thoroughly by the uglier trappings of wealth and fame, it only left Paris and Kim in the ring. Nicole was too busy starting to pop out kids and working on her fashion/jewelry line. Maybe the fact that she had already endured the most challenging and humiliating aspects of her addiction in 2003 and 2006 (both times when she didn't get *half* as much flak as any of the rest of us—not even in '03, when she was caught driving with heroin and, less momentously, a revoked license) made her fully rise from the ashes of being a worthless and aging party girl by '08.

With Lindsay a complete undesirable in the film world, she did what any desperate actress would do: turned to a guest appearance on a TV show. And what better choice than the role of a former high school mean girl turned pathetic fast-food worker on *Ugly Betty*? Admittedly, the show was my guilty pleasure at the time it was on, and I watched with special interest to see just how much worse Lindsay could get.

The answer came quickly, with her one-note delivery as Kimmie Keegan (who's, I guess, supposed to be like a jank version of Regina George). The answer was clear to the cast and crew as well, for Lindsay was not deemed worthy of fulfilling the planned six-episode guest stint. Tragically, LiLo could only make it to four episodes before getting the axe. On the plus side, at least she got to be featured in an episode called "Jump," the title being an homage to Madonna. Because this was going to be the only time she'd ever manage to be part of a project that could afford the rights to Madonna's songs (in this case, the shit from her *Hard Candy* album—you know, the one that featured Timbaland, the same man Paris and Lindsay quarreled over to produce their nonexistent albums—including "Candy Shop," "She's Not Me," "Spanish Lesson" and "Miles Away").

The rumors about a rift between Lindsay and America Ferrera were only usurped by the bizarre reports that she could be found in her dressing room obsessively cutting out tabloid photos of herself. And those photos were, in large part, thanks to her best career move of the year: "turning lesbian" for Samantha Ronson. One can only blame such a "turn" on her string of bad romance (*not* a Lady Gaga reference, I hate that cunt, too) decisions, speckled (like cum drops) with a roster of fuckboys such as Riley Giles. I get it, I've been there myself. But no one talked about *my* dalliance with Paris. Or Ellen. No, Ellen was too "well-liked" to be accused of cheating. Believe you me though, she's a fucking skank. And gives the ill na na head to prove it. Oh, there I go again, devolving.

Anyway, with Lindsay always claiming, "I'm a different person now," even to this fucking day when she's still a lazy asshole who just likes to stay in hotels and go to clubs (unlike the rest of us socialites who actually *work*), she didn't seem so "different" with regard to her Petty (Ugly) Betty levels in late '08, when she told *Bazaar*, "I have goals and I'm working to achieve them. I'm not hanging out with people who are out every night getting fucked up." This was, obviously, direct shade-throwing at Paris and Britney, a total besmirchment of that magical evening they shared together two years ago at the time of the interview. And Christ, what the fuck were these "goals" anyway, apart from being a model for her own leggings line so she could have an excuse to go topless? News flash: no one needs an excuse to do that anymore.

To boot, the shitty feel of the fabric of 6126 had no business being debuted at Fred Segal, holy temple of Cher Horowitz. I paid my latest assistant to go buy me a few pairs so no one would snap a photo of me within five miles of the product. And when-whatever-her-name-was brought them back to my house, I tried them on immediately to make my assessment: Wal-Mart material. Paris would *never* allow such an inferior piece of merchandise to bear her name. It just really goes to show the difference between a born socialite who already has the money to never come across as desperate in her business endeavors versus a social climber posing as an actress.

Still, Lindsay couldn't help her constant need to feign Paris-level wealth. This much was made clear based on her prom-themed birthday party that year. Paris, however, was not invited as they were in an ice-out over their pre-Grammy catfight. I, naturally, didn't get an invite either. Lindsay was content to forever keep me on the outside looking in, knowing full well that I would eclipse her if we ever actually met. But Samantha was very much present at the event, those "close" to Lindsay suddenly never remembering a time when she wasn't waiting somewhere in the wings. Though, technically, it was Lindsay who was always lurking behind Samantha's shadow at clubs. Their "relationship," in fact, was more of an alliance than anything else. A symbiosis centered on Samantha's musical selections and Lindsay's "appearances," as though her shaking her freckled ass to the playlist was somehow going to enhance it.

Frankly, I had long theorized that since Lindsay couldn't fulfill her lesbian fantasy of being with Paris (the way I had that lurid night so many years ago now), she had to settle for a lesser DJ (did Samantha Ronson ever win International DJ of the Year Award like Paris? I don't think so). As for the prom theme, I can't help but think that, on a Freudian level, it spoke to Lindsay's perpetual need to exist in a high school narrative in order to feel like someone important.

Dating a woman at that time also generally helped dilute the creep factor of dating any of the available men of the era. If Paris had gone lez, for example, maybe she wouldn't have had to date Benji Madden, twin brother to Joel a.k.a. Nicole Richie's boo (I honestly don't know how being in Good Charlotte got both of them so much pussy). And while it was evident to me that Paris just wanted to get back at Nicole for whatever non-offense she committed in '05, I knew she was also trying desperately to make Jared Leto jealous after not "securing him" post-public makeout at the Sundance Film Festival in January. But anyone who has made out with Jared (and there aren't many who haven't) knows that he isn't going to commit to anything beyond one "session," nor is he going to be impressed or threatened by any band other than his own. Paris was somehow too callow to comprehend this before embarking on a nine-month waste of time with Benji, but maybe she also thought it would somehow bring her closer to Nicole. It definitely didn't. Plus, Nicole was already well over Paris sexually shitting in her territory after DJ AM took the latter on as sloppy seconds not too long after Nicole broke up with him. Ah, poor, sweet Nicole, always being vilified and betrayed by those she's been nothing but open and candid toward.

I suppose that's why I continued being friends with her even after she wouldn't help me with my album, which I eventually decided to call *L.A. Slut Queen* and release on MySpace at the beginning of June. This was around the same time Lindsay was "super busy" being an "ambassador" for Visa Swap, some weird U.K.-based campaign designed to help non-socialites feel chic or something. It was geared toward people of no status, therefore no fashion sense, yet they were asked to bring their clothes in to collect points they could use as "currency" to trade in for other "vintage clothes." My God, it was so gauche. So naturally I had to get my latest assistant to bring the most hideous pieces I owned (mainly from the year 2004, when Ed Hardy was especially trending) to the trading point near my residence in London, just to highlight how ashamed Lindsay ought to be for allowing anyone, socialite or not, to clothe themselves in an inferior ensemble. It's just not what "ambassadors" of any sort of good cause would do. Yet Lindsay once again proved her out-of-touchness with reality by commenting, "The idea of swapping clothes, getting something for nothing and refreshing your wardrobe appeals to everyone," and then further insulting poor people who shop at H&M by mocking them for what they can't have with the donation of a Miu Miu bag, Issa dress and two pairs of Jimmy Choos. She could have at least had the decency to part with something a little more fashion-forward to assist the sartorially inept, like a Versace or McQueen item. But no, she consistently chooses to reveal her not so underlying selfishness at every turn. Typical fucking Cancer woman, like I said.

This is undoubtedly the reason why Samantha had to break it off with her in the end—one just doesn't imagine Lindsay to be very generous with pussy licking. Ass licking, on the other hand, is something she's all too adept at. Which is probably how she managed to get work in a new movie in spite of showing no interest whatsoever in anything except bullshit and fake attempts at getting sober. But, never one to shy away from a new club-type opening, or the potential to be photographed with Paris, Lindsay was spotted at the Apple Lounge by August. It was cute enough when it opened I guess, but it's really amazing that it could even still be around now, much like any of the other tickety-tack places featured on *The Hills*. And that even Kim didn't show up for the opening was telling that maybe Paris and Lindsay were very unclear about worthwhile establishments to attend in L.A. at this moment in time.

As Paris would confess to me one night soon after over drinks and *escargots persillade* at Comme Ça, she was trying to make nice with Lindsay in case "this shitty movie actually gives her a comeback." The latest shitty movie in question was *Labor Pains*, which did nothing to negate her reputation for being a full-time party girl with lines like, "You're a teenager, you should be out drinking and smoking," aimed at her younger sister in the movie. And no, one doesn't imagine it was much of a stretch for her to employ this line when considering how she must engage in such conversations with Ali Lohan, who, since that time, has become even more facially unrecognizable than Michael Jackson from his own original visage.

Paris continued, "But I know there's just no way that anyone's going to see it. Rick Schwartz already told me that it's probably going to end up just being aired on TV. Isn't that sad? And only one insurance agency would take a chance on insuring her coke-loving ass. She's basically a sitting duck after this comes out. Like, what has she even done since *Mean Girls?*" I couldn't exactly come up with a rap sheet that would be more impressive than Paris'—since she'd essentially done all the same things as Lindsay both personally and professionally, but without an IMDb page that was even half as heinous.

"I really wouldn't worry about it, Paris. She's going to crash and burn, like she always does." With that, I took a satisfied sip of my wine just as who but Kim with 50 Cent sauntered in. Even though she was supposed to be semi-monogamous with her steady Black fetish of the moment, Reggie Bush, everyone knew she had a little side thing going with 50 since the MTV Movie Awards in June. And, by the looks of it, Reggie must not have been acting according to her whims and desires for her to flout the so-called laws of monogamy so publicly.

She subtly sneered (as much as her latest procedure would allow her to) at Paris and me as she walked past—making a big show of linking arms with 50 while she did so. It very palpably occurred to me that Lindsay would be the least of our worries for the next few years. And I guess that five million dollars she had "settled for" from Vivid Entertainment for putting out her sex tape was really making her go hog wild with the body adjustments. She looked like a fucking Picasso with that non-cohesive shape, and I said as much to Paris as we ordered another bottle of prosecco, making it a point to elongate our dining experience so as not to give Kim the impression that she had made us feel in any way threatened by her sudden infiltration. We weren't. Not totally anyway. Because the most shielding thing about being a *born* socialite and having power for so long is that it can take you a minute, if not your entire life, to understand that you are no longer important, "socially pertinent."

In fact, some might say a true socialite can never acknowledge such an icky reality, which is maybe why Lindsay *is* something of an *esponente dell'alta società*, as they say in Italy—not that there have been many worthwhile Italian socialites if you ask me. Catherine de' Medici hardly counts. Though I do wish I could be even half as ruthless as she was sometimes. Maybe if I had been capable of her level of immorality and debauchery, I might have gotten to the top at some point. Had my own fucking fragrance at least. That I wouldn't have named after myself or some shitty adjective. It would have been something graceful and esoteric. Like Esoteric Grace.

Getting up from my seat to go to the bathroom for a pick-me-up, I passed by Kim's table to overhear her tittering, "I *promise* you won't be on my show. I know you like your privacy." It made me wonder why Kanye didn't get the same courtesy. Like, maybe he might not have gone bipolar without all the added stress of Kim insisting on staying in the spotlight, even after the theoretical "wake-up call" of her Parisian "near death experience" à la Cher in the parking lot/Tai at the mall. I don't truly believe he enjoyed media attention as much as Kim, even if he pretended to in the beginning, that part of one's career when everyone likes media attention. Even Greta Garbo.

Before I could make my way completely to the bathroom, Felicity Huffman, who was predictably dining with her gross piece/husband, William H. Macy, grabbed me by the wrist and hissed, "I've been trying to get a hold of your mother for weeks!" I failed to see how that was my problem, but I offered her a flash of my innocent megawatt smile nonetheless. "I think she's in Palm Springs, *Miss* Huffman," I was sure to iterate. What was the point of getting married if you weren't going to declare to the world that you were no longer a pitiable Miss past her prime? Maybe the only actress who ever got it right was Angelina Jolie when she at least hyphenated with Brad's last name to show that she cared. And that she didn't want anyone to think she was still single past thirty-five (that's the ultimate cut-off. Or maybe forty, thanks to Carrie Bradshaw getting married at that advanced age).

For whatever reason, Felicity was obsessed with my mother. More specifically, obsessed with using her as inspiration for *Desperate Housewives*. I guess the plastic woman who birthed me was no better example of such a character. As Felicity went on about how my mother's affair with Edward had to stop soon, otherwise my dad might get angry enough to cease providing, I thought back to the premiere of *Georgia Rule*, maybe the only movie Lindsay has ever done that anybody could take seriously, both in its time and in hindsight. As she herself commented on the red carpet, "I think the realism shows through, and that's important in film." As usual it was a "Wow Lindsay, you're so fucking poignant" moment, but then, that's what Garry Marshall, God may he rest, was there for. To pick up the slack from dumb sluts like Lindsay detracting from the quality of the work with her uninformed comments. Thus, Marshall better explained the script, written by Mark Andrus (who I fucked in his prime of writing *As Good As It Gets*), by saying it's "not always about likable people, but it's about how in your family, if there's somebody you don't like, they're still family." Much to Lindsay's chagrin. She really might have gotten so much further in her career without her overly invasive, trashy-ass gold digging parents (I don't know if there is a male word for gold digger, much like there isn't one for a male socialite. Do I have to coin every damn thing in addition to *hommeriche*? I mean, they say gold digger can apply to a man as well, but no one ever associates it with male propensities, especially thanks to Kanye's fucking '05 hit of the same name).

Amid Felicity's nonstop prattling, there was a brief pause that allowed me to find my out from the unwanted conversation with Lindsay's former co-star. But not before she also managed to squeeze in a little dig about Lindsay looking very "groggy" lately and had I seen her in town in the past month (for some reason, it was assumed, even by other famous people, that all famous people knew one another). Upon telling her, no I had not seen firecrotch, I exited stage right and made my way into the bathroom. Mercifully empty. Or so I was led to believe.

I entered the end stall and took out the much-needed vial of coke from my purse, snorting about four bumps before feeling something akin to satisfaction. I then went through the charade of flushing the toilet and opened the door of the stall to make my way to the sink and wash my hands, even though it wasn't really necessary. Gazing at myself in the mirror (as I often can't help), I noticed some residual traces of whiteness in my nostrils. I snatched a paper towel from the dispenser to wipe them away just as Brittny Gastineau emerged from one of the other stalls. Jesus, why is it that when there's one hooker in the joint, there's bound to be at least two more? Hookers run in packs.

Brittny was another inferior "socialite" because she was born in New York, and to a sportsman. That Jets guy, Mark Gastineau, who didn't even play on the offensive. Neither did Brittny really. She was always just along for the ride, kind of like...Britney. That's the only reason she consented to going to Lindsay's house one night in early '08, even though it was fairly apparent that she preferred to consort with her lesser sistren, Kim K. This was evidenced by both of them conceding to being photographed with trash "celebrities" like Jack Osbourne and Kimberly Stewart (each of whom were just coasting off the reputation of their respective fathers' shitty music) at Hyde in '06, when Kim was still desperate to be photographed with the likes of anyone and couldn't simply attract filmed "sit-downs" about skin care with someone such as Madonna.

However, Brittny showed without question where her true allegiance was in '09, when she was caught shopping with Kim at Harmony Lane on S. Beverly (though most people just call it Beverly, *I* like to distinguish). They were pawing through overpriced, subpar clothes that still hadn't found their voice outside of the early 00s well enough to even *begin* transitioning into the 10s. Most embarrassing of all, the establishment only had two dollar signs on Yelp before closing. Kim must not have learned to capitalize on the whole nouveau riche thing in time. Because, truth be told, flaunting wealth stopped being acceptable to the masses in, at the very latest, 2010 (with the rare exception of Ariana Grande being able to make incongruous white girl wealth "cute" with "7 Rings," but at least she worked for the cash money she was speaking so passionately of). No, to be sure, nary anybody among the common public wants to see others advertise the fact that they live a lavish style as a result of 1) essentially doing nothing and 2) that they've helped to sustain that lifestyle by profiting from the pathetic desire of Middle America to be like them, hence the existence of such things as KKW Beauty.

Maybe that's why it felt like all the glamor was drained out of Hollywood in 2008, symbolized by Lindsay "becoming" a lesbian. Because there's nothing more humbling than someone who is as big of a nymphomaniac as she is renouncing dick in favor of the "no frills" (yet totally complex) trappings of a vagina. And from what I could tell, Sammy baby was doing *all* the work—which is undoubtedly what contributed to the relationship's demise, apart from Samantha's mother, "Mrs. Ronson" a.k.a. Mrs. Jones, thinking Lindsay was gutter scum. Not just because Ann Dexter-Jones is a *real* socialite who got to dabble with that rare-quality British peen belonging to Mick Jones, but because she is a human who has eyes and could very blatantly see the damage Lindsay was causing to Samantha's reputation, ergo career.

We likely have none other than Samantha to thank for Lindsay's sudden interest in Dubai, for it was only because of the former that LiHo was ever even introduced to the potential "glitz" of that fake city, that Las Vegas of the Middle East. Of the awareness that the paparazzi couldn't track your every move mainly because it's illegal to take photos of anyone without asking permission first. Of course, it never occurred to anyone to ask Lindsay because she was even more of a nobody in the Dubai of 2008 than she is in the L.A. of 2019. That no one was paying attention to her at the launch party Samantha was DJing for Atlantis The Palm (or The Atlantis, if you will) made Lindsay as filled with rage as I was over losing my starring role in *Confessions of a Teenage Drama Queen*. Worst of all, Samantha herself, who was actually working, unlike Lindsay (fresh from a new slew of parole and community service violations with each passing day since her crowning July '07 PCH car chase), appeared rather embarrassed that this was the venue Lindsay chose to make it known to the world that their relationship was not just a rumor. She was clinging to Samantha at every flashbulb that went off exclusively on the red carpet of The Atlantis, barely giving Samantha room to breathe until she finally took her position behind the turntables at the after-party.

Ann was horrified at Lindsay's clinginess and desperation so early on in the dalliance. Or maybe it was more than that, but who knows? Because even now, Lindsay tries to downplay the relationship to the only talk show host who will still invite her on, Wendy Williams. Her fear of admitting to the world that she's bisexual (do I need to pull out the historic kiss with her mother as well?) is so strong, so firmly ingrained that she won't even do it in a landscape that practically flogs you if you're straight now.

I was there too, but I didn't want to make *a big show* of being there, y'know? My purpose was to be invisible and also to conduct a sociological experiment by dressing as one of the servers. It's really amazing how much the clothes make the woman, and can accordingly make her invisible because, truly, nobody looks at the help. A part of me wanted to go up into one of the rooms and change into a custom McQueen when I saw how woeful Ann was looking as she watched Lindsay down champagne glass after champagne glass in between taking frequent bathroom breaks. But I resisted the temptation to make my presence known. My mission was merely to observe, to "gather data," if you want. Ann also seemed to prefer the company of Nicole Richie or myself, likely wishing that we would just embrace the bisexual trend already and steal Samantha away from Lindsay. But that was never to be. In yet another contrast to Lindsay, when I say I love dick and only dick, I really mean it.

Oh, but back to my Comme Ça bathroom exchange with Brittny, who was oh so simpering thanks to both the effect of collagen on her lips and the satisfaction of catching me in the act of doing something *she* (and every other appetite-suppressing bitch in town) was constantly engaging in. Just because she had already blown her own rail privately in the stall before anyone else appeared and had had the good sense to snort it up in one fell swoop (admittedly, I was a sloppy snorter, Stevie Nicks understood), she thought she was so fucking superior.

"Tate. *So* nice to see you. Still trying to make Paris forgive you for being so embarrassing?"

I took a silent deep breath. She was baiting me with the intent to make me turn physical, but I could only do that in my mind, channeling the spirit of Cady Heron, to my dismay.

So instead I coolly responded, "Not really sure what you're talking about Brittny, but then, maybe you've gone a little cuckoo from spending all that time in Armenialand. Has Kim taken you to Glendale yet?"

Brittny rolled her eyes, taking out a tube of Christian Dior lip gloss that was some ungodly shade too dark for her pale skin tone. The goth look was so '01. Spreading it slowly in what seemed an attempt to be sensual, Brittny also managed to utter through her process, "You've definitely chosen wrong, Tate. You're letting the fact that Paris is finally paying some real attention to you distract you from this very important other thing: *no one* is paying attention to her anymore. She, Lindsay and Nicole are all marooned on an island called 00s history. And you'd do well to get off of it before it's too late to reinvent yourself."

With that, she smacked her lips together and was out the door before I could form a rebuttal. I felt dumbstruck by her abrupt, but logical and cohesive assertion. The same one Kim had already made in my presence. Though I didn't want to admit it to myself, there was motive behind why Paris was clinging to me so strongly of late. And now that Brittny had pointed it out to me, I couldn't help but look at her as an overly-into-it boyfriend type. It made me want to recoil, to play games as I would if Paris were a romantic interest, which yes, she had been in the past. But that was for a hot second and what was I really getting out of this friendship anymore? She didn't even want to acknowledge what was happening all around us, the walls that were crumbling in on the socialite world.

With October came the subprime mortgage crisis and, with that, every other global financial crisis came along for the butterfly effect (oh, how I still lament Ashton Kutcher wasting his youth on Demi Moore). While no, it didn't, like, "technically," affect anyone in my circle, it affected the very unfortunate reality that we could no longer parade our wealth around with half as much pride, because to do so would risk just what Kim did in getting tied up and robbed (a *vol à main armée*, if you will) in that hotel room in 2016. And no socialite (at least the kind born *in*to the lifestyle as opposed to the kind that clawed her way to the top with cheap-ass, inferior acrylics) *wants* that kind of attention. Nor does she need it because, if she's doing her job right, she already has it without invoking the press through tacky means like posting pictures of herself wearing rings that look better in a costume jewelry incarnation.

Believe it or not, I *am* actually advocating for socialites to start wearing costume jewelry out in public to fool their potential pillagers into thinking they have even the slightest chance of profiting from an ill-advised heist. I have yet to incorporate the foundation, or whatever it is one does for tax purposes in starting a foundation, but I will. Maybe this year. As, like, part of my community service or something.

Finding myself back at the table with Paris, her aversion to talking about real issues, like how shitty her line of pet clothing was (therefore not "recession-proof"), started to get on my last nerve. Only the coke was keeping me afloat now, especially as I looked from Kim K yukking it up with 50 to Felicity chewing politely with William. It seemed every other famous person in the establishment was with someone who loved and respected them, but I was with Paris, the girl who was premiering a show called *Paris Hilton's My New BFF.* Fucking pathetic, and honestly, a real win for Nicole. But maybe what was even more pathetic was that Paris had never even been to Dubai until *Paris Hilton's Dubai BFF* premiered in 2009. What kind of socialite was she?—who had I been looking up to all these years? Well, in between my weird jealousy over Lindsay. But hey, at least I could acknowledge that it was weird. A truly deranged or unhealthy person would not have been able to do even that.

Every day, I seek help for my foibles by going to Dr. Greenbaum, my latest and most effective shrink. Maybe because he's so...seasoned. And well-traveled. He just, like, really gets me, and in a way that I never even comprehended somebody I was paying to could. Not because, well, sometimes he eats me out when things start to get...emotional. But because he doesn't make me feel guilty or wrong about any of what I have self-diagnosed to be my sociopathic and narcissistic behavior.

In fact, he seems to think I might be able to aid him in classifying an entirely new disorder altogether. I just hope he doesn't name it after me, you know? None of that *Portnoy's Complaint* shit. I hope he calls it something more generic, like Socialitis or something. That's kind of cute in, like, a gross way. Oh god, I've gotten very off track here again. Let me just exit out of this lunch with Paris to get to the part where I'm back at my house, sitting in the sauna and thinking about what my next viable move is. Where my fucking place is in the not so brave new world where, like, ethnic people are taking over.

Not to be a cunt or anything (I fuck Black guys all the time, okay? It's not just "Kim's thing"), but Obama winning in '08 really caused the pendulum to swing in favor of not-white people anymore. And being that most "purebred" socialites are white, well, it got to feel like the end of days for relevancy unless you, like the Kardashians or the plot of *Get Out*, started grafting cultural elements from Black people for yourself. Better known as: cultural appropriation. Which *my* ancestors had never deigned to do, let me tell you. We were always our own people.

So for me to even think about prostrating myself to the level of doing something so desperate as to, like, I don't know get cornrows or, as Paris later would, pose for a Yeezy campaign emulating Kim, just seemed like enough to make me want to vomit up more than I usually would. Maybe that's the extra push I needed to get back down to a size zero though. The more I thought about it, the more I realized I had no choice. Adapt or become obscure. So I suc*cum*bed. I did it. I just fucking did it. The appropriation, that is. After that long, steamy session in the sauna, my idea for "light" appropriation was simple: streetwear. Specifically, Mishka.

But since Mishka just wasn't really a thing in L.A. yet, I thought it best to summon one of the New York-based designers (we never had sex...until he came over with the clothes) to bring me a few custom pieces that I could gradually incorporate into my wardrobe. That way, I couldn't be accused of "jumping on the Black bandwagon."

Since it was getting to be that most wonderful time of the year, Halloween, I also never would have dreamed of going to New York myself to have a fitting. Because Halloween in New York is just so…disgusting. The way people show their grotesquerie on the streets is something I never have any intention of being a part of. No, the Halloween of L.A. is all being whisked away in cars and secreted to locations that the wrong element can never find out about until it's too late. That's something I wouldn't trade for anything, least of all Mishka bullshit.

However, it was important for me to start making the effective strides for changing my "vibe." Between striving for an "organic" rebrand and being caught up in figuring out my Halloween costume, I had little time to think about what Lindsay might be wearing to the Roosevelt, let alone if I should totally start withdrawing from Paris now that her clout was being compromised as we all drew closer to the guillotine on our existence: the advent of the 10s. Anyway, I guess I just figured that a French maid costume was too classic for some other Hollywood ho to want to don in the Year of Our Britney Breakdown, 2008. That there couldn't possibly be any chance I would risk having a run-in with another whore in a duplicate costume.

<u>**Chapter 12: Panties in a Twist**</u>

*I*n spite of Paris' fervent protestations, I ran with the French maid idea. Oh how wrong I was, yet again. Besides, Paris was always balking at everything I did before she stole it for herself so that everyone else could steal it from her. They would never know that the true originator of that which they were grafting was Tate Carmichael: on-again, off-again L.A. pariah. This was why Paris could never let me go. My taste was too valuable. Because, underneath it all, she had even less than Britney, which was really saying something when factoring in that she was the apex of Southern white trash.

After banging the Mishka designer, whose name now evades me, but I want to say it was Mikhail or something foreign like that, I knew I needed to cultivate my pieces for the ultimate "make every man cum in his pants on sight" French maid outfit. I wanted to start at the source of where all true kink does: Frederick's of Hollywood. To some, it might signify total gaucherie, but to me, it was paying my respects to old Hollywood glam*our*. The kind of glamor you have to spell the British way because it's so glamorous. I wanted to bring that to my ensemble and then some. So, without shame, I drove my silver Bugatti Veyron (fuck Paris' cheap-ass Mercedes SLR) to McCadden Place, parked on the corner and had one of my fuckboys sit in the car to make sure no Hollywood High twats lurking around the area (as they always are because, if you aren't bound to be a star at that school, you're bound to be just another jealous little cunt) could try to fuck with it. My precious baby. Daddy had only just surrendered the keys fully to me, though he claimed we would share it. He was doing so much better now that he had taken a more high-powered, time-consuming job in London. It was not only great for his self-esteem—to be so needed and to make so much money (in addition to the natural amount we always had lying around in the bank)—but it took his attention away from Gwen's searing rejection. Her practically constant presence in Palm Springs with *Edward*. She really had no shame any longer at this point, especially since she knew that the masochist in my father would never divorce her. It would mean having to concede too many assets.

Sauntering into the Frederick's like it was my own personal closet, I carefully went about appraising the selection. My hand was particularly drawn to the silky black fabric of a pair of panties that had white ruffle trim sewn along the part where most women in America would have a FUPA. It would be just so wickedly delicious if I showed up to the party in this underwear, a black lace bustier, the requisite white mobcap and a duster in hand. I'd have to add some key accessories, like over-the-top diamonds, to allude to the fact that I had stolen them from my master…

In my sudden excitement over planning these details, the sound of the last voice I thought I would hear, nor would I want to, called out, "Tate? Is that you?" Knowing full well it was that faux sugary-sweet Hilary Duff, I turned very slowly, wanting to delay looking into her spurious mug as long as possible. And, sure enough, right when I made eye contact, I was blinded by the sparkle of her most recent teeth whitening. I almost wished I could ask who her dentist was, but I didn't want to admit that I wasn't satisfied with my own. Taking a deep breath to get it up for this social interaction, I cooed, "Hiiiiilaryyyy, what are *you* doing here?"

She rushed over to me, taking my falsified enthusiasm as a welcoming invitation to invade my personal space.

"Well, you know. A girl's gotta keep things exciting," she giggled.

What a fucking phony. Playing the blushing "virgin." As if she wasn't all too eager to suck whatever got in her eyesight. These days, I guess that meant Mike Comrie, which was in keeping with her boring-ass nature. He was fucking Canadian and a hockey player. How cliché can a goody two-shoes get? Like, how was it actually possible that the "edgiest" she could get was Joel Madden? And now apparently needed to cleanse again with someone as boring as

Mike. The name alone was enough to make me shudder. A boring name means a boring approach to bedroom comportment. And I simply couldn't be anywhere near that, even by proxy.

As Hilary unwittingly grossed me out with the images of her dull sex life that would require her to spice things up by going to Frederick's of Hollywood, my mind wandered to thoughts of myself (as usual). In my daydream, I was making various boys swarm all over me while "Womanizer" by Britney played in the background. It had just come out earlier that month, and I liked to reimagine it as more of an anthem for liberated, ho-ish women than philandering men. If Britney was any kind of true feminist, she would have come up with something of that bent instead. But she's from the South, so it's impossible for her to see things from this perspective, no matter how far we supposedly advance into this future that's female (a load of propagandist bullshit, by the way, mostly created by men). In any case, I enjoyed the song more than Britney's so-called comeback—as if her handlers were going to allow her the luxury of going into early retirement just because she went a little "cuckoo," as we all do. Though *some* of us possess the socialite grace to keep our emotions in control. We've certainly got too much to risk losing otherwise. Our dignity always even more important than access to our bank accounts (which, if you think about it, kind of go hand in hand).

One can't say the same for Lady Gaga, who materialized from the bowels of the Lower East Side and into public consciousness that year with "Just Dance." While everyone might have been taken in by her "weirdo" shtick enough to want to dress as her "futuristic" incarnation that Halloween (see: the *Pretty Little Liars* episode, "The First Secret"), I got a warm, fuzzy feeling inside just relishing my commitment to class. A feeling interrupted by Hilary Duff, who I had forgotten was talking to me as she had to snap her fingers to get my attention again.

I countered with, "Oops, sorry Hils. I just remembered that I'm late to my eyebrow shaping. See you on Halloween maybe?" Before she could agree or not, I dashed out of there, unaware that I still had the panties in tow.

As I hobbled back to the Bugatti in six-inch Louboutins (again, it makes no sense that the Bling Ring didn't target me), I had no idea that the dignity I held so dear was about to be severely compromised. The guy I left in the car (I'll call him Evan because that's my stock name for any boy whose name I can't remember) looked like he was really dehydrated so I opened up the refrigerated glove compartment to offer him a chilled Perrier before putting the pedal to the metal—like any girl who is good in bed, I love to speed. But right as I was hitting the gas, Evan asked, "What's with the granny panties?"

Looking over to see that the underwear had fallen onto the parking brake, I apprehended that I might be apprehended for my accidental shoplifting. That's right. I, Tate Carmichael, *actually* accidentally shoplifted as opposed to lying about it to save face the way Lindsay would with that not even cute necklace. One that only cost a paltry $2,500. What self-respecting celebrity doesn't have that much to spare? If you're going steal jewelry, go big or go home. Treat the theft like a fucking Hitchcock heist movie at least. But no, not Lindsay. She's constantly keeping it low-class. So any who, I was driving in my usual daredevil way and had barely gotten halfway to Hollywood and Highland when the ominous sound of an American siren (I just really think the European ones sound so much prettier because they're like a mirror of the pace of life there) started wailing behind me. I knew I had taken an expensive item but I didn't imagine it could possibly warrant a police chase, so I kind of shrugged at Evan and just kept driving, accelerating my speed and making a sharp left at N. La Brea, weaving in and out of traffic like a mad woman.

"If it was just a mistake, then what the hell are you doing?" Evan demanded, not exactly helping my stress level and proving himself to be more bitch boy than fuckboy.

"I'm panicking, okay?!"

"Just pull over," he instructed.

"No!" I screamed. The more someone tells me to do something, the more I don't want to do it. It's the born rebel within me. I kept on going instead. I was in a fucking Bugatti. Did the police *really* think they could catch me? What arrogance. I easily high-tailed it away from them—all the way to Malibu. Even with the distraction of a cowering, distraught Evan hyperventilating in the front seat. His cowardice made me laugh to myself as I blasted the volume to "When I Grow Up" by The Pussycat Dolls. "Careful what you wish for, 'cause you just might get it," they cautioned. Lindsay would have done well to heed those words, wanting to be famous so badly as a child only to be turned into a tabloid trainwreck.

Pulling up into the parking lot near Sigma Chi at Pepperdine, I giggled to myself. I outran the police as Paris, Nicole and Lindsay never could. Just one of so many infinite ways in which I was superior, yet constantly overlooked and underestimated. It was actually ridiculous that life was designed to fuck over those with true talent and sparkle. Even though Paris is always spouting bullshit like, "Don't ever let anyone dull your sparkle." Well, she's dulled mine. And she let Kim dull hers. Let her guard down long enough to allow for a complete takeover of her former clout and authority.

This much was made crystal clear (or are we forced to say "krystal klear" during the new reign of the Kardashians?) as Halloween approached and, with it, the various parties at which people were expected to come dressed in different attire every time. Kim wasn't the originator of this concept, but she did take it to the next level. What's more, Kim's devotion to being as basic as Paris was evident in her choice of costumes—one night a flapper, another Wonder Woman (bitch please, that is so done, on both counts). As for me, I wasn't going to budge on my French maid decision, opting to wear it at every event I graced with my presence…after giving head to most of the frat boys at Sigma where I took a break to compose myself after that harrowing police pursuit. What can I say? Unlike other girls, I don't play the *innocente*—that's Italian for innocent, in case you couldn't guess—about loving to lick cock as though it's a caramel-centered lollipop therapy treatment.

Alas, the issue with this commitment to the costume quickly presented itself when I heard that Lindsay was dressed in something very similar from Audrina Patridge, who, though in possession of a socialite's name, did not possess a socialite's aplomb. She only wanted to come to this tacky thing because Marilyn Manson was hosting. Like every girl looking to roughen her edges, somehow Manson was always the go-to. Except in the case of Rose McGowan, who made him look like the bitch he truly was (and is) behind the veneer. Audrina didn't stand a chance with him, of course. Not even for a clandestine little hookup. Which she would've been game for since her "thing" with Justin Brescia was such a non-thing, just as Justin himself was such a non-thing. Plus, Audrina was very much in her ho phase in '08. We all sort of were. I was still enjoying the last year of my twenties, thirty feeling all too far away in 2009. I still had plenty of time before having to fret about being a little more modest. Not by much. But like, in a way where I was, at the bare minimum, not posing nude for a mirror selfie while my child was in the next room.

Though Paris had promised to show up with Nicky by eleven for the Halloween party, they were nowhere to be found, and I was losing my patience for my date that evening, Chace Crawford. I felt Ed Westwick would have raped me or something had I chosen to go with him, his real personality not being too far off from that of Chuck Bass. Sure, I like a guy who knows what he wants, but I also want what *I* like to be a factor. So Chace it was…even though he, too, was something of a mirror of his *Gossip Girl* character: totally bland. I caught myself almost calling him Nate at times, to the point where I just had to stop addressing him at all. All this emotional fraughtness was only compounded by whispers of how I was wearing the same costume as Lindsay. Tending to my woes at the open bar, who but the "master of ceremonies" himself, Marilyn, came up to me to inquire, "Do you make house calls?"

Playing along with his banter, I responded in an offensively cliché French woman's accent, "But of course, I live to clean. To serve. Wherever I may be summoned."

Marilyn grinned. "Well then, I have an urgent mess that needs to be…made. In my hotel room."

Looking back at Chace, who was talking to Zac Efron (the two were likely going to give each other some sort of pleasure that night), I shrugged and said, "Show me the way."

Because my luck wouldn't be *my* luck without the adjective "bad" in front of it, Audrina saw me slip away with Marilyn holding my hand. It was Audrina that spread the word of my tryst that night, which led to the final nail in the coffin (no, like, goth pun intended or whatever) of his already fledgling relationship with Evan Rachel Wood… And yes, I had an inkling about *why* it might be fledgling even then, but I've never let something like "scruples" prevent me from fucking an overt creep.

Up in Marilyn's room, I pretended to dust for about two minutes (which is kind of a lot and probably speaks to a more deeply-rooted fetish he has) before he finally seized on my body and disrobed me, starting by pulling my stolen panties down. He slowly made his way toward my clit with his mouth.

And, right as his tongue hit my more important set of lips, an abrasive knock at the door interrupted my instant wetness. *Readiness.*

"Open up! This is the LAPD."

I didn't really think things like that were said outside of the movies. But I guess L.A. *is* the movies, so what did I expect? Brian (at this point, I think we were intimate enough for me to call him that), however, was not so quick to surrender to the piggies (I'm giving a nod to that part of Brian's name inspired by Charles). He wanted to finish what he started with me, so he ripped off the rest of the already barely-there outfit—which was really just a black lacy bustier—and led me into the bathroom where we could continue. About five minutes later, I felt myself getting close, but it was at that point that the police had managed to at last bust the door down (also just like they do in the movies). It didn't take them long to find the "evidence" that had led them to me in the first place (those damned Frederick's of Hollywood panties) and decide to cuff me right at my instant of orgasm. My nipples hardening, I screamed not from the pain of being arrested for such a petty crime, but for the pleasure of being fucked by Marilyn Manson. I'm just glad it happened before he became truly fat (and also, you know, before he got #MeToo'd).

As TMZ rushed to me like sharks to a drop of blood while I was being shoved into the cop car waiting at the back entrance of the Roosevelt, I was still seeing stars from the orgasm. I was in a haze that made me unaware of just how shameful it was that I was being thrown into the clink for stealing an item that amounted to the price of a lip gloss from Jessica Simpson's Dessert Beauty line (I know for a fact that several lower-level celebutantes had to go to the hospital for attempting to test its "edibleness"). This was by far a new nadir for me and the various mortifying scenarios I had found myself in since Lindsay's rise to fame and my attempt to outshine her with the sheer obviousness of my class. Somehow, said class never wanted to make itself known to the public, but solely behind closed doors to those lucky enough to spend intimate time with me…that's not a sexual innuendo.

Coming to, in terms of grasping the full weight of my actions, I could see out of the corner of my eye none other than Lindsay herself, snickering with Paris and Nicky at the sight of my fresh media frenzy hell. I supposed it was *my* turn to pick up where Britney left off now that she was slated for such a swift rebound from her "mental breakdown" (always code for: too many drugs). With her album about to come out, all negative attention needed to be redirected, even if she was declaring, "All eyes on me in the center of the ring, just like a circus." Those eyes were, in actuality, directed at me, it appeared. Well, fine. It had been a while since my name was in the tabloids to such a profligate degree as it was in 2004, due to that that misunderstanding about my minor dalliance with Fabrizio, the Italian deckhand. Yes, I fucked him, but I wasn't *with* him. They really didn't have to blow it so out of proportion. Furthermore, if I had done such a thing in the present day, I would be applauded for my ability to look beyond the class divide.

I tried to be optimistic about the arrest. Maybe it would be somehow beneficial to reinvigorating my as-of-yet unstarted career in either film or music. Or attract a reality show offer. There just *had to be* some higher purpose to the shame. And as I was hauled—nay, *mauled*—into the twenty-first precinct (I specifically requested to be booked in Beverly Hills, so as to be given the same courtesy as any socialite), I wouldn't even allow it as a consideration in my mind that this further ill repute would not *somehow* translate into gold *somewhere* down the line in the near future. That's why I'm smiling so The Joker-like in my mugshot, okay? Not because, as certain publications wanted to insist, I was found with "unheard of amounts" of MDMA in my system. How could they even try to peddle such an egregious and blatant lie? What kind of ill-bred monster would even dream of taking MDMA on Halloween when everyone knows that's a Christmas drug? I was being targeted in a most gruesome way, and I must have done something terrible in my past life as a courtier (other than banging married men) to deserve this maltreatment.

I stayed in the holding area for far less time than I would have to for my purported stalking of Lindsay, with one of Daddy's (I'd stopped calling him Gary lately) lackeys coming to rescue me almost instantly. Daddy was in London, of course, which was all the better. The last thing I wanted to hear was one of his endless lectures about responsibility and maturity, only serving to make me feel worse than I usually already do about the way things have turned out for me.

The lackey, a twenty-something paralegal named Dillinger (poor thing), used his trench coat to shield me from the paparazzi (for the only reason to own a trench coat in L.A. is for this precise purpose). The garment was my lone comfort amid the flashbulbs (so to speak) and video cameras going into overdrive as we ran into the back of a waiting Lincoln Town Car (ah, how I miss those days of Town Cars, even though Mr. Big made them kind of unfashionable in the beginning of the 00s).

I took a deep breath, still in some strange version of my French maid's costume that basically included fishnets with no underwear (they had been confiscated), high heels and my tattered bustier. *That's* what I had been photographed in, and that's the image that every ex I wanted to make think I was doing just fine would see the following morning on the front of every rag from here to New York. And probably London, so Daddy could get a nice glimpse of what his little girl was up to as well. All the while, I could only pray that no one would mention that, yes, I was in the same costume, though not conceptually, as Lindsay. That was honestly my biggest concern. It was the only piece of good fortune from those twenty-four hours that no one seemed to mention her being at the party at all. Worse still, Brian didn't even bother to call me to ask if I was okay.

Where the fuck was *his* image plastered everywhere as a means to shame *him*, huh? All he got was a small mention for being the "other party" in the hotel room with me. I was livid about the overt double standard.

Chapter 13: Sticky and Sweet in San Diego

*S*itting cross-legged on my canopy bed listening to "She's Not Me" by Madonna, I knew I needed to get out of town again. Every time something this awful happened to me, it was my automatic reflex. The only cure I could think of for my impossibly icky feeling. I'm not going to be a fucking *basico* and say I had the "mean reds," but I did. Except I wasn't suddenly afraid and didn't know what I was afraid of. I very much knew my fears of the moment were grounded in becoming irrelevant, on the same path as both Lindsay and Paris).

As I contemplated if I should go far or stay in California, my iPhone 3G, which I had Bedazzled with an image of a narcissus flower because I'm just that talented and honest about my mental condition, sounded the ringtone for Winona Ryder, which I had set as "Downtown" by Petula Clark in honor of *Girl, Interrupted*. Naturally, I had thought about calling Winona myself as she was the only celebrity of my caliber who had been arrested for shoplifting (everyone, including me, was too young to remember that Farrah Fawcett had done it at one point, too, but Gwen was sure to call me up from Palm Springs in between Botox and getting eaten out by Edward to offer that to me as a consolation). But I also didn't want to assume that she would feel empathetic toward me, so I didn't.

To hear her fragile, bird-like little voice on the other end of the line offered me far more comfort and reassurance than I could have possibly anticipated. Especially since I assumed she preferred Paris after making a cameo in the same movie as her the year she got busted for shoplifting. There was something kind of sophisticated and beautifully calculated about the fact that she chose Saks for her "heist" though. Like it was just middle-class enough to be relatable, but not so outlandish and appalling as to be totally unforgivable, as it would have been had she decided to swipe merch from a place more haute couture-oriented. I guess my shoplift was sort of the same, except Frederick's of Hollywood isn't relatable to the sexless potatoes in the Midwest. Ergo my vilification.

Winona assured, "I just want to say I really know what you're going through. But you're going to be fine. Better than fine. You didn't even steal in the four digits' worth, so you're a petty theft at best."

I somewhat took offense to that title, but bit my tongue. "Well you're just so sweet to call Winona, I really do appreciate it," I cooed in a better baby prostitute voice than Paris ever could as the final beats to "She's Not Me" led into "Incredible." Winona, picking up on it instantly, asked, "Are you going to the *Sticky & Sweet Tour*?" Hmmm, now that I thought about it, I *had* noticed a few comp tickets lying around for the California dates, but I certainly wasn't about to go to Oakland (Madonna likely felt the same but was being paid about a million-plus dollars to be there) and I didn't want to stay in L.A. Then it struck me. Election night in San Diego at the Madonna show? What could be better?

"Well…yeah," I confirmed. "I think I'm gonna head to San Diego tomorrow."

Winona sounded disappointed. "Oh. I see. I already have tickets to Dodger Stadium on the 6th…"

I sighed. "Sorry, I can't make it. Gonna stay south for a while. Maybe go to Mexico after."

Winona was silent for what felt like three minutes before she finally concluded, "That must be nice. To have all that freedom." She tittered. "You think you're free? I'm *free!*" she joked in a creepy way that indicated she was still jealous that Angelina Jolie had chosen the better role in *Girl, Interrupted*. I also think she was acting passive aggressive all of the sudden because she was essentially restricted to the parameters of L.A. for random, possible reshoots or additional scenes for *The Informers*, a film nobody liked even half as much as *American Psycho*, or maybe even *Less Than Zero*, which is saying a lot (granted, *Less Than Zero* has plenty of camp value that oughtn't be underestimated. Maybe *The Informers* will be regarded the same somewhere way down the line). But shit, it wasn't my fault that her chosen profession was to be a glorified slave, constantly at the mercy of someone else's schedule.

This is precisely why I wanted to, like, counsel actors to parlay their fame into other things, mainly life-altering endorsement deals that would afford them ample free time and money to do whatever they wanted without being the puppet of some expectedly psychotic and narcissistic director. Jennifer Aniston had figured it out, why hadn't Winona Ryder? It just affirmed my belief that actors love the pain, it's what they're married to more than their fucking "craft," a word I can't stand to hear used for any art, but especially when applied to acting.

On the plane (of course I took the private jet, I'm not flying fucking Southwest, recession or not), I thumbed through the latest issue of *Bazaar*, featuring none other than a motherfucking spread on Lindsay in the November edition. Of all the fucking people to choose from. Why not Michelle Obama or Madonna herself? I couldn't understand how she managed to cling so effortlessly to a spotlight that had long ago stopped showcasing that she might have any actual talent. Then again, I had to keep reminding myself that maybe Lindsay was shrewder than I thought. Maybe she had been repurposing herself this entire time so as to be post-00s-ready. That is, ready to live in a world where everyone truly was famous for being famous. A part of me did want to believe she could orchestrate something so elaborate, that it took her that many years of meticulous self-destruction to finally be able to beg for a reality show on MTV that would be pitifully billed as a "*Vanderpump Rules*-style" narrative with a Grecian twist or whatever. But no one is that much of a mastermind committed to the cause of embarrassment.

Lindsay was never embarrassed about the things that she should have been though, like "shyly" admitting in this grotesque *Bazaar* interview, "I'm the biggest loser *Gossip Girl* fan. I love Chuck Bass. I want to be his friend." Sure, in the post-#MeToo world, that's pretty shameful…in '08 there is nothing more contrived she could have said. The worst thing about the "admission" was that it made it all the more evident that she was using Samantha for more tabloid fodder, having exhausted her party girl antics angle long ago. She needed a new way to frame herself for the critical purpose of garnering attention. Bisexuality was it.

But any girl who "loves" Chuck Bass can never be a true bisexual (though he is rather effete when you examine him). And if you ask her about that relationship now, she just simply fucking writes it off as though it was nothing; chalks it up to "living in L.A." When, if her publicist had any brains (but maybe she doesn't even have a publicist at this point), she would be overplaying the shit out of her ahead-of-the-curveness on "fluidity." I sighed heavily to myself when taking into consideration just how stupid and non-capitalizing everyone else was in comparison to me. Would I ever be rewarded for my non-efforts at superiority? Gazing out the window at the expectedly stunning California landscape, I prayed that Madonna would notice me in the front row.

***

My first stop after leaving my items in the room at the Hotel Del Coronado (a part of me didn't want to stay there because it was Hilton-affiliated but, like, what isn't? I had to stay there to honor the memory of Marilyn) was La Jolla. I wanted to find an endlessly bougie ensemble for the evening, to really stand out in a way that none of Madonna's decidedly unfashionable fans would (they were always just wearing, like, t-shirts. With her on them. It wasn't very inspired, and I wanted to brighten the environment for her performance). So I went to the Design District, figuring there would be a chance to find both a unique piece at a boutique and perhaps a unique piece to take to the show. Madonna would probably also appreciate a straight man's presence in the crowd as well. And there was really no one straighter than Bill Murray, who just so happened to be ambling down the sidewalk in his strange manner (he kind of walked like a cripple) past Pomegranate, where I was also just emerging from with my bounty (or as much bounty as could be had in a place as sartorially challenged as San Diego).

He looked me up and down, smiled and said, "Hello Tate." We had met about three years ago when I was auditioning for the part of Lolita in *Broken Flowers*, a part that somehow went to this other bitch named Alexis Dziena. Whatever, she wouldn't do anything much after. Like I'm supposed to be impressed by a bit part in *Nick and Norah's Infinite Playlist?* So yeah, Bill knew me. Quite well. I guess maybe I should've fucked Jim Jarmusch instead of his lead actor, but, God, Jim is just so asexual. Maybe it's because he's been not-married to the same woman for so long. It's none of my business, I guess. What is my business is that I probably would have been Lolita had I fucked the right person, yet, as usual, I couldn't resist the man that was perfectly wrong for me and for the occasion. But, maybe, just maybe, fucking Bill was about to pay off in the form of a date to the show.

We finally got close enough for him to kiss me on the cheek, letting his lips linger about three seconds longer than what could be deemed reasonably appropriate for a "friendly" greeting. I only encouraged it by leaning in eagerly to receive the *besito*.

"What are you doing here?" he demanded, grinning. "This town doesn't exactly feel like your speed."

I grinned. "That's kind of why I'm here. I need a break from L.A. Again."

"Marilyn didn't call you, huh?"

The mention of that name was suddenly fucking up my hotel vibe. Rather than reminding me of Norma Jeane, it now felt like the name Marilyn was perverse and wrong instead of glamorous and iconic. "Um, actually, no. It has nothing to do with my Halloween 'debauchery.' I'm just here to see Madonna. Her *Sticky & Sweet Tour*. And also, like, be somewhere low-key for election night. People are getting way too fucking buck-wild with their political ardor right now."

"Did you vote?"

I chortled. "Of course not, Bill. That is so fucking plebeian. And, I mean, democracy is all an illusion anyway, right?"

Bill put his hand on my shoulder. "I didn't know Woody Allen was holding auditions for a new movie."

"Huh?"

"Sounds like a pseudo-intellectual line from one of his scripts."

I glared at him. "Haha. You're so clever." I punched his shoulder in that playful, "I'm such a friend" way that was really filled with a shit ton of sexual tension and foreplay.

Bill's body must have responded to it as he offered, "Let me take you out for dinner."

"What, right now?"

"Yeah, it's late enough. By deep Southern California standards. We're all old fogies here."

"Oh god. Only really old people use that phrase."

"Then you know I'm not lying. It's early bird special time."

I looked down nervously at the shopping bag I was carrying. Picking up on my constant fear of gaucheness, Bill said, "Follow me, we can put that in my car." It was as though he knew I didn't want to call my driver to alert him to the fact that I was already whoring it up.

Bill, in typical Bill fashion, drove something modest: a silver Prius. It was environmentally-friendly and all, but it certainly wasn't the easiest vehicle to fuck in the backseat of. Which we did, like rabbits reunited. Bill was so much more open and free in his California period. I really hated it when he became so Brooklyn-centric. It sort of tainted him forever for me. Which I guess is why I moved on to his son to spite him. Even though it was really only spiting myself to bang a Greenpoint restaurant owner. Ugh, I truly am a textbook masochist.

Zipping up his pants with what resembled a Glasgow smile, Bill assured, "I still want to take you out to dinner, you know. You're the most beautiful thing I've seen in this place in years."

I rolled my eyes. "Save the charm for a more wide-eyed ingenue."

"Is that what you're calling yourself these days?"

***

At Trattoria Acqua, we sat near the window, overlooking the ocean view. It was almost *too* dripping with romance. And as the waiter, Paolo, imported straight from Italy (who knows what part), poured us their most expensive strain of Sangiovese (not that such a strain of grape could ever result in being more than $450 to $500 a bottle, really), Bill gazed at me with genuine interest. It made me anxious. He was going through his second divorce at the moment, to another basic named Jennifer (his first wife was named Margaret, there's clearly a pattern). He proceeded to unload all his emotions on me about the struggles with that, which really detracted from the mood because, like, the last thing I wanted to hear about was anyone's financial woes. It's so unattractive. But I nodded along, biding my time. Waiting for the right moment to invite him to the show. It would really help my reputation right now to be seen with an older, respected actor so as to cleanse my current association with a shock rock ugo.

When, at last, he finished whining, I got my entrée to make the inquiry. "If you want to cheer up a little, you're welcome to come with me to the show tomorrow," I said with as much nonchalance as I could feign. Bill tilted his head slightly, as though sizing up my acting abilities. Was I as nonchalant as I seemed, he must have been wondering. All the while, I clenched my legs together as a means to will him to say yes. Will Bill. He took a sip of wine and savored it for what I thought was an hour before he finally agreed, "I could do that. It might be nice to get out for once. I'm always at home these days."

I unclenched, feeling my confidence return. "Are you sure? I don't want this to affect how much money you have to give Jerri."

"Jennifer."

"Whatever. Women can be shrews. And if it gets out that you went with me to this concert…things could go further awry."

He arched his brow. "Tate, my life has already gone as awry as it can at this point: I'm an actor." With that, we had sealed our fate. "Now," he continued, "why don't you tell me what you're really doing here?"

Feeling more comfortable than I ever had with another man since…ever…I began to confess, particularly the more the wine started flowing.

About an hour in, I suddenly found myself blabbing, "And that Lindsay is the biggest cunt of all. I can't believe she had the nerve to call Paris a cunt on camera. I mean, how dumb can a person be? And then this whole Kim thing. God. How did *that* happen? How did we *let* that happen? I'm just so fucking stressed right now and I don't know how to get things back to square one."

Bill stared at me like I was in a straightjacket. "Do you have any idea how vacuous you sound?"

I was made to feel a complete fool when he chose to respond that way to all the strife I had expressed to him. Like I was just another dumb little rich white girl to be mocked because, I don't know, someone wasn't blowing my leg off with a machine gun in Africa or something. Like, Jesus, do problems need to be that severe for people to take your pain seriously? Evidently so. Even when you're as shallow as Bill Murray, who was even shallower for pretending not to be with that whole "I'm just a regular, goofy guy" act. An everyman of cinema. Fucking spare me (which is, incidentally, the name of a bowling alley I opened near Lucky Strike, where I spe-cifically stipulated that no "work outings" of any kind could be held there as it made me sick to my stomach thinking of people having to be subjected to forced "fun" of that nature, so don't ever tell me I'm not a fucking humanitarian).

Bill's outburst had thrown me, but I didn't want to lose him as a date to the concert. So, in a rare and unprecedented move, I kept my cool. I swallowed my pride along with my Sangiovese and said, "That's your feeling, I suppose."

"No, darlin', I think it's pretty objective. You need to get your head straight. Maybe do some charity work in Africa. And just so you know, Lindsay Lohan is not actually from Africa, in case you're confusing her with her character in *Mean Girls*, so don't worry about being called some kind of 'copycat.'"

He was really pushing my buttons now, and I don't ever wear anything with buttons, not even metaphorically. I had to weigh my options carefully. Did I want to throw a tantrum? Wouldn't that feel so much more satisfying than biting my tongue just because I didn't want to be photographed alone at a Madonna show? Yes, I decided. It would be.

I maniacally drummed my nails (embellished with diamond accents on my hot pink acrylics) against the white linen tablecloth, carefully deciding what I was going to say in response now that I refused to censor myself for the sake of having an old white dick accompany me somewhere. "Bill, I've got to run," I announced suddenly in my breeziest voice. "It's been, well, rather terrible spending time with you, and I've got to cut it short."

Bill guffawed. "Enjoy your lonely rich girl's existence, and good luck finding someone as generous as I am to listen to your petty problems for more than one second."

I stood up gracefully and sensually, I could even see in his eyes that he was regretting that he had sent this pristine body running. "I don't think I'll have any trouble, *Bill.* Enjoy the rest of your day."

Exhilarated by taking the high road and not causing a scene in the manner that I had originally intended, I learned something very important about myself that day in La Jolla: I had matured, transcended. I was so much more evolved than all the teen-oriented drama that Hollywood was always shooting its load over. That did not mean, however, that I was about to surrender my basically lifelong quest for justice in terms of seeking retribution for all Lindsay had taken not only from me, but from so many other just above aesthetic par girls in L.A.

The next night, I entered Petco Park from a secreted back entrance using my privilege as a rich and attractive person of importance and notoriety. I didn't need to announce my presence to Madonna, one of her dancers simply emerged from among the many recesses of the underground stage area and guided me toward the "VIP area," I guess. That little back room where there's champagne and her various friends and hangers-on commingle before and after the performance. Mercifully for me, there was an eligible man already drinking some of said champagne, and clearly feeling loose enough to quickly sidle up to me and make his introduction.

"Hi there. I'm Adam." Of course I knew he was Adam. Levine. The douchiest guy in "rock 'n' roll." But I had to hand it to Madonna for managing to attract one of the most eligible "straight" bachelors of the year to her show. It really was a testament to her magnetic quality. The kind that even my money couldn't buy.

"Hi there," I returned, taking the glass of bubbles he poured me and relishing an inevitable opportunity to outshine the Grammy after-party rumors of '05 that declared he'd had an orgy with Paris and Lindsay. I needed to get well wasted if I was going to become sticky and sweet for him though. And by the time we careened to the front row for "The Sweet Machine" intro, we were already all over each other. It was exactly the kind of publicity I had wanted and didn't even need to end up trying for. Not only would it make Marilyn realize his desertion had no effect on me, but it would also make Bill see that he had wrongly treated me like shit, that there were plenty of other dudes willing to put up with my alleged "frivolity." Oof. Fucking Bill. I really wish he hadn't gotten into my head like that. It was detracting from my enjoyment of Madonna announcing that Obama had won the election. The Bush era was over. And the white man's era, too (for about eight years anyway).

As though Madonna had won the presidency herself, she then gave a victory speech, which sort of washed over me in waves as Adam stuck his tongue down my throat and his hand down my shirt.

Chapter 14: Labor Pains—From Not Working

_T_he next few months were an average alcohol and coke-addled blur for me. I found it difficult to keep up with Adam, but I did anyway. I also found it difficult to keep up with La Vida Lohan, even though I had heard a few things about her tantrums getting much worse as it became clear she was just as annoying as a "lesbian" to her suitor of the moment. Though Samantha wouldn't be sticking around for the drama much longer. Who could blame her? She had already withstood so much in just the brief period of a year. Like all DJs, Avicii included (God may he rest), Samantha had a delicate sensibility, just wanted to stay at home and watch a movie at the end of the day—or rather, night. Lindsay most certainly did not, even despite having supposedly achieved what every straight girl dreams of: a domestic situation.

I, conversely, had settled in quite nicely to the whole Sid and Nancy act with Adam. Tatam was our celebrity couple name, and it suited me fine. Also we were way more discreet and tamer than Sid and Nancy with our drug use, but it was very much the thing that made us have common ground. Because, honestly, I really fucking hated Maroon 5's music, and was a little bit ashamed to be dating the lead singer when I wasn't totally inebriated out of my mind. Luckily, one of my many rich person's skills was being super refined and calm at any degree of intoxication. That's why I never got caught passed out in the front seat of a car like Lindsay, only to be forever compared in meme form to Bernini's "The Ecstasy of Santa Teresa." How she always manages to land on her feet in such ways as to be compared to one of the great masterworks of Italian sculpture is beyond me. It makes me think that Woody Allen was right when he whispered into my ear at some party in London in '04 (before I knew he was just feeding me lines from the *Match Point* script), "I don't care that you're beautiful, I only hope that you're lucky."

It was almost as if, in that moment, he had verbalized to me what the universe could not: I was born unlucky. Sure, I had money and I was hot, but where everything else was concerned, it was largely useless to me to be in possession of these attributes if it was only going to lead to humiliation that would have been far less visible if I were an ordinary civilian. I almost started wishing that I wasn't famous at all the night after Woody said that. Just goes to show how fucking forceful his negativity can be when he's not trying to talk you into darkened rooms to "discuss art."

I told him I was his dreaded philistine archetype, the dumb blonde that ultimately just serves to make one of his lead characters realize he's better off with a dark-haired woman because at least she can somewhat carry on a conversation or pretend to be interested in what [insert pedantic character's name here] has to say. See? I'm very laden with depth. I watch Woody Allen movies as a California girl, for fuck's sake. That used to *mean* something. But then #MeToo went and fucked that up also.

The more I tried to tell him I wasn't his type, the more he tried to woo me. I think I had almost forgotten about his ardor until a bouquet of flowers showed up at my house sometime in late March, a period in 2009 when I was already pretty fucking elated because of how Lindsay finally managed to chagrin herself past the point of no return with the most indescribable peek into the mind of the drug-addicted European (or is it Asian, technically?) she would eventually transcend into. The source of my elation was, in case you forgot, an overwrought forty-two second "commercial" of Lindsay spouting out random "buzz words" for Fornarina (if you haven't heard of it, I understand) that conclude with her laughingly saying, "Fornarina," as though even she herself can't believe this is happening. That she actually deigned to freely admit in a post-Bernie Madoff-scammed world, "Will Work 4 Food." Or, based on her rail-thin appearance, will work for as much crack cocaine as I need to survive through this thing called celebrity. Ah, poor Lindsay. I nearly felt pity for her that year. She really was an exemplar of how some people just can't hack it when they're thrust into fame as opposed to born into it. You have to be groomed for this genetically, it's not something you can just "become." And Lindsay was ample proof of that.

So anyway, I was already chirpy as it was without getting this bouquet of flowers—miraculously, Queens of the Night; Woody really was suave—but this put the cherry on top of my somewhat hyper-emotional month thus far. Mainly because Adam was starting to become too insufferable to bear. I was going to have to end that soon, before I also risked him cheating on me anyway. Plus, like every damned white guy, he suffered from that common affliction, Pencil Dick Syndrome. It was time for me to move on. Not to Woody, hell no. But Woody might lead me to someone else. Jewish men are neurotic sure, but they're not the same as white guys. Their dicks are more workable. So maybe if I encountered someone in his circle while I was in New York—the reason he had sent me those Queens of the Night was to invite me to the TriBe-Ca Film Festival for a screening of *Whatever Works*— I could make everything come up roses. Or just make myself cum.

I was eager to get out of the L.A. fishbowl. Lizzy Grant might have said that there was more anonymity in the City of Angels when I first met her (yeah, I caught the Arlene's Grocery show in February, but I felt mostly sketched out by being at Arlene's Grocery in lieu of somewhere more tailored to my caliber), but that bitch was fucking wrong. She's been wrong about a few things. Especially lately. I can't get into it now, because we're not there yet. But just you wait. She was *not* her carefully curated self until *I* gave her a hot tip on how to be.

And now that I was going to make my grand announcement as an "anonymous" friend to *Us Weekly* (I always felt that *Us* was the perfect middle-class tabloid) about my abrupt breakup with Adam, the fishbowl feeling was only going to intensify. It was better for me to leave town after blessing them with this juicy tidbit than to stick around and wait for the paparazzi to seek me out and discover who I might fuck next. Yes, there's no better PR strategy than to depart after having caused an explosion that will dispense the gossip-packed debris in your wake. So that's just what I did, having Rosita or whatever her name was pack some basics into one set of luggage while I pulled aside some custom ensembles to go in my Louis set (to be clear: the classic pattern, not that outdated white background with the color logo one).

During my rather steady relationship with Adam, Paris had started hovering around me a little bit more, suddenly reassured of her faith in my stock.

That, and, well, Kim was not giving her the fucking time of day. She had come off another pathetic high of playing interviewer on the E! red carpet for the Grammys, likely salivating over Kanye West from afar when he, Jay, T.I. and Lil Wayne performed "Swagga Like Us" with M.I.A. (I wonder if she regrets allowing those goons into her orbit when she could've carried the whole damn thing herself). And maybe she actually salivated right onto his dick backstage at that time for all I know. I put nothing past her. Anyway, I didn't go. Why would I attend an event where "4 Minutes" was beat out for Best Pop Collaboration With Vocals by Robert Plant and Alison Krauss? It would have made no sense. Though at least Adam didn't win for Maroon 5's collab with Rihanna—that would have forced me to stay with him longer due to such newfound pull.

So yeah. Paris. A little on my dick again, but for the first time maybe ever, it didn't matter to me. She was trying so hard to turn that inane persona of hers into something of substance that she even let some small-time music video director (I don't count Regina Spektor on one's resume as getting your foot in the door of "big-time") follow her around to cobble together some footage for a faux poignant documentary called *Paris, Not France* (*so* clever, right?) that was going to be released to "the masses" that summer in her attempt to start rebranding as someone who knew she was totally vacuous all along. I wonder what Bill Murray would say to her over dinner in La Jolla.

Whatever Paris' attempt at a fresh angle for the upcoming 10s was, I didn't really want to be a part of it. No, I wanted to be my own person in 2009. And considering that everyone had disbanded—been forced to scatter like roaches when Kim flounced into the room and suddenly touched the light switch with her fat ass—it was something of a wide-open power grab during this period. It was the most liberated I could ever remember feeling. Like a weight the size of 90s Kate Moss had been lifted.

I think those around me could sense my rejuvenated confidence as I stepped off the jet in New York and was shuttled by a driver to my current preferred apartment on the Lower East Side (Williamsburg wasn't really happening for socialites until 2011). Because even before I got out of the car, Jared Leto was practically bombarding me as he "accidentally" crashed his bike into the driver's side door to get my attention. I don't know why he thought I wouldn't give it to him regardless. He's Jordan motherfucking Catalano. Always has been, always will be (thanks to the myriad poseurs that keep rediscovering *My So-Called Life* and thinking they've unearthed some hidden gem that no one else has ever heard about—give me a fucking break. It's like when dumb bitches think *The Simple Life* is "vintage" *Keeping Up With the Kardashians*. I cannot stand the incompetence of the youth, though I do still consider myself one, and I have the tight vag to prove it…courtesy of the magic of a labiaplasty).

I had watched him in that show with Nicole and Paris—and I guess Kim was there too—when we were our most authentic Lolita selves in the mid-90s. God, to be wealthy enough to pay for someone to have an adequate brain to create a functioning time machine (instead of that goddamn faulty one that Stephen Hawking tried to pass off on me I'm still basically acid-tripping from. I gave it right fucking back to his con artist ass. Sued him, too. He didn't fool me for one second with that "condition" of his as a means to get sympathy or "a pass"). But wait, I was happy in 2009, not yearning once more to return to the past for a do-over. And with my confidence affirmed by Jared in his unseemly state on the ground, automatically giving me the literal upper hand as I lifted him daintily but effectively, 2009 was only getting better by the minute.

Jared joined me in my already furnished apartment (I had enlisted this highly sought-after transgender interior decorator named Yvonne to finish it up about a year prior, ergo all the gender-allusive lamp bases) so that I could patch him up. For once, an activity my mother had forced me to do (be a Girl Scout) resulted in something positive…me appearing to be nurturing and maternal by effortlessly dressing his wound, getting really sexual and fetishistic with it by licking the blood off his knee first. Yeah, that's right. Billy Bob Thornton-era Angelina Jolie ain't got shit on me. I was way raunchier in my gothicness. People never acknowledged me for that either, not even when I was caught with my goddamn stolen panties down while fucking Marilyn Manson.

His bent bicycle in the corner (you would have thought he wouldn't be so faux hipster as to have owned a Huffy) and his fragile aura before me, I got the sense that I would be in New York for longer than I anticipated. Well past the closing date of TriBeCa on May 3rd. This meant I was right: Woody really had brought me a new lover. Jared and I began our affair right then and there, and with him refusing to get on top of me so that he didn't hurt his precious knee while we fucked on my pink satin sheets (I was a firm believer in specifically having satin sheets in New York, even though I tended to have more sex there and it made the dry-cleaning bill Daddy had to pay for astronomical—only plebes will try to tell you that you can machine wash such fine linens. Honestly, the things that poor people have to tell themselves to believe that their life is fine).

He was neither spectacular nor subpar, which I guess is what constitutes someone (read: a straight white male) "great" in bed in 2019, but in 2009, when I was a little bit more finicky in those last months of holding fast to being in my twenties (I was going to turn thirty as May 17th rounded the bend), I found him totally forgettable. If only Paris could have had a similar experience instead of pathetically clinging to that image of the two caught kissing at Sundance, which shows her being the one very clearly more into it than Jared. And even though Jared was more ancient than I was (that is to say, he was thirty-seven), I knew he had banged Lindsay when she was in her sexual peak during the filming of *Chapter 27*. That was, like, one of the zeniths of her sluttery. So I knew she was barely even trying with Jared, but still somehow impressing him with her then-tight pussy. It wasn't to remain that way for much longer, as you already know from "the list" that made the rounds in 2014 after she "casually" wrote down the names of every guy she had fucked on a Scattergories paper and tossed it in the trash in 2013.

What a calculated bitch, knowing goddamn well it would crop up again right when she needed some pitiful tabloid publicity—the very thing I myself try to stray away from but somehow always end up receiving despite my best efforts. And I feel that the image of them together in bed probably greatly detracted from my own performance (it's hard for a girl to get as wet as possible when she's got any mental portrait of Lindsay sloshing around in her mind). But I did what I could to stay on top (yes, I know I don't need to say literally, but…literally) and I think he was pretty fucking pleased, my anxiety over being better and more desirable in bed than Lindsay aside. I shouldn't have even doubted myself on that front. I could out-act and out-fuck that bitch any day of the goddamn week, any moment in goddamn history. I was foolish to be insecure, and I wonder if things might have worked out between Jared and me in the long run had I been surer of myself, possessed the ironclad poise and self-possession that I do now.

Jared refused to attend any events with me for TriBeCa, as things started to get heated between us whenever we didn't have the dilution of sex (which is, as you might not know due to the fact that you're reading a book, the place where one always wants heat, often at the cost of a toxic emotional dynamic for the sake of the physical). He said I was using him for publicity, that I just wanted my picture in *Page Six*. God, as if I ever wanted any affiliation with a publication so misogynistic as the *New York Post*, the very paper that could get away with labeling Lindsay, Paris and Britney's wild ride as a "Bimbo Summit" in 2006. It infuriated me that Jared really thought I would even need someone as two-bit as he is to stay in the limelight. All I had to do was walk down Rivington and it was, "Tate! Let me get a photo with you!" or "Tate! Are you making a cameo on *My New BFF*?" or "Tate! Did you hear Kim and Paris aren't talking anymore?"

The one question or exclamation I didn't ever seem to get while on the streets was anything pertaining to Lindsay, so unmentionable had she become. Even the media had grown weary of bringing her up just to confirm that she was still a hot mess who had willingly destroyed her own career for the sake of being a part of Regina George's (a.k.a. Paris) ephemeral "in" crowd. And now that Kim was the new Regina, the new queen bee, Lindsay had fucked herself over for no reason. She couldn't even secure a permanent foothold as an A-list member of the party girl scene, where you were only as good as the amount you charged for your appearance fee. In 2015, Kim could get $40K. Paris could barely get $20K, Howard Stern liked to point out during an interview with Kim and Khloe because he's a bigger cunt rag than any of us combined, his catty nature proving he's just a passive aggressive blonde waif inside that Jewish husk. And anyway, I heard Paris gets a million dollars every time she DJs, so fuck Stern. Except, like, ew, please don't fuck him. I did so that you don't have to.

To prove just how much I didn't need Jared, I started going out with other guys more famous than him. James Franco (another sword that entered Lindsay's sheath), Robert Pattinson, Penn Badgley (remember now, *Gossip Girl* was still a huge deal, hence Lindsay's gross gushing over Ed Westwick as Chuck Bass). It was a different dude every night until

Jared finally couldn't take it anymore and showed up to my apartment—or broke into it. That, I actually found pretty hot more than I did concerning or offensive. It probably got me wetter than Madonna when she got smacked around by Sean ('cause you know he fuckin' smacked her, I don't care what she tried to claim in 2015 when the whole Lee Daniels tango went down. Oh god, I just realized now I'm going to have to pay for a libel lawsuit because Sean is so uppity about being labeled a domestic abuser. Everyone really has gotten so fucking soft in the post-10s).

At first, of course, I was a little disturbed to see that the door had been busted open. Mainly because I thought I was living in a luxury building with higher quality security and infrastructure than that. But fine. It just goes to show you that every class must contend with the problem of cheaply-made products in America. So, cocking my pepper spray (I replenished the supply at least once a week in a custom-made, pink diamond-encrusted bottle), I emboldened myself and approached the open door. I thought I was being rather quiet, but my heels were clacking pretty conspicuously on the marble. I could hear someone breathing—seething, really—the same way a bull does before he's about to charge. I closed my eyes as I stood in the doorway, ready to aim and fire. Which I did, blindly spraying indiscriminately like a male squid doling out sperm packets before looking up to see Jared screaming like a banshee.

"What the fuck, Tate? It's me. It's me! Your fucking boyfriend!"

I stopped spraying and hysterically wailing the second he ended on that "d" in boyfriend. "My *what*?" I demanded.

Rubbing his eyes in agony, he grabbed me by the shoulders like he was doing an imitation of Val Kilmer's performance in *At First Sight*. Actually, Jared's "performance" was probably better than that.

"You heard what I said. Now I'm fucking sorry for saying that you were using me. I know you weren't. And I want you to cut the shit with these other douchebags and be my fuckin' girl."

How could I say no? Even in his unsightly red-eyed, red-faced state, he was still Jordan Catalano. If he had cheated on me with a Rayanne figure in the form of Paris, I would've gone crawling back to him for more, just like Angela. I was an ugly girl on the inside that way. Desperately seeking validation.

After we both orgasmed for the first time together a few days later, things truly started to get intense. We were inseparable. I was terrified. Every time I thought that I couldn't possibly open my heart to that degree ever again, someone *came* along to disprove me. With Jared, though, I think what was left of my emotions all went into him. It was unsettling almost how much I could feel the butterflies in my stomach whenever he was near. That, too, helped with my bulimia. And, speaking of, an invitation from Amy Winehouse to visit her in Saint Lucia that August tantalized me to no end. Even despite the pure happiness bubble that had developed from just spending time lying around with Jared during the mornings and afternoons when we were both still coming down from the coke after another night spent at Mehanata. Which is, by the way, the club where I told Lizzy Grant straight to her face that she wasn't going to make it very far without a nose job and some collagen. Where are my fucking royalties for that?

It didn't help that I chose to tell Jared about this Saint Lucia plan while he was particularly irritable on an afternoon in July when he still hadn't consumed the coffee I worked so hard to make (it was made in a moka pot, all that twisting and turning. That's *a lot* of physical labor for a socialite). When he was still semi-coked up. In fact, after trying to casually slip the topic into the conversation as I massaged his dick, he glazed over. That was his way of expressing extreme rage. It was even worse than when he yelled at me or backhanded me across the face (which, as I mentioned, only served to make me wetter for him…just another way that I was suited to providing inspirational motifs for "Del Rey" to write about. You know, the stolen *Ultraviolence* material, especially the title track. I knew she always wanted Jared for herself and she couldn't even get him when they eventually did a Gucci commercial together).

To make everything even more stressful for me, Jared had already asked me to come with him to the Venice International Film Festival for the first official screening of *Mr. Nobody*. It would have been a dream of course, had my ex, Rhys Ifans, not also been a part of the movie and therefore present. I didn't want to bring this up as a reason to Jared for not being able to/not wanting to attend, so instead I positioned it as needing to help Amy get through her attempt at continued sobriety (which we all knew was a farce). Also, it would really upset Paris, having likely assumed that *she* would be the one to be called upon in an emotional emergency by Amy considering their so-called iconic photo together with Kelly Osbourne back in Amy's heyday. Then again, Paris was trying her best to remain distant from *has-beens*. That's what all has-beens tried to do to ignore that they themselves were, that's right…has-beens. And with Kim starting to make even more cameos in shows that Paris might have able to once upon a time (you know, *America's Next Top Model*, *CSI: New York*, that type of shit), her break with reality was manifesting on "reality" TV. That she had to find a new best friend that way was almost as sad and tragic as Lindsay in the Fornarina commercial that even Japan would have been too embarrassed to let air in its country.

Anyway, I was all for has-beens, and when Amy died in 2011, I would be rewarded for the loyalty I displayed in '09, asked by Mitch to say a few words at the ceremony and then getting in every British and U.S. rag for my close relationship with the fallen chanteuse. That's always what European people called singers when they died, like a show of reverence that was too little, too late or something. Jared, for some reason, was not understanding of my Taurean loyalty. My devotion to friendship no matter how much it might diminish my own star. It was a curse, really. And one that only helped assure my downfall in the public eye.

My Louis bags all packed the morning of August 3rd to head to the jet, Jared finally let his guard down, revealed to me one last time that he had an unwavering vulnerability beneath it all. Sure, he was snorting some coke off my glass coffee table while he showed said vulnerability, but that's fine. Vulnerability is vulnerability no matter what you're doing while showing it. He at least felt invigorated enough to get up, push me against the wall and fuck me one more time as a plea for me to stay with him. But honestly, I didn't want to go to Venice, that's what it came down to. The place creeps me out. It's so disorienting. There might have been a certain satisfaction to letting Rhys see me with Jared, but more than anything I feel it would have just been awkward, and that Rhys, being an Englishman, would have found a way to belittle me in such a way as to make me feel like I was ugly, poor and dating a toad. Compounded by the baffling and bewildering setting of Venice, I just don't think I would have been able to take it. It was something Jared wouldn't have understood, so after he gave me my last orgasm, I shouted at him, "Did you make Lindsay and Paris cum like that too?"

He thought I was going to let him forget about his little *bisou* with Paris at Sundance in '08, but another curse of mine is having the memory of an elephant (though, thank God, the frenetic metabolism of a chihuahua). The Lindsay tryst obviously happened during *Chapter 27*, even though he tried to claim he was in character twenty-four hours a day. These weren't his fucking Joker days, I don't know why he had to try so hard to pretend to be a "serious" actor when he had already been in enough serious films by then: *American Psycho, Lord of War…Phone Booth*. Maybe it was because *Chapter 27* was the first film he really had to carry as his own actor. Still, I had no faith in his bullshit. He would've fucked Lindsay in or out of character, and she probably got off on him being all fat and Mark David Chapman-y. She was a weirdo like that. A fellow slut from another hut.

Jared glared at me. Stared daggers for bringing up the unspoken source of contention between us: that he had fucked two people in my circle and it was a challenge not think to about that when we ourselves fucked. Fortunately, he was too self-involved to put together the pieces about my own history with someone in his current professional circle: Rhys.

In the midst of gathering my last little accoutrements for the trip, Jared threatened (like a drama queen), "If you walk out that door, don't bother coming back."

"Of course I'm going to fucking come back. It's *my* apartment."

Jared rolled his eyes. "You know what I mean, you fucking smart ass."

"How dare you call me smart? I'm no such thing. I allowed *you* to enter me, after all."

With that, I all but ran out the door so that he couldn't get in the last word. I only hoped he wouldn't stay there too much longer as I was planning to call Lupe (I think I called all my cleaning ladies Lupe by that point because of *Will & Grace*…or was Karen's cleaning lady named something else?) to fumigate the whole place with her magic, and I wouldn't have put it past Jared to try to have sex with her to spite me. It was what we did, us rich folk: fucked others to get back at each other since none of us could use our money to make the other feel powerless. That was only something you could do with lower-income people like Tara Reid.

While I fled the U.S. once again for greener, more tropical pastures, Lindsay continued to stay as public as she could by going to an Emmys after-party (she clearly wasn't nominated for her work in *Ugly Betty* the year before in order to be able to attend the actual ceremony) at the Chateau Marmont. Patently not satisfied with the amount of attention she was getting (and with no Samantha to yell at anymore after the breakup/restraining order), Lindsay thought it would be cute to throw beer cans at the paparazzi. Which made her former weapon of choice in '06, an empty pizza box, look even more "classy," as Paris would label it (drenched in IG shade, naturally).

Not content to make a small news item with beer can-chucking, Lindsay seemed determined in her bid to be a colossal walking anti-drug advertisement when she made a bigger splash at the Ungaro show at Paris Fashion Week to start the month of October off with a wet fart of a bang. Everyone stood agog at the fact that this tweaked-out bottle blonde former actress could genuinely think that heart-shaped pasties, bright pink "Jasmine" pants (you know, the palace kind) and shapeless silhouettes on the dresses—that is, when they weren't practically glued on as an homage to the cheesy clubwear that you can still find at Charlotte Russe (if you can still find a Charlotte

Russe)—were billable as "fashion." One critic politely called the offerings better suited to a diffusion line, while others were more straightforward. Like the *New York Times*, which kindly commented that Lindsay's involvement was "something akin to a McDonald's fry cook taking the reins of a three-star Michelin restaurant." Did you really think I was going to miss the setup to such a disaster? Fuck no. It was time to get out of Saint Lucia.

Though "sobriety" was noble and all for a couple months (but of course this meant Amy and I were at the bar every day), I was bored. I needed a major city's landscape to get my name back into the headlines with the rest of the hopeless white girls trying to compete with the Armenian mafia. Paris (the city, not the person) would be ideal for such an endeavor. It was the thing that brought everyone back into the limelight. Even Kim, who was losing her touch before that jewelry heist during Fashion Week boosted her up (I still believe she hired her "robbers," just like most people with any brains do). Thus, I made arrangements, bidding adieu to Amy and telling her to finish her fucking album already before she became remembered for nothing other than having shitty taste in men and being a drug addict. She claimed she would. As you know, she did not. But I tried to help…there's just only so much you can do for a person who wants to stay off the rails. In this way, Amy and Lindsay were kind of similar, it just seemed that Lindsay had the Woody Allen luck philosophy more on her side than Amy. Because God or whoever knows Amy was more talented, yet somehow Lindsay has risen from the ashes again and again despite her unbridled non-ability.

When she was younger, sure, she could pass herself off as a "dynamo" because everything you do when you're a child is more impressive by the simple virtue that you're making way more fucking money than any adult. The older you get, though, the less you can coast on the alleged "talent" every-one thought you possessed when you were a kid, and it suddenly becomes clear that you haven't progressed artistically in any way, but have instead devolved (I think it's safe to say *Labor Pains* was a devolution from *Mean Girls*. Or even *I Know Who Killed Me*, which had, at the very least, midnight movie kitsch value). I was ready to see Lindsay fall on her face once and for all with this upcoming guaranteed-to-fail fashion show for Ungaro.

Jared had called me several times during my absence to confess that he missed me, but I couldn't bring myself to invite him to join me in Paris. It would have been reopening an unnecessary wound. Why bother getting sucked back in by all that good sex when I knew it couldn't last? That he would probably end up fucking Kim next for all I knew about the depths of star-fucking both parties were capable of. Accordingly, I mulled over a new escort for the occasion. For the important reentry into the spotlight that my appearance at Fashion Week would mean. I didn't want it to be just another American actor…that wasn't going to lend me the distinction I needed to ensure totally outshining any other socialite at the event. I also didn't want it to be a French man because, well, they're little bitches who usually aren't even that good in bed.

Then it occurred to me that I hadn't really dabbled with an Italian man of late (I'm not counting Fabrizio the deckhand). Not since that unfortunate time I let Roberto Benigni put his hand down my dress at some fundraiser in L.A. in the early 00s. Maybe it was time to give the nationality another whirl. The first man I thought of was Roberto Saviano. Also, I can't help it that every Italian guy is named Roberto.

He was getting a lot of buzz because the film adaptation for *Gomorrah* came out in February and there was a huge mafia bounty on his head. Still is. To get him for Fashion Week would be an incredible coup. I went about the business of contacting him through my European publicist, himself an Italian man who knew everybody's business if they lived in England, France or Italy. Sergio was instrumental in helping me stalk Roberto, "encountering" him at his favorite coffee bar in Milan to strike up a "meaningful" conversation and enough of a rapport to warrant extending an invite to come to Paris with me. He played it aloof at first, but I knew he would say yes. At the end of the day, a blonde American girl is an Italian man's kryptonite. And don't you ever forget it, if that's your flavor. I highly recommend dyeing *your* non-lustrous dark hair the right shade to taste that kind of power.

With the gossip columns and fashion writers already running their mouths about the scandalous decision of Mounir Moufarrige to appoint Lindsay in a last- (*very last-*) ditch effort to breathe some sort of youthful resonance into the fledgling brand, everyone was ready to watch the burning Haus of Ungaro burn down just a little bit more that week. Roberto had no idea what he was in for, but I could tell that the entire experience was giving him a new idea for a novel.

When the expected battalion of jank was finished parading the designs created through the "advisement" of Lohan, she came out holding hands with the real designer, Estrella Archs, who looked more than slightly ashamed and seemed to be dragging Lindsay down the runway with her. Standing there awkwardly with Estrella at the edge of the stage, it made me think of how Lindsay randomly showed up onstage at a show of Lily Allen's back in April at The Wiltern to attempt jumping in on the mic to sing "Womanizer," Allen's favored cover of the time, and a song that Lindsay had definitely argued over with Samantha during one of her DJ gigs (Lindsay wanted to hear it, Samantha did not). This was all Lindsay appeared to know how to do to stay in a klieg light that was bright enough for her: she had to jump in on someone else's mic despite herself being incapable of exhibiting anything worthy of getting said mic time.

Ungaro was the zenith of this metaphor, and soon after it would be *Machete*, a "film" in which Lindsay was given no other choice but to embrace parodying herself as a dumb bitch/slut, albeit with the false description of being "a socialite with a penchant for guns." Oh fuck off. She would never even hold a candle to *my* daddy's secret gun collection (secret because, for the purposes of living in L.A., he had to pretend to be liberal). It just went to show that Lindsay had always wanted to be one of us. That's why she destroyed her acting career once she was rich. She wanted to live as destructively—and as though there was no limit to her funds—as a real socialite. But she fucking couldn't, ergo this endless series of cringeworthy "gigs." In fact, maybe the one thing I will say for Lindsay is that she sort of pioneered the gig economy. Or at least put it a little bit more into the public consciousness as a concept.

Smiling with Roberto on my arm after the show, I bathed not only in the flashbulb lights, but also in Lindsay's blatant sadness. That she was trying to pass off as sheer joy. What a fucking joke.

It was almost like you had to feel humiliated yourself for being that close to her aura of shame. Roberto told me after, when we were back in my hotel—and had gotten our fucking session out of the way—that it was as I had suspected: seeing the barbarity of it all had, indeed, very much inspired him. He wanted to get to work right away, and felt that it would be best to get to a point of isolation to do so. This meant going back to Italy, the most isolated place there is. I really don't fucking know why people romanticize it so much when all there is to do is eat like a cow and then try to get to some facet of civilization in a car when you're not based in Milan (I don't really like Rome, so I'm not including it).

But Roberto was hopelessly Italian, even though most of his countrymen wanted him dead. For some reason, God only knows why, Italians always remain loyal to their blood even when it turns on them. And it will always turn on them. Betrayal is part and parcel of being Italian. That's why you couldn't have paid me to go back into that country at that moment in time (I would, however, be paid to do a Ferrero Rocher ad in Piedmont about two years later. So yeah, you could actually pay me to go back).

I only wished that he wasn't such a writer, so driven by his need to get his thoughts and ideas out onto the page as soon as possible to the point where it interrupted his personal relationships. We might have had a wonderful Parisian romance if he wasn't a little slave-bitch to his goddamn "craft." Oof. I just can't with writers who call it that (in addition to, as mentioned before, actors). As though they're performing some sort of magical witchery when all they're really doing is masturbating, splooging their fucking neuroses out onto the page. Well, good riddance to Roberto then. I was better off. I only wished I could have been seen out on the town with him a few more times to get the maximum mileage out of the purpose of my journey, which was to get back in the public eye. Seeing Lindsay verbally flogged was just an added bonus for my trouble.

After that, she jumped at another off-brand chance: narrating and participating in a BBC (but like BBC3) documentary called *Lindsay Lohan's Indian Journey*. The title made it seem less exercise in humanitarianism and more attempt at homage to Bill and Ted. There was also this weird, like, meta tinge of melancholy to the whole thing considering Lindsay herself was a child laborer. Anyway, she dipped out of America to shoot that shit in December, which meant ringing in 2010 would feel even sweeter without her energy-sucking presence.

Paris was going back to Australia for New Year's Eve, almost as a *fuck you* to her time with Kim there in '06. When Kim was still at her side as her lapdog assistant, deluding herself in subsequent interviews by insisting to everyone from Ellen to Oprah that she was a "celebrity closet organizer." I really don't see how that sounds better than being Paris' assistant. I rather think it sounded slightly more dignified to be an "aide" than a person who has to touch other people's grody last-season shit. But again, Kim was no top-level socialite. In truth, she really dumbed down what it meant more than Paris, who explained to everyone that she was only playing a character while on *The Simple Life* for the sake of making the then-untapped-into medium of reality TV more interesting. She knew how to attract viewership before the suits at the networks themselves did.

At the same time, I think she just feels a hair ashamed about how vacant she came across in retrospect and has been using the "I was playing a character" excuse as a way to make the display of dumbness somewhat less immortal. Yeah, well, me fucking too. I'm playing a character even now. The one that leaves her body while she's trapped in prison because everyone here should never have been born. In any event, what I'm saying is that: there was no one in the inner socialite circle who was planning to stay in L.A. to celebrate the end of another year. Even Nicole was out of commission. Increasingly going full-tilt mother, capitalizing on that venture by designing a custom line for...I'm taking a deep breath before I say it…A Pea in the Pod. She had really lost her edge more than anyone, to be honest. It was rather sickening, and not in that *RuPaul's Drag Race* sort of way. It all just left me feeling a bit somber, coming to the revelation that I had no friends or even a boy toy to keep me company at a time of year when it mattered most. When you were forced to take a long, harsh look at your life. As such, I decided not to accept a recently divorced Guy Ritchie's invitation to come to London, where, gross, my dad was going to be with his new twenty-something girlfriend. No thanks.

The only other person with a movie out at that end-of-year time that I could potentially fuck with was Terry Gilliam. He was sort of hot to me for renouncing his U.S. citizenship a few years ago as, like, the ultimate statement against living in a country run by George W. Bush. Little did he fuckin' know. And yeah, he was married to the very woman who permitted him the luxury of renouncing his citizenship in favor of absconding for Britain, but what did marriage really mean to any director? Affairs, that's what. Still, I thought it best to go for someone more age-appropriate as part of my New Year's resolution not to have an Electra complex. Daniel Craig, then a very age-appropriate forty-one, sprung to my mind as an option to fulfill my apparent fetishism for British men. He was coming out of another long-term relationship with a producer woman no one had heard of and therefore no one would care if I was seen on his arm in Primrose Hill. That he didn't even have a movie out that year also accentuated this "I'm so humble and not at all opportunistic" vibe I wanted to strive for more than anyone else in my original camp of friends seemed to be.

To that end, 2010 was to *really* commence Kim and her whole family's repugnant bid for world domination. It was in 2009 that, much as I hate to agree with that little Instagram troll, pop culture died (maybe because Michael Jackson did; that was the beginning of the end, 'cause pedo or not, he still represented a certain era itself dying). And all that remained were the Kardashians and the lingering ramifications of Lindsay's poor decision-making in 2007.

<u>**Chapter 15: "What a bitch, taking your
hamburger. I mean, what was that?"**</u>

*K*im continued effortlessly down the path of endorsement deal success as 2010 began at a steady clip for her in terms of power and financial clout increases. What was most appalling of all, even to those who tried their best to defend Kim in saying that she was a totally different "brand" than Paris, is that Kim recreated Paris' Carl's Jr. ad campaign of 2005, but with—most insultingly of all—a healthy slant. Like any motherfucker is buying salads at Carl's J. And like anyone is buying that a member of the Kardashian Klan would ever dare set foot in there after already spending enough of the early and mid-00s living off the crumbs of photo ops at various Coffee Beans throughout Los Angeles. No, no. Kim was done with being a bottom feeder of the social hierarchy. She was now to *become* the social hierarchy. And though it took a few demeaning gigs in the interim (like a stint on *Dancing With the Stars*) before her eventual ascent to the reigning queen of "reality" and social media, 2010 was the year when the shift really saw its completion.

Considering what a slow start January got off to, what with J.D. Salinger finally croaking being the only really noteworthy thing of the month (what? You didn't think a dumb bitch socialite could read *Catcher in the Rye*...it's much better than watching *Chapter 27*), Kim came out of '09 swinging with this "augmented reality"-packed promotion, "tantalizing" people to engage with the commercial by touting "The Ultimate Salad Lunch Date," during which extreme nerds could chat with her on a webcam on January 13th if they bought one of the wilted salads between December 30th and January 12th. Something about it smacked of the porn industry to me. But Kim was more prostitute than porn star, even despite her sex tape (in which those pained expressions make me wonder if she should give up Black dick. No guy wants to see the girl he's fucking looking like she's giving birth as opposed to orgasming).

I was still gallivanting about in London, even though my passion for Daniel Craig (I feel obliged to call people with a last name as a first name by their full name, do you know what I mean?) had cooled since our New Year's Eve kiss. He wasn't very good in bed, I'll just say it. Not that the Brits are generally known for their adroitness in this arena, but something about Daniel Craig's technique left me feeling particularly hollow inside where instead I should have been full...of James Bond semen. To say that Daniel Craig left a dryness in my panties would be more of an understatement than saying that Obama had "aged" by the end of his presidency (the man went from hot as fuck to gray old man in those scant four years). He tried to insert himself without any finesse whatsoever, and then he had the fucking nerve to not even cum. He just kept thrusting for what felt like eternity into the small hours (I won't call them "wee") of January 1, 2010.

So it was that I slunk out at about nine a.m., when I knew no one in their right mind except the most depraved paparazzo would be on the streets to see me leave his house. I should've probably just grabbed a flight (a.k.a. taken a private jet) back to Los Angeles, and yet...something about London had a hold on me. Even though Madonna had effectively deemed it over when she finalized her divorce with Guy, who was still after me even though I had rebuffed him several times now, I just found it so...proper. So much more charming and civilized than Paris, a city that holds an allure to people that I still don't understand, and most certainly not after it deigned to let Lindsay in and participate in that haunting fashion show.

Resisting every urge I had to go crawling back to Rhys, I instead booked a suite at the Four Seasons, which I know was a bit middle-class in many ways, but I still esteemed it for its old school prestige. It had a nicer ring to it than a Hilton. I checked in, got settled and took a hangover nap at around ten. I was starting to feel the signs of my age, clearly. I could never share these feelings with anyone, of course, least of all Paris, who was just slightly younger than me (or is it I?). Nicole was too. Only Kim could have maybe understood what I was going through, midlife (for a socialite) crisis-wise. I could never talk to her about it though. She didn't even see me as worthy of allowing into her orbit now that she was Miss Carl's Jr./Mrs. Bush (not George W., Reggie). I hadn't been as blatantly snubbed as Paris, who was "content" to do what would become a trend for her in 2010: foreign commercials. Starting with this really nonsensical one, at least in terms of decent casting, for a Brazilian beer called Devassa Bem Loura. I didn't know what it was then and I definitely don't now. I just heard it was supposed to be "witty" because the translation meant, loosely, I suppose, "very blonde bitch." That, Paris surely was. And still is (have you seen her relentlessly throwing shade at Lindsay even now as the firecrotch pathetically *still* tries to make this "comeback" we've all been hearing about happening since 2006?).

Then there was her absurd Israeli lotto commercial. I guess the point is, a lot of faux celebrities were suffering because of the continued effects of the recession. It's just as much of a challenge to be rich—if not more so because of the expectation to sustain one's lifestyle—when the economy goes to shit. In Lindsay's case, she was already accustomed to performing endeavors that were of a compromising and unseemly nature (I can't emphasize the Fornarina commercial or Ungaro show enough), so one might think that any real work that came her way would have been something she'd cling to desperately…by not being such a coked-out fuck-up. That the lead role in a project called *The Other Side* was offered to her primarily because there was no one else interested in gambling on a screenwriter's directorial debut (whatever happened to David Michaels anyway?) was taken for granted by Lindsay.

In her delusion, still ironclad to this day, she imagined that they asked her because she remained sought after, hot shit. But no, it was because she was full-stop shit that they extended the opportunity. Yet another one that Lindsay would squander after her 2010 headlines began in typical chagrin, not the least of which included being accused (in what would continue a longstanding history of the rich white girl propensity for stealing to feel alive) of taking a $35,000 Rolex from a friend who had come over to her house for a party. That's like way worse than what happened to Carrie Bradshaw in "A Woman's Right to Shoes." And then she had to throw ice at Samantha Ronson at Trousdale. All of this occurring after one of the most degrading series of paparazzi photos in Lindsay's very storied career of degrading paparazzi photos: the cactus tripping.

It happened early on in the year, in March— after Saint Patrick's Day, mind you, so there was really no viable excuse for "raucous" behavior. I was still trying to get my bearings in London when I saw the photos splashed across *The Daily Mail* and other tabloid-like publications. It was similar to a comic strip or one of those flipbooks leading up to a catastrophic denouement. As usual, in her state of constant denial and pathological liardom, Lindsay would tweet that the paparazzi had pushed her. Na bitch, we all know your drunk and high ass tripped and fell because you were drunk and high.

With this in mind, Lindsay was eager to take on the whorish role of April in *Machete*, not only because she could play her trashtastic self with little effort, but also because she got to shade her daddy by having a father in the film that was obsessed with her and wanted to fuck her. We all know that's where some of the source of contention is with Michael. He just wants to bang his daughter and can't, and she, like, lords it over him. It's beyond the Electra complex, and now that I think about it, it makes a lot of sense that she fled to Mykonos to become a "businesswoman," Greece being the epicenter and origin of all fucked-up and incestuous narratives.

But Lindsay was already sucking on that European titty in 2010, when she, seeming to want to cash in on her image of being a hooker, was convinced she was going to play the part of Linda Lovelace in a movie that *still* hasn't been made—

I'm not counting that separate Amanda Seyfried affair—entitled *Inferno.* In fact, an inferno was the place Lindsay seemed to enjoy inhabiting for the duration of 2010. With the intention of "promoting" her still unmade movie about Lovelace, Lindsay went to Cannes in May. Underneath it all (like the No Doubt song), I think she knew it was just a glorified excuse to party somewhere that didn't make it seem so much like she was a trainwreck due to the lustrous, drenched-in-riches (and rich people) backdrop. She had to have been aware, amid the recesses of that sharper than she lets on mind, that no one was going to hire her for a lead role ever again. Unless it was for Lifetime in the form of *Liz & Dick* in 2012, the year the world and Lindsay's career finally and truly ended.

I, too, decided to take a little trip to the Côte d'Azur, but I, like the refined and sophisticated socialite that I am, arrived late to the festivities, with only about two days left of screenings. Lindsay, by then, had already started to see some unpleasant writing (in creepy chicken scratch font) on the wall regarding her "good time gal" days. It came, really, in late 2009, when she seemed to masochistically welcome her formerly good-natured judge's decision to extend her probation by another twelve months— despite the very overt track record of Lindsay not giving a single fuck about volunteering her bony ass to anyone other than a guy that might have drugs (or a girl who looked like a guy that might have drugs). Lo(han) and behold, the judge soon saw that her decision had been in vain, revoking the probation while Lindsay was coking it up in Cannes…all in the name of promoting her "film," of course. And if there so happened to be a yacht or two or more involved, who was she to refuse? Like Rory Gilmore before her, it's impossible to resist the many temptations that a yacht invokes in a "spirited" "young" woman.

It was, to everyone left still watching, a very blatant fuck you to the judge, Marsha (a real ball-buster of a name), who revoked the probation when it became clear Lindsay wasn't that keen to attend her mandatory weekly alcohol education program, which she dipped out on while still in Cannes because she "lost her passport." Oh Lindsay, always thinking the simplest, most non-creative excuses are going to get her out of things, even the now permanently ingrained contempt the public has for her. At least, any public that still bothers to keep up with her sad little affairs, like a reality show on MTV.

So it was that Marsha responded to Lindsay's claim of losing her passport with the withdrawal of her probation and a bench warrant (so tame), accompanied by the disappointed explanation, "I couldn't be more clear about the priority of this case and getting things done. She should have made sure she either didn't go to Cannes or, if she went there, she should be back two days early. If she wanted to be here, it looks to the court she could have been here… She's not here. There's really no valid excuse." But in Lindsay's mind, like the minds of most faux socialites, the only valid excuse she needed was that she wanted to do something. Or rather, *didn't* want to do it. I can't say I blame her for avoiding these alcohol "education" classes. It was probably more enjoyable to put those drug suppositories up her asshole (quite wide from all the railing, I've heard).

I sat back and watched it all unfold from my perch on the terrace of the Hotel Carlton Intercontinental, where I usually like to stay during the festival despite how teeming it is with other "stars" stealing from my own publicity. This year, to my advantage, it wasn't exactly burgeoning with high-profile clientele. For fuck's sake *Uncle Boonmee Who Can Recall His Past Lives* won the Palme d'Or. It wasn't like a fucking Tarantino flick was in the mix. But an Xavier Dolan one was, and let me tell you, he veers more toward straight than gay or bi, as far as I can tell—don't believe what you saw in *Heartbeats* with that love triangle bullshit. If a pussy is presented, he'll take it over dick. That much was clear when I brought him back to my hotel room (he was staying at the shittier Radisson Blu).

Smoking an e-cigarette (I was kind of ahead of the game on that as well), after he was finished going down on me, I turned on the TV to avoid telling him that he hadn't fully sated my needs. That was the thing about guys who were sensitive: all willingness, zero primal instinct or intuition. Meatheads could definitely give better head if they could just get past the hurdle of not wanting to press their lips to the same kind of lips that pushed them out into the world. Alas, no one said life was fair, did they? Not even for socialites born into far better circumstances than your relegated-to-reading-to-seem-interesting ass. Any who, when the news reports started flooding in about Lindsay and her pathological lying being taken to new heights (not a single person believed she lost her passport and couldn't get back on time), I could feel the joyfulness welling up inside my *chest*. Probably since I can't feel anything in my stomach because I've had it stapled so many times (all in the most avant-garde methods, mind you—and none that have left so much as even a trace of a scar, thank you very much Janet Jackson).

Xavier, who was annoying me to no end by now because of his lack of interest in what mattered (mainstream Hollywood) and the absence of his ability to pleasure me physically, came up behind me as I fake-smoked at the balcony.

"What are you so happy about, eh? Could it be somebody is in love?"

Fucking disgusting. I don't know what it is with low-class guys, especially directors, always thinking that women are having, like, some sort of visceral reaction to them. The only thing "visceral" happening to me was that Lindsay was getting dropped from *Inferno* in the most self-destructive way possible. Like, she couldn't even sustain the roles that were tailor-made for her anymore—movies about whorish trainwrecks. All because she was such a parody of a whorish trainwreck. 2010 was shaping up to be something real special indeed.

It didn't take very long for her to revive the SCRAM bracelet jokes of '07 when the MTV Movie Awards rolled around on June 6th and she was accused of setting it off during an after-party. Quite a tumble for Lindsay, to have to go from thinking she was a star attraction at Cannes to settling for slumming it as an after-party hanger-on at anything put together by MTV. Paris, Nicole and even *Kim* didn't show up to *that* function. And I was certainly still too busy overstaying my welcome in Europe as I usually tended to do once I set foot on that soil, which somehow always provided me with someone to till mine… Don't judge the metaphor. I've watched our gardener work while I sipped a low-cal daiquiri by the pool, I know some horticulturist lingo. Plus, I like to make use of plant imagery considering how many fucking quaint suitors still think giving flowers is cute when every socialite would prefer the dual pearl necklace Samantha Jones got from Richard Wright on his private jet as an initial *cadeau* to prove whether or not he's even worth continuing on with for something as lengthy as a six-month to one-year trial period.

Paris' fall from grace persisted along the same timeline as Lindsay's, though not nearly in a shame spiral so flagrant. Granted, she wasn't without her own little summer snafu in the form of getting caught doing something très Lindsay, which was to say "doing drugs" (as if weed counts) at a very public venue: the FIFA World Cup. I get she was, like, trying to make her international thing happen the way *I* had in terms of causing scandals by showing up to some shitty soccer game between two countries I don't even think she's ever even fucked anyone from, but why do it in South Africa? No one was even getting information in the same rapid way about it in 2010 that would have made it advantageous enough for the effort. Me, I like instant results with my scandals. Not to rely on some literal wire to convey it from all the way down in a part of Africa where there's not even any Black dick to fuck. But she probably, in her dumb blonde way, kind of assumed all of Africa must be filled with Black men. I can't fault her for this "logical" thinking. Once a socialite gets something in her mind that a place or a person ought to be a certain way, she simply can't remove it from her rigid brain.

Nor could Paris remove the idea that to smoke pot publicly, just because it was somewhere as "lawless" and "uncouth" as South Africa, could possibly be illegal.

Whatever was going on in that bird-brain of hers, she was clearly rooting for the Netherlands to win, if she was even aware that they or Brazil were playing. Her lack of shame over being escorted from the Nelson Mandela Bay Stadium was, at the very least, felt by her semi-contrite publicist, Dawn, who claimed, "I can confirm that the incident was a complete misunderstanding and it was actually another person in the group who did it." I wonder whatever happened to Dawn anyway. Or all of the publicists from the mid- and late 00s. I'd like to believe they're all diabolically plotting their tell-all reality show (because only someone like me is dumb enough to write a tell-all *book*) somewhere. Just biding their time for the right moment, the right level of resurgence in interest. Lord knows that's what I'm trying to do with the perfectly-timed release of this incendiary "piece."

Ah, and speaking of pieces, maybe you're wondering whatever happened to Xavier. Did I cruelly eject him from my life as I seemed to with every foreign blonde cad (yes, I'm talking to you Rhy Ifans, who I will never forgive for shaming me no matter what, especially when I'm so clearly financially and physically superior)? Surprisingly, not just yet. He had a certain *je ne sais quoi* and a *joie de vivre*—and not just because he was fake French in that he was Québécois. That's different than being just plain Canadian though. Somehow less tacky. If it came down to me having to introduce him to Daddy, this would be his only saving grace. Which of course I never would because Daddy wouldn't approve of anyone who might actually be able to love me more than *he* did. But yeah, I decided to keep him around, to bring him back to L.A. with me like a little pet, where he would be my date to the VMAs. It was always best to bring someone non-music industry involved to the affair. And I could tell Xavier was fiending for some more mainstream legitimacy, despite his filmic claims of only listening to "esoteric" offerings like The Knife. Please, the only thing people enjoy from The Knife is "Heartbeats" and if they say otherwise, they're pretentious little fucks from Europe.

Tragically, the awards show was dominated by one of my least favorite undercover whores, Stefani Germanotta. I don't know how she managed to rise through the ranks faster than Lizzy Grant, as they were both hookering it up on the Lower East Side at the exact same time. Boring as usual, the only juicy part of the ceremony came when it was over and Kanye tweeted, "I'm sorry, Taylor." Talk about too little, too late. So while everyone ooh'd and ahh'd once again ad nauseam over the fucking "Bad

Romance" and "Telephone" videos (it truly is incredible what the masses will be duped into believing is "high art"), I passed the flask back and forth between Xavier and Paris, who had decided to keep a low-profile (by her standards) after the whole South Africa ordeal. Xavier was getting on my nerves the entire time, finding a constant opportunity to express ingratitude by complaining that I was a corporate Hollywood slut who clearly had no taste whatsoever in music or anything else. That's when I decided to go home with a Black Key. Xavier was fun or edgy or whatever in France I guess. But in L.A., he was a liability, an uncomfortable reminder that there were actually people out there who wanted to make art instead of just sell shit posing as art.

In another part of the globe, long before J. Lo and A-Rod were causing a stir on the island of Capri, Kim was having the best summer out of all of us there in September (she didn't have to be bogged down by Kanye and his Twitter storms yet), despite being photographed solely with her shrew of a mother while they both stuffed their faces. She really was building an evidence-based case for the joys of being fat—yet another way in which she literally reshaped the socialite game. It was almost as if, even more than that heifer Anna Nicole Smith (RIP—rest in prescription drugs), Kim was rewriting what women, and therefore men, saw as beautiful.

I would never fall for that, fuck no. You weren't going to catch me with my ass hanging out with *any* trace of cellulite on it. I don't care how much of a "trend" it was. Because if you haven't learned by now: trends come and go. Conventional forms of beauty are forever. That's why they wanted to punish us "basic blondes" (at least Paris and me…Britney was kind of busted-looking when you got right down to it—no conventional beauty there unless you can classify it as Southern White Trash Glamor. I think that's why Brit Brit was the saddest of all to see the Ed Hardy trend go).

So as Kim fortified her already-plump physique with Italian food, Lindsay attempted to see a silver lining with the release of *Machete* earlier that month. For the most part, it got mediocre reviews. But at least it spawned a theme bar in London with Lindsay's nun poster as the centerpiece. She'll always have that going for her: being an inspirer of kitsch (read: a patron saint of fuck-ups who want their own trashiness to be embraced, if not by society, then at least by a middling 00s celebrity). Rather than attend the premiere, however (you know, like any shrewd actress already scraping by on minimal publicity as it was might try to do), Lindsay decided to use her newfound freedom from rehab/jail (again) to get photographed with an energy drink and driving a Maserati (she is so transparent with the way she spends as an automatic reveal of the fact that she has no money, starving for it by the time she gets any significant amount so as to blow the wad on something incongruous like an island called, shocking, Lohan).

But, who knows, maybe she was mildly ashamed to be a part of the film? Somehow found it all "beneath" her despite her minimal appearance in it. Then again, in her defense, the majority of 2010 movies were largely unsatisfying. It was as though the universe *wanted* to provide us with further evidence that pop culture died in 2009 by making a James Franco-starring vehicle the primary "buzz movie" of awards season. Did anyone *other* than Jonah Hill (who has and always will be in love with Franco) watch *127 Hours* in its entirety? No, they did not.

Lindsay, at best, could say that she had achieved the "honor" of being mentioned on *TIME*'s blog (emphasis on *blog*) for having one of the top tweets of the year with, "The only 'bookings' that I'm familiar with are Disney films, never thought that I'd be 'booking' into jail... Eeeks." Oh the horror that comes with a false sense of self-awareness. It can be so damaging. Like the way the public and the media interpret you to the point where you—the actual you—doesn't even exist anymore. Still, I could feel no sympathy for her. She was no master at her "craft," but she was certainly a master at squandering opportunities. A socialite can only be so understanding of fuck-ups until starting to wonder if maybe the fuck-up in question *wants* to be a martyr, or simply doesn't comprehend that only *real* socialites can make the same mistakes over and over (and over) again without punishment or stigma. That is, unless you're me.

Things had been relatively tame and dignified for "my personage" throughout the year, with the "eminence" of dating an "indie" movie director forcing the formerly chastising media to see me in an entirely new light. The sort of light that Lindsay could once receive when she wasn't relegated to low-budget movies. A casting agent had even taken notice long enough to reach out to me personally. He got me an audition for the lead role in *Beastly*, which, eventually Mary-Kate managed to use her "built-in audience" to get. She did me a favor though. If I was going to be in any bastardized remake of *Beauty and the Beast*, it was to be the movie called my life, which found me somehow in the arms of Harvey Weinstein himself by the time October rolled around and I was feeling unsettled by the fact that Lindsay was *still* somehow managing to get articles written about her in *Vanity Fair*, offering the same assurances made about how she had changed. I couldn't fucking understand how she kept doing it, managing to keep her name in the headlines despite no viable film credits to be found since 2004. And then I ran into Harvey at some soirée inside The Standard (the Downtown one, not that inferior West Hollywood one *Sex and the City* made famous).

Unlike most girls who would later narc on him, I could see that Harvey was clearly just a lovable teddy bear beneath that toadish exterior. That all he wanted was to use his power in exchange for the commodity of sex the way men in the industry had been conditioned to believe was the "way of the world" in Hollywood. He was only carrying on tradition when you get right down to it. He was very old-fashioned, pulling an Edward Lewis in *Pretty Woman* when he offered me champagne and strawberries in the hotel room he had ready and waiting and didn't even need to try to lure me into. In fact, it was *I* who suggested we take our "business conversation" upstairs.

Word about Harvey was already rampant throughout the small island nation of Hollywood, and I had to admit I was very curious about what information I might be able to pump from him... while he pumped me. Chiefly, I wanted to know why Lindsay hadn't been blacklisted to the utmost degree that she so richly deserved to be. Through a series of acrobatic bodily and emotional gestures (it can be quite a challenge to work with a portly body in the boudoir while also pretending to seem engaged), I got Harvey to admit that *he* was the only reason Lindsay could still lay claim to her title as "actress."

"She gives me whatever I want, when I want it. She's always been sexually docile to me. I can't bring myself to give her the axe," he confessed.

It was then I stopped gagging on his cum long enough to spit it out in extreme disgust. "You've *got to be* fucking kidding me."

Getting up off my knees, I proceeded to methodically dress. He was no teddy bear, he was a pathetic ghoul who misused his money to the point of not even thinking of getting gastric bypass surgery. Such an easy fix to one of his main problems in life: that fucking paunch. Maybe if he didn't have one, he wouldn't need to rape girls in exchange for movie roles to get them to "like" him.

Taking a perfume bottle out of my purse as I approached the mirror before departing, I daubed some of Paris' most recent fragrance, Tease, on my neck (she said it was inspired by Marilyn Monroe, because all teases and hoes are inspired by MM, ergo the 6126 leggings line), made sure my nipples were practically popping out of my sequined halter and zoomed the fuck out of there. Harvey called out, "Tate! Don't go."

I arched my brow, "It's either *me*...or Lindsay." He made the mistake of choosing the latter. That's the mistake they've all have made, probably even you.

Taking a break from boys, men and sex in general after such a foul series of experiences, I decided to focus on the only constant male in my life as the holidays approached: Daddy. Gwen had, by this point, taken up even more official residence in Palm Springs as she continued to wait for Edward to die and give her all of his assets even though she had absolutely no legal bearing on them once Edward's ex-wife and only daughter got their paws on the Last Will. I had to say, a part of me respected Gwen's steadfast allegiance to debasing my father, abandoning him in a far crueler way than actual abandonment by dangling the promise of an eventual return. Maybe I inherited some of my own cunty ways from her. That's why I couldn't totally begrudge her style; she was the reason I was so indoctrinated with ruthless survival skills. The kind that led me to the conclusion that the current state of Hollywood could not abide, that it had to go back to "*Mean Girls* with coke and paparazzi," as a girl from Lindsay's so-called inner circle once put it. And the only way to make that happen was to fan the flames of the brewing rivalry between Paris and Kim, since Nicole was clearly out of the game, doing her goddamn fashion shit and being married to even more of a has-been than Paris herself.

So maybe I helped the rivalry along a little bit, not that it even really needed my gentle, custom-manicured hand to do so. But I was getting bored, needed a project. Since I didn't get cast in *Beastly* and all. That's when I made the bold decision to flagrantly betray Paris in a manner I never had before by strategically choosing to ingratiate myself in Kim's good graces in time for the holiday season. More specifically, I needed to ensure I would get an invite to the Kardashian's now famed holiday party. The one that Paris couldn't get back into until 2016, when she pathetically posed with Kim in an even more lackey-like fashion than Kim ever did with her. It was honestly so uncomfortable that I can, with complete confidence, tell you that if you ever wanted to torture me and/or extract a piece of vital information, all you would probably need to do is hold up that image to me for about five seconds before I surrendered. I just really can't look at it, it's too painful. To see someone who was once so unquestionably "the queen of everything" reduced to this kowtowing state. It was like watching, I don't know, Madonna do a duet with Justin Timberlake or something.

Whatever might have been Paris' motives for posting the photo on her own Instagram (at least it was Kim who put up the photo of them at Riccardo Tisci's birthday party in Ibiza in 2014), she was very obviously desperate. And I could never look at her "no plastic surgery" face the same way again. I knew Paris would really have to take a close, harsh look at herself in the mirror once she found out that *I* had been invited and she hadn't. It would be a real stark assessment of just how lacking her power was. That Kim had, in essence, just stolen her fucking (Carl's Jr.) hamburger the way Christy Masters stole

Michele's (you know, in *Romy and Michele's High School Reunion*). Paris would never have a back brace to stick magnets to, naturally, but I guess her lazy eye before all the corrective surgeries was sort of, like, equivalent to that. However, I wasn't going to be the Romy to her Michele—there to say, "What a bitch, taking your hamburger. I mean, what was that?" Because 1) Paris started out as the bitch to Kim and Lord knows payback is just that and 2) I know exactly what "that" (bitch) was: Kim beating Paris at her own game by copying everything she had done but doing it better by making it less white at a time when being white was about as chic as Fornarina.

The only way to secure my place at that coveted party, of course, was to fuck Rob. This was when the family still somewhat respected his pussy choices before he completely destroyed all credibility with Blac Chyna. And he had them all salivating so hard for that hot second in 2012 when he allegedly banged Rihanna. Though I'm pretty sure she must have been roofied in order for that to have any credence to it. In my case, as you might have gleaned, I'll fuck anything if it suits my political purpose. I'm like Mata Hari that way. Or Marie Antoinette (except Louis wasn't exactly known for wanting to bang all that often, so maybe that's a bad example, except the part where she's a decadent diva not deemed worthy because of her heritage. I suppose that would make Lindsay more like Marie. There she fucking goes again, stealing everything I want).

Rob was a willing and oblivious accomplice to my schemes, genuinely interpreting it as sheer "coincidence" that he should keep "running into me" at strip clubs and coke dens (sort of one and the same) all over town. Titillated by our "common interests," it didn't take long for Rob to lick the bait I had cast out in very shallow waters. This was at the beginning of the end of November, the perfect time to "casually" procure an invitation from him when I "drunkenly" gave him my sob story about having nowhere to spend Christmas because my parents were selfish fucks with no regard for my psychological well-being, which is why they would both be away during the holidays in London and Palm Springs, respectively. And each one of them with significant others who were somehow more important to them (meaning able to give them some strange illusion of immortality) than their only spawn—the one person/thing that was supposed to provide their life with meaning yet somehow didn't. Or was insufficient in doing so, I wailed on to Rob as he stroked my hair in front of the stripper we watched mount the pole to "Your Love Is My Drug" by Ke$ha (who was not yet Kesha).

Hearing it made me want to call her up and tell her that letting Dr. Luke abuse her on the reg really wasn't a fair trade for these beats I could just as easily create for her on GarageBand. Or like, maybe I could get Claire Boucher to show her a few things about how to make one's own product without relying on a man who couldn't be bothered to give himself a stage name that was even worth constructing an alter ego for. Like, at that rate, just fucking keep Lukasz Gottwald. It's edgier. But since Ke$ha was still Ke$ha instead of Kesha, she wasn't ready to hear she didn't need to endure this abuse, least of all abuse from someone born in Rhode Island. Also, I was one of the only people who really knew about it, apart from everyone who worked in the studio and on the music videos that came off of *Animal* and all the way up to *Warrior*. But when your paycheck is contingent upon someone else's verbal and physical abuse (because you're a fucking plebe like Lindsay or something), you tend to turn the other cheek while someone such as Ke$ha gets pummeled like a battered wife taking a punch for the collective entertainment of little tween bitches who have no respect for what it actually takes to exude that sexily sloppy persona that only Ke$ha could carry off (Jules Stein and William R. Goodheart Jr. know Willa Ford couldn't).

My sympathy for Ke$ha aside, it seemed like Rob was buying my own tale of tragedy enough to pity me. Pity gave way to him consoling me with one of the increasingly coveted invitations I had been seeking all along. To Kris "Jenner" Kringle's Kardashian Khristmas party. Okay, I made up that name, but they should probably adopt it at this point. It's what the people want—that "subliminal" use of the letters KKK (which Khloé didn't use so subliminally when she posted that meme of her, Kim and Kourtney with the caption, "the only KKK to ever let Black men in"). And yeah, the Kardashian family would probably peddle white pointed hoods if they were offered a handsome enough endorsement deal to do so. That's what still makes them America's favorite family— our sad and lamentable excuse for modern, ultra-capitalist royalty. However, Jackie O Kim is not, despite trying to be for that *Interview* photoshoot in 2017, when all bets were off on politics because the Orange One had already "won."

Let it be noted that *I* was the only socialite among us who never had anything to do with Tiffany. Ivanka, sure, I could tolerate now and again in the days of '07 when she was getting on the bandwagon of "celebrities" starting their own lines (though mainly snorting them). But only if there was an over-the-top after-party at the Trump Tower and I happened to be in New York, even though everyone knows that L.A. is infinitely superior and more undercover elitist. I also couldn't avoid her at Paris' album release party in '06 when she seemed to be literally everywhere I turned. That fat fucking face of hers harshing my mellow.

Lindsay would eventually settle for seizing photo "opportunities" with Tiffany in Mykonos for the sole sake of promoting her inevitably shitty reality show for the only entity as irrelevant as she is (MTV). This was a moment that occasionally made me think twice as to whether or not I truly believed she had stolen my life. But yes, I stand firm in my assessment. Because it was me—always me—who was supposed to live this luxurious post-youth life in Europe that still connotes being youthful. But now if I had the desire to open up a nightclub or create an island named after me, how could I? It had all already been territory covered by Lindsay, the least worthy, least deserving out of every "00s queen" to have made this corny escape under the pretentious guise of "wanting, nay, *needing* to be a better person." When I think about what a fucking phony she is, ugh. It just makes me feel way too in touch with Holden Caulfield, therefore my white male energy.

All I have ever truly wanted in this life— apart from constant orgasms—is to be recognized for *my* efforts in the face of appearing to be doing nothing. *My* ability to reinvent and resuscitate my public image with my talents in the party arts. But somehow, some way, Lindsay has managed to monger all the credit for quote unquote enduring…via the mindless holding-out-for-relevancy tactic of using credit *cards* to help keep her foot in the VIP area.

She gets the credit for being "an underdog" and now an OG of pop culture, miraculously turning tabloid fodder into the stuff of lore (even though the "Bimbo Summit" was only iconic because of Britney and Paris). She's a retroactive "martyr" for withstanding abuse at a time before Instagram, a time before "celebrities" could control and manipulate the nature of their false image. I suppose Paris has rather done the same thing, except she isn't quite as much of a laughingstock thanks to the power that comes from endless reserves of cash and making a side career out of shading Kim for all of the blatant ways she has stolen from *her* life and art. That is, when she's not also bending over to lick Kim's back(side) while talking shit behind it.

But oh yes, getting invited by Rob to Kris "Jenner" Kringle's Kardashian Khristmas party. Once he was bored enough with me crying to the beats of Ke$ha at the strip club (meaning he just wanted to get back to looking at the naked woman in front of him without me killing his boner completely), Rob offered me a place chez Kardashian. Not just a place at the table, but a place in his bed for the night, which meant I, too, would be waking up to all the free social media publicity that came with being a Kardashian in the age of their ceaseless ascent. Paris was going to be unable to control her lazy eye from twitching at the sight of it. And, sure enough, I did receive a conveniently-timed text from her on December 26th, "innocently" asking, "U coming with to Mexico?"

For whatever reason, 2010 was the year that everyone wanted to go to Mexico for New Year's Eve. I really have no idea why. Cabo is just so blah, and basically recreatable with the right lighting and décor in El Pueblo de Los Angeles. Lindsay, needless to say, was not among the "elite" to jump on this caravan that Paris had pulled together. Ultimately, the caravan was to distract herself from being repelled by Cy Waits, her nasty beefcake boyfriend du jour. She couldn't admit this (even if only internally) until she lost her phone on a drunken bender and then had to reconcile the fact that, without this device to keep her amused, she actually had to *listen* to what Cy was "saying." It was enough to make her cry (and, as you might have seen when she was being driven away by a cop car from the courthouse in '07, that looks even more unsightly than *Kim* crying).

Her tears streamed tenfold as a direct result of how I had declined her invitation. Not just a "polite" rejection, mind you, but a text that said: "Fuk no. Enjoy your bootleg holiday, bitch. I'm going to TAO with Kim." She had no words to express in return. For what does one say to no longer being of use to pop culture? It's literally the only thing of value as an American to be: in the public eye. A "creator"— or somehow an important part of the "cultural lexicon." And as far as I could tell, even Nicky Hilton (who had to show up in Mexico to console her pathetic older sister as she couldn't get anyone else of note to come) was of more interest to the public as 2010 came to a close than Paris herself.

I, of course, found myself in the eye of an impending media hurricane for my escalated dynamic with Rob, who was unashamed to be caught in very compromising positions with me while the paparazzi zeroed in on us like a moth to a lamp (ah, but the moth meme wasn't even around then). While I thought that Kim would be glad Rob traded up so well from the usual hookers he "dated" (I was an *un*usual hooker), I was already starting to sense a bit of hostility coming from her in the weeks leading up to the party, as though she was trying to scare me away with insulting pull quotes stated in front of other members of the Hollywood elite. Like, "Oh yeah, Tate is coming. I forgot... The party is going to be *amaze* this year. I usually have to keep the details under wraps from non-VIPs. But yeah, since *Tate* made the cut this year, it seems non-VIPs have been privy to a lot..."

I fucking hated her. She was the worst kind of self-superior twat because of how low in life her station had been before. Granted, she might not have been a shoe size eleven sporting Ivanka Trump-brand stilettos the way Paris once did, but she was still way overcompensating for how far below she had commenced on her path toward "greatness." Now she felt obliged to pay everyone back for all those decades spent down at heel at a time when it was still the Aryan socialite's reign. And I was a part of that recompense—in addition to the fact that she was still embittered about her failed attempt to blackmail me at the club after catching me *in flagrante delicto* with Joel when he was supposed to be with Hilary. *Also,* I do find it strange that Joel was more concerned about Hilary discovering his indiscretion than the press having a field day with his pedophilia. He really should have gotten way more vitriol from the media about his predilection for underage snatch. But back then, it was a white man's paradise for such fondnesses. They really had no idea that the 00s were to be their swan song. The end of their epoch of unchecked power (even though, yes, they're all still in control, they just "let us" make fun of them much more freely now).

Though I wanted to rip Kim's fucking throat out as the party approached (so as to keep her from continuing to publicly disparage me with such free-wheeling insolence), I knew she was the one in control—at least for now. Once I was at that party, however, it would be all gloves off as I proceeded to hold obscene PDA court with Rob, who was eager and willing to be my plaything if it meant I made whatever weird concessions he wanted in bed (and believe me, Bruce Jenner turning into Caitlyn was far more normal and expected than anything Rob wanted to work out psychologically between the space of his sheets—and if you had a mom like Kris, surely *you'd* have some shit to work out, too). While I waited to gain the upper hand, I bided time, much in the same way Lindsay believes she's been doing before making her grand "comeback."

I even took the affront of Kim sending the least important of the purebred Kardashians (everyone knows the Jenners are half-breeds, therefore lesser than), Khloe, to "help" pick out an outfit that would be in keeping with the theme of the soirée: "Off With Their Heads—A Tribute to *Alice in Wonderland*." True to her stale ways, Kim was already preordained as the Queen of Hearts. To give her some "credit," at least she didn't feel the need to make her rotisserie of ensembles entirely fairy tale-themed or whatever after wearing her basic-ass "sexy" Red Riding Hood (she ain't little, so I can't add that part at the beginning) costume to Heidi Klum's Halloween party. But I could tell she was piggybacking (piggy that she is) off of Heidi's motif. Alas, no one else could seem to fathom that she truly ought to be faulted for her lack of originality, least of all Rob, who was starting to get on my last nerve, Gretchen Wieners-style.

Except, Paris. *She* could fathom it. Paris of all people knew that Kim needed to be more than just wrist-slapped for how she was profiting so well from stealing everyone else's act. But I couldn't confide in Paris. Not at this time. She was too inconsequential at the moment for me to fuck with and I needed power. So much more power if I was going to banish Lindsay from ever even daring to step back into this world, even if said attempts consisted solely of laughable tripe like *Machete*.

Thinking this to myself as Khloe (who, by the way, I can't be bothered to bequeath with an "é" at the end of her name…as if she deserves it, does she think she's fucking Beyoncé?) "gave me the honor" of "taking me" to Adele's of Hollywood as though I couldn't go there my damn self (it's not like I hadn't in the past, being the master of disguise in the bedroom that I am), I toyed with the notion of going as the white rabbit. For that's exactly who I wanted to be in this five-act play called *Chasing Pertinency*: pulled out of a hat as the victor all along of the bounty I deemed to be "the most media-savvy (and worthy) of them all." Then it dawned on me that things had gotten so bad, even during this still pre-woke period, that I wasn't "permitted" to go as something (someone?) slutty for Halloween. That's what it was to be an early twenty-first century princess vying for the affections of her increasingly disloyal subjects in a post-00s world. You had to be "sneaky slutty." "On blast slutty" was no longer so embraced.

White rabbit it would have to be then…but an undercover sexy white rabbit—no quotation marks around sexy because I was actually hot and not fat. Or, excuse me, "voluptuous." Khloe, being the Kardashian that she was, couldn't have been more pleased with my choice as, in her mind, it didn't pose a threat to the careful menagerie of whoredom she was curating with her sisters. She had no idea just how much I would be the star of the fucking show with Rob as my unwitting pawn in the role of an ace of diamonds (a card far too generous for his particular brand of non-intellect, for there was nothing "sharp" about him).

After the "salesgirl," if that's what you can call anybody who doesn't work in Beverly Hills, rang us up and made the correct decision in remarking on who *I* was (and will forever be no matter how non-chic being a white socialite becomes) as opposed to Khloe, still largely a nobody without Kim by her side, I received an accordingly undercutting backlash the moment we went outside. Where she pretended "not to notice" that I hadn't yet gotten into the car. This easily allowed the driver, per Khloe's assurance that everyone was in the vehicle, to nearly take my Louboutin, and the foot inside of it, off with his rock-hard tires (a tidbit: the Kardashians specify that a certain amount of air pressure needs to be in the tires of every car that drives them around, possibly because they feel the vague threat constantly looming that one of their enemies wants to take the air out of them…the tires, not their sac-filled bodies).

Playing the perpetual "good sport" at this game Cady (still the better version of Lindsay, and the only one between the two of them who would ever achieve redemption and public forgiveness) would address as "Girl World," I laughed the incident off knowing full well that it was intentional. I even took her up on her half-hearted invite inside the house to show the rest of the litter what I had chosen as my costume. Paris could *never* have endured this type of horror. The bitch cannot swallow shit the way some of the rest of us socialites have to. That could be why I'll always love her and hate her at the same time. The emotions are practically born of the same "mechanism" (the heart, I guess?). I actually really wanted to call her after the whole ordeal, but knew that it would not serve me well in the long run. The whole point was to show her just how much she had erred in never taking my side in any of the tabloid bullshit with Lindsay, Britney and Nicole. Well, now she would see, really *understand*, just how much she had fucked up. Because it was my turn to leave *her* in the dust with this au courant crew. Au kourant Kardashian krew, that is.

With the night of the party upon me, I had to deal not only with the stress of starting to go into hair and makeup about six hours ahead of time, but also the knowledge that there would be plenty of blonde girls, USC and UCLA ones, in orange jumpsuits paying "tribute" to Lindsay's latest brush with the law. This is when topical costumes can be the worst, constantly serving to remind you of some frenemy in Hollywood you would really rather not have to think about. But I took a deep breath, delving into my meditation first thing in the morning to assist my mind in handling what was sure to be an intense and long night ahead. The meditation was also supposed to assist my mind in ignoring how I caused a huge scandal by stealing Madonna's go-to makeup artist, Gina Brooke, that day. That's right, I got her to do my face for the event. Madonna, after all, was planning to wear a Barack Obama mask in yet another case of being controversial for the wrong reasons in her post-*Hard Candy* years. And another example of how having children can really make you lose your edge. I shudder to even think of ever ejecting anything out of me and having to give it some of my hard-inherited money. Besides, no matter how rich you are, not even the best plastic surgeon can undo the damage to one's body (and pussy tightness) wrought by a spawn that ultimately just wants to accuse or kill you.

I explained this to Gina, who was asking me if I planned on having any parasites of my own with Rob. It was a question that required all of my strength to answer without blowing chunks for so many reasons. Instead of expressing how grossed out I was by Rob, I explained this other element of, you know, just not wanting to. She seemed to understand…she was a "young person" after all. And I don't think anyone who was approaching forty and suddenly aware that she hadn't done anything with her life really wanted kids. Which I guess is why Lindsay talks about having them so often lately—she thought she had done something with her life. Practically stealing them off the fucking street just because they're refugees—refugees who still know better than to think that a life in one of Lindsay's low-budget hotel rooms is preferable to their current placeless state. Actually, now that I'm saying this, I realize Lindsay is a Hollywood refugee with utterly no place to go where she'll ever truly be accepted. This has *got to be* the reason why she keeps opening up businesses. So she can walk into a place and pretend she belongs because it "belongs" to her (or whoever her dubious investors are that somehow still thought it was worthwhile to get their dick sucked by non-*Freaky Friday* era Lindsay).

Tonight, I was going to feel the same way: like a foreigner infiltrating fake Armenian territory with Rob as my only passport and ally. It didn't help that when he showed up to my house to pick me up in his black Lambo like the douchebag prince that he was, it turned out he hadn't even put his costume on yet, which meant we wouldn't be able to walk into the party at his house properly as a "pair." I wanted to start sobbing, but I couldn't undo all the work Gina had just finished, lest she refuse to make me over ever again. In lieu of botching my maquillage by shedding a tear over his incompetence, I demanded that Rob go back home, change into his costume and *then* come back to get me *tout de fucking suite*. He looked appalled. Or as appalled as someone with so few brainwaves can reasonably appear. His mouth agape, he closed it, then opened it again as though he might say something, then walked out. Within seconds, I heard the tires of his car screeching out of the driveway, exiting as only an uncouth meathead would.

Gary, who had witnessed the whole thing while perched in the doorway of his study, came out to console me, complimenting me on how I had managed to make the white rabbit "so damn sexy," fingering the gold-plated pocket watch dangling near my garter as he wrapped me in his arms. Oh god, why did Daddy have to be the best man I would ever know?

"There, there *petit lapin*. He'll come back. And when he does...I'll fucking kill him for not treating you well."

But Daddy was wrong. Rob didn't come back that night. In his defense, he had initially intended to. Except that when he got back to the Kardashian Krib, the party was already in full swing and he was effortlessly lured by another whore of the year, Megan Fox, who was having second thoughts about her marriage to Brian Austin Green. She wanted to try out her bisexuality that night and Rob happened to be there to watch instead of being where he should be, which was to come fucking collect me in his ace of diamonds card getup. And I, having a sense of pride that no one else seems to, was not about to show up to that party by myself. I was not Cady Heron, comfortable rolling up alone and dressed as an "ex-wife." Which left me with no other option but to stay at home watching scary movies with Daddy, who would only ever let us see classic *giallo* ones like *Suspiria*. It was his rule. Italian horror movies only. Sometimes I hated that being rich also meant being pretentious. But it wasn't fucking supposed to if you lived in L.A. I guess Daddy never got the memo (remember memos?).

The next day, however, everyone else got the one about me…being snubbed by Rob and the entire Kardashian Klan. It was yet another fucking tabloid nightmare that only Lindsay would be able to help mitigate with her own constant barrage of trainwreckery.

Chapter 16: The (Truly) Lost Years

*O*f course, Lindsay would end up proving useless to me in the scandal bait and switch department. For 2011 was somehow the *one* year she caused little to no drama (by her standards at least). She didn't even bother with making a low-budget movie in 2010 and then *not* bother to promote it in the subsequent new year. But she did, for my unwitting sake, steal a very cheap ($2,500, chump change for a socialite) necklace from Kamofie & Company, a place you would never catch me dead in because Venice will never be a kosher location for a Beverly Hills girl no matter how many Lana Del Rey murals they put up. Even *that* bitch prefers the Hollywood Hills when she's not pretending to live in Echo Park.

It was February and, by this time, my falling out with the Kardashians remained still-constant TMZ ammo. But, sensing a lull in interest if they kept pushing it too hard, TMZ then decided to blur some of the tired headlines about my rift (like "Rob Still in Fight With Tate Over Being Late For a Very Important Date" or "Kim Won't Go Down the Rabbit Hole Anymore With Tate at Hollywood Nightclub") in favor of talking about Lindsay's overall patheticness for not being able to afford the necklace. Whereas, in Winona's case, it wasn't pathetic, so much as a bad cocktail of prescription drugs and sheer boredom.

Goddamn, I don't know how she does it, but she's such a complex and interesting androgyne.

Despite this little media distraction, I still felt inclined to keep a lower profile than usual, sending my newest "aide" (a polite term that the socialite community had begun using to refer to their Mexican maids) to pick up my takeout from Bottega Louie, because no, you can't convince me that Downtown L.A. is "happening" either. At least not enough to actually be seen there. On the plus side, all the anxiety this was giving me served as a boon to my bulimia. I mean, like, vomit all over the fucking place. Thank god for my aide to clean up after me at every unexpected spewing. At the same time, I was too depressed *not* to eat. Though I know that's quite shameful to admit. I really don't like to talk about any of my human qualities, what with the pedestal that rich and beautiful people such as myself get put on.

In a way, this would have been the perfect time for me to reach out to Lindsay as a sort of peace offering. As a means to show that I had more compassion than the average cunt-bitch socialite—which, of course, I do. But then I thought, you know what? *She* should be reaching out to *me*. Fucking begging for my comfort and counsel. And yet, it wouldn't be in Lindsay's character to attempt not squandering an opportunity. It was the code she lived by, and still does. Thus, I turned to my forever "friend," Paris, as I always do when I'm in crisis. I could tell she had been expecting my call. She could be infuriating like that. Always waiting to be vindicated. And, thanks to being rich, she consistently was. Not that I was helping to break the cycle with my humiliating obsequiousness.

I shuddered as I heard myself apologize, "Paris I was so wrong to have ever tried to go over to the dark side with those Kardashian Kunt Rags. I don't know *what* I was thinking. I was blinded by Rob and, oh, I don't know, maybe I actually thought it was love. Can you understand that?"

I could hear her nails being clipped by her manicurist on the other end of the iPhone. She never failed to get them done at this exact time on Tuesdays. Sensing a way in, I asked, "You know, I could really use a touch-up on my nails…would Phuket be available to do mine also?"

Cowering to the sentimental fact that I still knew her routine, Paris capitulated, "I sup*pose*. She won't be done with mine for about another hour though. Should give you plenty of time to get in whatever low-budget vehicle you're driving these days."

And just like that, I was back on the right side for the wrong reasons (desperation and ostracism). Lindsay could not say the same. What's worse, she seemed to still be wearing John Galliano even after February 24th, when he was arrested in Paris (Paris,

Paris—always Paris!) for those illustrious anti-Semitic comments toward a Jewish woman with an Asian boyfriend (though no one seemed to care that he was slapped with the threat, "Asian bastard, I will kill you"—oh Asians, truly always sidelined in every regard). It was, like, she had genuinely lost all sense of how to take social cues. And once you go Winona, of course, you can never live down that stigma in any store you enter, even if your reputation for driving "mishaps" (to use understatement) still outweighs the one you have for shoplifting.

Paris was telling me all about it at our latest manicure session (I was now fully reingratiated into the monotonous female friendship tasks centered around grooming). "It's so tragic, I mean, honestly, people aren't even donating their Gallianos to fucking Out of the Closet right now, let alone, like, daring to be seen wearing anything of his long enough to be photographed. And you know it takes her forever to get noticed by the press at this point, so she's clearly desperate for any sort of attention. Which is why she's always getting the negative kind. It's honestly sickening, like, I cringe when I think about it."

Before I could get my chance to agree so as to prolong further trash-talking, Paris continued, "And what the fuck does it all come down to?: her goddamn daddy issues. Like, God, how *tragic*. And predictable."

And then it dawned on me: Paris was actually upset about losing Lindsay as a friend. Because, as you, friendless reader, probably already know, you don't talk about someone all the time if you're not secretly kind of obsessed with them (except for me—I'm not obsessed with Lindsay, I just actually despise her). Then, another stroke of genius: why don't I initiate some type of way for Paris and Lindsay to be able to hang out together again despite her social pariah status *du moment?* Since I knew Paris would never admit to *wanting* to see Lindsay, I tried to make it about me. Through also making it about her.

"You know, it wouldn't be a bad look to offer Lindsay a little bit of charity by inviting her to the opening of your boutique..."

At this time, Paris was prepping for the opening of her third handbags and accessories store in the Philippines. In the mall of some hole called Davao City (she had already opened two in Manila, the only place worth shaking a stick at in those islands if you don't give a fuck about deep sea diving, which only one's boyfriend should). So she had to expand to other markets in the area without becoming oversaturated. It was thus that I suggested something of a girls' trip.

Paris arched her brow at me. "I wouldn't be caught dead in any city with that firecrotch."

"Not even, say, Cairo?"

"What the fuck are you talking about Tate? Why don't you just get to the point?"

"Do you even know who Hosni Mubarak is?"

"Another trust fund kid who's finally legal?"

"No, Paris. Ugh."

"I don't have time to talk about this anymore, I have to meet up with Nicky so we can give each other our honest opinions about what we're wearing to Madonna's Oscar party."

Paris sighed and glanced admiringly at her new stiletto nails (I was personally of the coffin persuasion when it came to acrylics, and I usually liked to adorn them with some type of flourish [such as a stencil of a labia], but Paris was almost annoyingly classic in this and all regards). Suddenly remembering I was still there, she asked, "You're going too, right? Or did Kim ruin all your credibility with Madonna? You know she doesn't like reality stars."

I resisted the urge to demand how, then, did Paris get invited, knowing already that the Hilton name was more viable for getting into such affairs. Or at least less associated with sleaze and scandal than the Kardashians'...for the moment. Pausing to think about how to come up with an excuse for not going—other than no one had asked me—I found myself staring at the light beads of sweat on Phucket's forehead as she concluded putting the final touches on my nails. At least I wasn't her.

That's the only way it could have been worse in terms of what was happening to me. Which was having no choice but to admit to Paris that I wasn't "worthy" enough to be admitted entry into the single most important social event of the season. Madonna wouldn't even end up being forced to acknowledge Kim as a cultural phenomenon until her 2018 party. As one "source" put it to *Page Six*, "Madonna didn't want that element. But last year she felt she couldn't avoid them anymore."

2011, thankfully, still was safe from full-fledged Kardashian reign over every facet of pop culture, even something as formerly legitimate as the Oscars. And it made me wonder why, indeed, I wasn't considered as a significant enough attendee to have made the guest list. It was then I knew who I would have to call in order to get me in, having enough faith in him and our past to assure Paris, "Of course I'll be there. What do you think I am? A nobody?"

Paris bit her tongue in response. That fucking whore.

Back in the supreme safety of my own room at Daddy's, I stared at my naked body in the mirror as I called up Orlando. Sure, he was still doing his best impression of a husband in that sham marriage to Miranda, but the two hadn't even been fucking more than once a day since they were robbed by the Bling Ring. That was two years prior—Miranda could be so fucking dainty that way, as most Victoria's Secret models seem to be. It's like, Jesus, you can be thin and still be a little bit more durable, like mentally, you know? But apparently bitches of Miranda's variety didn't know. Bitches like Lindsay, on the other hand, *did*. Even when she was at her anorexic peak, she could take a bit of trauma with a grain of "salt" (read: cocaine). Maybe that's why she did what she was about to do that night: go all in on the self-humiliation front.

But before Hollywood was about to be appalled anew by Lindsay's latest shame-fest, I was having déjà vu all over again by prostrating myself before Orlando in *private* shame. This time, by putting him on "video phone" while in the nude. Mind you, this was during a year when being nude on a phone format made everyone look pixelated. Regardless, I was still a hot-ass bitch even in flesh-colored pixels. So obviously, he was titillated by both my body *and* the prospect of getting caught by Miranda at any minute.

In the midst of pretending like he wasn't touching himself as he panted in between words, Orlando demanded with mock outrage, "What do you want from me now, Tate? Though I think I can guess."

"Oh? Then tell me what I want, Orly," I said in my sexiest baby voice. He was still a sucker for that, too. The walking cliché of a British man that he is. One can only imagine the lengths Katy now takes it to with him. I could def envision her wearing a diaper and a bonnet while doing it as well. She just seems like the type who would incorporate costumes into the bedroom as a substitute for missing being on tour. What with no one wanting to pay to see her anymore.

Orlando accurately guessed, "You want me to get you into Guy Oseary and Madonna's party."

I rolled my eyes, hating that I needed him, even after all these years. "Well, can you?"

He stared at the pixels that most resembled my nipples and took a deep breath. "For you, Tate, of course. You know it's you that I've always been waiting for."

Such enthusiasm was a little *too* much for my taste, so I deflected the romance of it by saying, "Okay Orly, let's not get sentimental. This isn't the time. Fuck you later?"

I could see him shuddering in near orgasm already over the thought. "I wouldn't be getting you in if that wasn't the implied tradeoff."

I blew him…my best Marilyn Monroe-esque kiss as I said, "Good, then we're both on the same page."

He gave me the details of the location and what the theme was going to be so I wouldn't look like an uninformed prat by showing up in totally normal couture. The next step was tying my wagon to Paris' since I couldn't exactly show up with Orlando when taking into account his married state. I *could*, however, shag him senseless in one of the ten thousand available rooms in Guy Oseary's lavish abode. One supposes it really does pay to be Madonna's manager despite the undeniable bouts he must have with her illustrious "fastidiousness." But, let's just say it, you have to be a bitch to reign—unless you're me, and your bitchery seems to get you nowhere but downhill.

To my shock, Paris was totally welcoming of me coming over to Nicky's (she had only just started dating James Rothschild, so she wasn't a complete milquetoast at that point) and getting ready there together. For some reason (can't *imagine* why), I thought she might pull some Plastics bullshit on me and tell me something to the effect of, "On Sundays we can only get dressed together as a duo," but she was almost weirdly eager to have me over to judge her ensemble. It crystallized for me just how useless Nicky was as a sister. There was almost a vulture-like quality to her in that her eyes were so dead they were unreadable. That must have been pretty hard for someone as vivacious as Paris. Then again, one can't even begin to calculate the difficulties of having such an "outgoing" (a euphemism if ever there was one) younger sister when you were just trying to maintain even a slight modicum of the family name's former twentieth century dignity before its twenty-first century legacy came around to bite it in the ass in the form of Paris.

Paris continued to surprise me that evening as she showed herself to be super attentive to helping me look my best (as thought that was ever a problem for someone with enough natural beauty to have still never needed plastic surgery, even in my current geriatric state of being thirty-five). While a certain part of me was living for her "generosity," the shrewder part of my brain—the one that knew Ashlee Simpson was going to be a flash in the pan, though I so badly wanted her to succeed in the long run—was aware that there had to be some underlying motive. I never could have imagined it would have anything to do with Lindsay, especially since all of Paris' focus should have been on taking down Kim for stealing her entire shtick, including the release of fragrances based on her own "essence." What was that supposed to entail, huh? Baby prostitute mixed with the stench of unwashed crotch? Christ knows, but Kim would soon put out her third goddamn fragrance in April: an offensively overpriced bathwater called Gold.

You know what Paris was releasing for *her* third perfume? A sophisticated product called Heiress in 2006. Because she doesn't lower herself to the tickety-tack level of pretending to be Beyoncé's form of "white-Black." But at least Beyoncé is actually Black, whereas, for whatever reason, Kim and/or her mother got it in their pointy heads that being tan equated to being "passable" as "the right" 2010s race (something Ariana Grande would also eventually be infected by).

They were clearly correct in their surmisal. And, somehow, not enough people give them shit for appropriating everything (save for stooping to a fried chicken ad, I guess) from Black culture just because they only let Black dick enter their expensively waxed pussies. But in any case, no. It was definitely not Kim preoccupying Paris' mind on that Oscar evening in 2011, so much as Lindsay. She seemed to know something about what was going to go down that I didn't. And from the looks of that faintly detectable furrow in her brow, whatever it was spelled disaster. Stepping out of her house in my pale blue/somewhat green Alexander McQueen dress from the '05 spring collection (maybe I was capitalizing on him just a bit in the midst of his surge in popularity after his suicide…hence, the upcoming Met Gala that would kick off the Savage Beauty exhibit), I let whatever thoughts of Lindsay I had melt away. I just knew that the night was going to be unforgettable. If, for nothing else, because I was going to fuck not just Orlando in one of Oseary's rooms, but also Christian Bale and James Franco (he didn't bother attending his own D-list party at the Supperclub, where Lindz ended up, poor "child"). And let me tell you, both are easily cajoled into pretty much anything when drunk enough (ass eating included—probably because the rumors are true: all actors are basically gay).

While I was enjoying the many-splendored perks of my Hollywood Influence Renaissance (and, by the way, every day one still finds herself relevant in Hollywood is a renaissance), Lindsay was summarily ejected from the "secret" entrance for gate crashing. What's worse, her honor was defended by no better than Josh Brolin. *Josh* Brolin. Truly cause for Lindsay to have fled to Dubai right then and there over the shame. But no, being the long-standing harborer of delusions that she is, she banished the embarrassment away like it was Napoleon to Saint Helena. Lindsay was so adept at deflection and delusion that she could blame her association with Terry Richardson as the reason for not being let into the party. Alas, since this was still pre-#MeToo, people weren't all that skittish about such ties.

Vis-à-vis pre-#MeToo, it goes without saying that old, pock-marked dick Harvey was at the party that very night trying to get into my shimmery, diamond-encrusted thong (yes, it's as painful as it sounds)…again. I was obviously busier with hotter pursuits than that, but he wouldn't stop buzzing around me like a goddamn hornet. I really wanted to murder him that night and probably could have. That party is the perfect place to kill just about anyone you want to in H'wood because, chances are, there's at least twenty other people who want to kill the same person, ergo too much motive for the police to pinpoint any one culprit with ease. And, as we

all know, the LAPD is much too busy shooting up Black folk like Nicole Richie to bother for very long with entertainment industry murder mysteries. I guess what I'm saying is that I had experienced a missed opportunity to "neutralize" Harvey that night as I wouldn't attend Madonna's "The Party" again until after Ronan Farrow claimed all the glory for taking him down.

And while I was riding high that evening in Orlando's Porsche (he's really good at driving while intoxicated, I promise) as he tore down the winding stretch of road that David Lynch had to make seem extra creepy with *Mulholland Drive*, Lindsay's fate made me smile. Try as I might to resist relishing other people's pain, I had simply gone through too much of my own to be a "bigger" person (who wants anything of themselves to be bigger anyway when we all know that petite is forever timeless?). Lindsay deserved even more humiliation than that as far as I was concerned. She had gotten so fucking arrogant in the '03-'04 glory days that saw her ego balloon to the point of never being able to see beyond that era, convinced that no time had passed at all and that her "stardom" was still germane to the present (except it was about as germane as Jermaine Dupri).

People might ask me why I'm so hung up on it. Why I bother obsessing over a person if she's so unimportant. The fact is, it's what Lindsay *represents*. She was the prototype for Being Middling Yet Always

Failing Upward. *She* was the one who opened the floodgate that allowed nothing but riffraff to pour into the 00s and post-00s Hollywood scene. And not even *blonde* riffraff (no dye job could ever conceal her redheadedness…not with *those* freckles). For me, she would forever embody the beginning of the end of the glamor and class that had once meant so much to my socialite world. So there you have it, it's not a very complex psychological analysis of my "obsession" (though "personal vendetta" feels more accurate as a term), but it's the truth.

As the rest of 2011 roared ahead with the usual tabloid fanfare, it was the movies that came out that were most memorable to me. Even more than Kim once again whoring it up by getting married in August to Kris Humphries because he had the same name as her mom and, of course, for publicity (you all know how long that marriage ended up lasting). I was struck by how openly nihilistic society was becoming with the release of *Drive*, *The Skin I Live In*, *Melancholia* and *Damsels in Distress* (yes, I watch high art films apart from just *I Know Who Killed Me*, you presumptuous asshole). I think I was also one of the few people to see Madonna's second directorial effort, *W.E.*

We'll just pretend The Weinstein Company didn't produce that and essentially everything else. Even mainstream offerings like *Bridesmaids* and *Bad Teacher* seemed to be pointing at a collective societal shrug that shouted, "No fucks given!" And whenever society starts to give less of a shit about anything, the crème de la crème people like Paris and I suffer the consequences. Mostly for our commitment to and focus on aesthetic and pristine presentation, which everyone else pisses on and balks at it, not knowing how much work and effort goes into it. They who walk around wearing formless "gender fluid" clothing (the biggest scam the fashion industry has ever pulled off) and looking as slovenly as Billie Eilish. It's no longer a world fit for or even *worthy* of elegance. People don't know what to fucking do with it, it's such a foreign language to them now.

So maybe, in terms of being a trashy, classless ho, Lindsay was slightly ahead of the curve before any of the rest of us could see the trend coming. Yet, for a while there, she really did try to exude attempts at being tied to the "old world glamor" of celebrity, remarking in a late 2018 interview with *PAPER* (with the pathetically poseurish a.k.a forever-associated-with-Kim headline, "Break the Internet"), "'I was always running around my house singing Madonna songs or watching Judy Garland,' noting that she and her grandmother, an early radio soap star, would watch classics like *Murder, She Wrote* and *Gone with the Wind* together. 'I was obsessed with Shirley Temple. Maybe it was just in my genes?'" Much like overt insanity and noticeable predilections toward absolute whoredom, I reckon. Oh shit, you're not "allowed" to slut-shame anymore. My bad. It's just, like, what drove most of existence in the 00s, so I'm only giving you a "slice of life," as it were.

But before 2018 and yet another flirtation with a "second" (a.k.a. ten thousandth) chance, Lindz was pretty busy with community service at the morgue or whatever. Her statute of limitations on shame continued to know no bounds when Donald Trump, the same man who made lewd comments about trainwrecks like Lindsay being the best in bed long before his presidential campaign, wouldn't give her a spot on *The Celebrity Apprentice*, commenting, "Lindsay has to straighten herself out first. And I know Dina, she's a really lovely woman. I don't think she gets very much credit—she's tried. I know Michael a little bit. It could happen in the future, but right now we need to see Lindsay get straightened out." Then again, Dina said it was Donald who approached them in 2010 to "star" in the show to help bolster ratings. As though Lindsay has ever been much help with that when it comes to TV. To that end, one of the few things she would do as 2012, the year the world ended and we all chose to ignore it, rolled around was host *Saturday Night Live* for the fourth (and I'm assuming last) time.

Tragically, she had nothing whatsoever going on at that moment to promote on the (formerly) valuable airtime that *SNL* provided. Her little attempt at a short movie for Art Basel, *First Point*, wouldn't be out until June, nor would her further career-deadening role in *Liz & Dick* air (*on Lifetime*) until November. On a side note, *First Point* is probably some of her best acting—when it's not upstaged by Sasha Grey—due to the fact that it forces her to remain silent while relying solely on the score from Daft Punk's Thomas Bangalter (not the most bangable of the duo) to tell a story, evidently about a vacuous female surfer. It's also probably more effective for "art house" purposes than *The Canyons*. But yeah, without *something* to shill that was out already, it made for a rather clunky *SNL* appearance.

I had the misfortune of being in the audience to witness it as I was, that month, banging Jon Hamm semi-regularly. He had to make a cameo referencing how unfit Lindsay still was to manage much of anything, least of all a meaningless appearance on a show that stopped being relevant around the time Chris Farley died. So he was there for the camera to cut to when Jimmy Fallon "jokingly" assured Lindsay that, if she couldn't handle hosting, Jon (who I liked to call "Hamm Sword") was on standby to take her place. But if she actually had fucked up, Hamm Sword wouldn't have been there to pick up the slack because, early on in the show, we snuck out to get drinks at the St. Regis, which I thought was a bit hooey, but he insisted was romantic. I would have rather fucked him in my own apartment than get a hotel room *there*.

I told him as much, yet he was adamant about the St. Regis, almost like he wanted to be caught, like he wanted to accelerate the end with Jennifer Westfeldt (but that wouldn't happen for another three years in 2015).

God, suddenly I realize that this entire tawdry narrative is like a literary version of Lindsay's fuck list, the one she "accidentally" left lying around the Beverly Hilton Hotel for convenient discovery in 2014, when, again, she had little else going on to drum up much media attention. Save for her "hard-hitting" "docuseries" on the OWN Network, "aptly" titled *Lindsay*. An unfortunate foray into reality TV that evidently gave Lindsay the license to forever refer to Oprah as her good friend that she calls upon for advice all the time. Yes, I'm so sure Oprah gives a fuck about Lindsay's white girl problems—primarily tied to financial woes involving not being able to start another doomed-to-fail business. Just add it to the Scrooge McDuck-level pile of money substituted by delusions in Lindsay's case.

When I awoke the morning of March 4th to the tune of Lindsay's *SNL* appearance being panned on the internet (I always scroll before processing any of my other surroundings, as I'm sure your living-in-*Fahrenheit 451* ass does too), I turned over in bed to find that Hamm Sword had disappeared. I thought it strange as I was not accustomed to being left behind in the boudoir. *I* was usually the early absconder, the one with the heebie-jeebies. A term, incidentally, that sounds like it could have been the title of a Lindsay Lohan movie during her Disney apex. Where the fuck did he go? I suddenly felt like Diane Keaton in *Looking For Mr. Goodbar*. Was he going to pop out at any second and either 1) kill me or 2) announce that he had infected me with a sexually transmitted disease? The answer turned out to be neither. I didn't even find some kind of sentimental note (or a callous one, like Madonna did in the "Bad Girl" video) as I made my way toward the bathroom to begin grooming. I really thought I would though, that he was in the age bracket to do something like that. Turns out, he was just in the age bracket to be a cad. I never even heard from him again, and I certainly wasn't about to be the one to reach out and ask what the fuck happened to make him treat me like any average whore (as opposed to a high-class one).

I remember little else of 2012 other than that slight, plus further confirmation of the world's end when Pope Benedict XVI, that old-ass neo-Nazi, got elected to the papacy (I pay attention to Catholicism because it's the only entity that appreciates decadence and debauchery as much as a socialite). And it was a slight that cost me the avoidance of many a *Mad Men* premiere party, let me tell you. At least until 2015 when *Master of None* seemed to be the only show anyone cared about. At that time, Aziz was even more of an egoist prone to thinking women were having a great time "hanging out" with him when, in fact, they were craning their necks to see where the exit was. It has nothing to do with him being Indian, all right? It's not racism. Unless there can be racism against the nasally intonation of one's voice, unceasing in its need to "communicate" nothing at all.

It was in 2015 that I started to give up on men anyway, which was fortunate, since that's when all of the hottest 90s movie stars in the purest sense of the word started to get way too leathery to be interested in. I turned thirty-six that year, so maybe my sex drive was waning. I'm not Madonna, for fuck's sake. Though, confession: I've been no stranger to consulting with her go-to doctor for vaginoplasties.

Lindsay's sex drive, in my estimation, must have been waning as well. Because I don't feel that a person would make little lists on Scattergories paper about who they've fucked in the past if they're doing much fucking in the present. Whether that meant she was truly over the idea of sex and the status it was supposed to generate (depending on who it was with) was beyond me. Maybe she just couldn't get anyone to fuck her anymore. Then again, 2014—the year of the list—was also the year of her West End debut in *Speed-the-Plow* and where, as you might remember, my sure-to-be-deemed-as-an-epic story began. You see, it should come as no surprise that, like Jared Leto playing

Mark David Chapman (saying "Holden Caulfield" would be too obvious), I am writing all of this down from a certain institution. That is to say, naturally, a women's correctional facility in some part the Golden State that no one ever talks about, or would even assume could possibly be in California. What, did you think I was going to let them keep me in London? The sun never shines through the prison windows there.

I would've much preferred the glitz of Sing Sing, but alas, this isn't *Breakfast at Tiffany's*. Mainly because I've never needed to prostitute for money to get something as prosaic as lodging in New York. But you see, when Daddy found out about my, once again, blown-out-of-proportion "antics," he finally did cut me off after all those formerly idle threats. I really wish he had done it sooner so as to not have given me such a false sense of security. But anyway, before I get to rehashing my one and only encounter with Lindsay, I have a few other things to add about the state of the world now, in a time Bret Easton Ellis calls post-Empire (I know quoting a white man doesn't give me much credibility but at least he's gay or whatever [when he's not tantalized by me], and it's not as though I'm defending the likes of Donald Trump and Harvey Weinstein, as Lindsay has).

Maybe it has something to do with the keen perspective that comes with age, particularly when you've lived as well as I have, and, in turn, endured the naysaying of many detractors who would prefer that you live as shitty and impoverished of a life as they do (which, now, thanks to "tough love" enforced much too late in the game, I can safely say that I do). Or maybe I'm just bored off my fuckin' ass with no twenty-four-hour distraction of a phone or fear-mongering news headlines (like "J. Lo and Cardi B to star in stripper movie together"—okay so someone from the outside occasionally keeps me up-to-date [I won't say who], which is how I manage to remain *au courant*). It doesn't really matter *why*—as most shrewd people have learned by now. Like Randy (Jamie Kennedy, who is so not worthy of that last name) in *Scream* said, "It's the millennium. Motives are incidental." The only thing that matters is the Y factor (I'm saying Y because X isn't a play on why, so shut the fuck up and keep eating your bon-bons while you masturbate to my life's trauma and nonstop sexual encounters, often interchangeable).

That Y factor being: how much money would someone give me to write a tell-all about the bullshit of the twig-bitches-turned-fat-bitches (yes, I'm body-shaming the Kardashians once again) that have somehow been anointed as tastemakers for the very non-virtue of having money? The answer is: not that much. But it's what comes *after* the publication of a book—what veterans of "the biz" still call source material—that matters most. That potential for option money. A reality TV series. A Netflix series based on the reality TV series. Because I am finally at the same point as Paris, Kim and Lindsay (though somehow not Nicole): ready and willing to whore out whatever is left of me that's sanctioned as even remotely commodifiable.

Chapter 17: "Kim Kardashian's ass is nothing but an empty promise"

You really are the platform on which this whole family has risen," Jimmy Kimmel said to her, kissing her ass like people used to with Paris. Kimmel is talking about, of course, how Kylie is a "self-made" billionaire thanks to her makeup line. Ignoring the part where she's "self-made" the same way Paris is, Kim's obsequious lilt throughout the entire interview reaches a crescendo after Kimmel asks, "You're almost a billionaire, aren't you?" She pauses to weigh the answer, deciding to respond with, "My husband is, so that makes me one, right? Close, by proxy." She should get that fucking tattooed on her forehead. CLOSE, BY PROXY. Because *every*thing that plastic surgery-dependent ho has done is a result of proxy. And not just with Paris, but starting from the very lineage that courses through her veins.

That Tom Kardashian, their uncle, was able to luck out by having a wife "chic" enough to serve as matron of honor at the wedding of Elvis Presley and Priscilla Beaulieu was the beginning of the streak of "Kardashian luck" that would be cultivated solely from clinging to other people's stardom. Even Kris herself, when she was still Kristen Houghton, showed no shame about the "latch-on." You might say her sole knack in life was the ability to understand that the only way to elevate her white trash station was to cleave to someone's higher status. That turned out to be, of course, Robert Kardashian, which doesn't say much for what she was able to attract apart from a pro-golfer named Cesar Sanudo, who she happily cheated on after meeting the wealthier "Bob" at a race track. It's unclear whether they retreated to some bathroom or his car to bang right away or not, but if the "OH SHIT" necklace she was reported to be wearing at the time of the encounter was any indication, she was likely down to bone wherever Robert suggested. And he was very into "suggesting" things, the misogynist prick. No wonder his daughters, both legitimate and ill (Khloe shade, duh) have such terrible taste in dick.

That Robert's favorite movie was *The Stepford Wives* (fortunately, he didn't live long enough to see the Nicole Kidman version) was telling of his obsession with molding women into his little dolls and controlling them. Unlike Priscilla (yes, he had a yen for her after her marriage to Elvis, and even ditched Kris at one point to be with her), Kris was willing to endure being the plaster of Paris (once again, it's always Paris) for Rob's oppressive sculpting. Because everyone in that family has a price for their soul. And Kris' would turn out, in retrospect, to be pretty high when considering how low her daughters would be willing to go.

In effect, Kris wasn't about to put on the "fake smile" that Ariana insists no one should for the sake of keeping up appearances. That's why "Mama Kris" made her smile genuine by overtly sleeping with other men, starting around the mid-80s (something that was pretty apparent to Robert when Khloe was born during a timeline that didn't compute for him to be the biological father). Yep, Mama was a rolling fuckin' stone, knowing the full weight of the power of ho'ing it up all over Beverly Hills. Her karma, one supposes, was Bruce Jenner. But that endurance of poverty, in turn, begat Kendall and Kylie, the aforementioned billionaire of the "Klan." She reaped what she sowed again and again in terms of usage of her pussy. Kim would be most like her in that respect—even if Kris was the one who "urged" (read: slapped her around) to explore that side of her nature in greater depth.

Maybe even Paris helped her further cultivate that (back)side of herself as she took the "poor" fatherless child under her wing. Like literally, I think they became inseparable at a party where Paris felt compelled to "ironically" wear angel wings. Oh Christ, who can remember it all now? I think I've just spontaneously blacked everything out since I've decided this is the end of my saga. My saga which no longer remained one-sided after I at last confronted Lindsay. That night outside of *Speed-the-Plow*. Having had the time to *really* ruminate over the all too "cosmically aligned" events of said evening, I've come to the conclusion that Lindsay must have blatantly framed me. After all, she has no "deranged" fans, let alone any fans at all that would risk arrest just to make an attempt on her life. I myself would be taking a big risk on writing a book heavily centered on her were it not for my still inexhaustible resources of income (what I have access to at the moment I've decided to nobly use for publishing this work and paying for the necessary promo ads on Instagram to spark any remaining sentient being's interest in reading).

No, it didn't add up at all. Until I realized that, all this time, while I was spurring on my metabolism by despising her, she had her own plans to completely topple me. I had believed she was so blithely "unaware" and self-involved that she scarcely remembered who I was when I wasn't spotted with Paris or Kim. In fact, as I calculated in between getting a tattoo of the Versace logo (little did I know, Michael Kors would buy it and render the label irrevocably déclassé) on the back of my neck and reading all the celebrity biographies the prison library had to offer (so as to help me establish the tone I wanted for this little tome), I was smacked with the mental clarity I needed to fathom it: Lindsay had set me up to make me look like more of a pathetic has-been than she was.

She had outwitted me in a classic move of playing it aloof, letting me believe I had the upper hand during the roller coaster called the past two decades. On that closing night in late November of her (as always) poorly reviewed performance, Lindsay's strategy was made clear all along. She had used me to deflect unwanted attention from herself. When I thought about it, it was uncannily strange that every time she had one scandal, I seemed to be slapped with another, far more embarrassing one. It was *too* coincidental. And yeah, I'm from California and I can buy into a lot of hippie-dippy psychobabble bullshit about happenstance, but I could feel in my nonexistent gut that I was right about Lindsay. She had been the dark force behind my ruined potential all along.

***

To my shock, the only person who has come to visit me in prison during the five-ish years I've spent serving out a ten-year sentence (vastly commuted as Daddy came around to helping me ever so minimally) is Orlando. I found out who my real friends were, that's for sure. And the only one among the lot is my dear, sweet Orlando…who was certain to keep me apprised of all important events occurring on the outside. Like, apparently, Donald Trump becoming the president. Did not see that coming. To cheer me up one day, Orlando brought in an issue of *The Sun* (I'm very international, as you know by now). In it,

Lindsay was quoted as saying, "I know Donald Trump, he is a nice person. He's a New Yorker and my mom knows him. My dad was a broker when he was younger, so I know that part of the world. I like Donald as a person… They are just making too much of a spectacle out of the election and they're being mean. People are too mean towards Trump." Who knows? Maybe, in her twisted mind, she thinks she helped him win the election.

Orlando continued to provide me with many delicious tidbits of gossip from "the modern world" despite having to witness my deteriorating appearance. I mean, fuck, I hadn't even been permitted the simple human right of a daily blowout in ages. I might have been forced to overthink my physical demise if 'lando hadn't brought me a particularly titillating gossip highlight in late July of 2017. Almost exactly ten years after the nail in the coffin of Lindsay's career with that second DUI of '07. Thanks to Orlando, a Grinch-sized grin spread across my face when he pushed his phone up to the glass so I could read a *Billboard* interview with Paris about her "exceptional" DJ career, what with being the only American female who had a summer residency in Ibiza. And somehow, even still, Lindsay, forever intertwined with Paris and that "Trashy Golden Age of Celebrity," came up in the conversation when the interviewer asked, "You know Lindsay Lohan tweeted asking you to come to Mykonos for her birthday. Did you see that?" Paris, in her best form, replied, "I didn't see it… I like, doubt that Britney or Beyoncé are either. I think that was a little bit random but you know, trying to promote the club over there or whatever."

I could tell Orlando was getting hard watching me get hard over Paris' continued commitment to slamming Lindsay. Of course, it would have been nice if she had found a way to bring *my* name up. To defend me in some way. But until this book comes out, I reckon I've faded entirely from everyone's consciousness. God, I don't know what I'd do without Orlando. Though he was real quick on the draw to mention his engagement to Katy Scary (probably because he's actually gay, and that song of hers, "Ur So Gay," was about him in the long run). This meant he wouldn't be able to visit me anymore (he claimed, but I had a feeling the conjugal visits would restart sooner or later). He also told me he never really slept with Lindsay. He wanted me to know that "fact" above all else, asserting (with his dramatic flair), "Lindsay lies about everything. About losing her passport while partying in Cannes, about her SCRAM bracelet 'malfunctioning' at a party thrown by Katy where she swears she wasn't drinking. You can't trust anything she says."

"Oh no?" I said, arching my brow. "Look, I don't care if you slept with her or not. The only thing I care about is that, for the sake of humanity, there isn't a second season of *Lohan Beach Club*… Maybe you can do just one last little thing for me, for old time's sake."

If you thought the favor was going to be burning down all (one) of her Greece-based businesses, you clearly haven't gotten to know me very well at all. What I wanted was access to watching *Among the Shadows* (or *The Shadow Within*, if you prefer). I needed to get one final confirmation that Lindsay would never be able to resuscitate her film career (though Zsa Zsa Gabor knows she might still try with music—anything to creep the fuck back in), while, at the same time, constantly managing to finagle parts in *something*, however low-budget and under the radar. I'm happy to confirm for you, so that you might never have to suffer a "film" so bad that even the color correction serves as a source of vexation, it is categorically worse than the supposed benchmark for bad movies known as *Gigli*. It should be at the top of the list of worst movies ever rendered to "screen" (or rather, direct-to-video outlets), well above *Glitter* or *Crossroads* or *Swept Away* or even Lindsay's own *I Know Who Killed Me*. But then, it doesn't even deserve to be classified among that kind of camp.

Feeling slightly devoid of more than several brain cells after enduring the entire fucking thing—not just the trailer, like the one critic from *The Guardian* who could barely be bothered to "review" even that instead of suffering full-tilt—I, at the very least, got the corroboration I was seeking. Of her illegitimacy not just as an actress (of that we had all long been well aware of), but as a socialite. Yet somehow invoking the same special treatment that only a rich bitch like myself once used to get. But, naturally, this only made me more perplexed as to how she could still secure any film role, even in a movie produced by a very blatantly clueless Italian who seemed out of touch enough to think Lindsay Lohan was in any way a "household name" in 2019. It wasn't even one in 2015, when the movie first went into production in Brussels. *Brussels*. What the fuck has ever been shot in Brussels? Except, I guess, *Mr. Nobody*. But Jared Leto can make low-budget locations work because of his beauty. Lindsay cannot.

During one of her incalculable stints in 2010 trying to make a "return to the spotlight" despite never really being gone from the public eye, Lohan "frankly" offered herself up for a *Vanity Fair* spread, "contritely" insisting, "…I'm not getting any younger." The slore was twenty-four when she said this, adding, "I want my career back. I want the respect that I had when I was doing great movies. And if that takes not going out to a club at night, then so be it. It's not fun anyway. I don't care. It's the same thing every time." I read those lines over and over while waiting for my nails to dry in the comfort of my living room, back when I had rightful access to an on-call manicurist. I kept racking my brain trying to think of these "great movies" she was talking about. And then it hit me (…baby one more time). It wasn't really Lindsay's fault that she was this delusional. She had been bolstered up in an age that had made her genuinely believe that throwaway comedies like *Life-Size* and *Confessions of a Teenage Drama Queen* (which I still maintain I should have gotten the part for, ergo altering the entire course of socialite history) were poignant and meaningful. She was but a reflection back to the black hole of a society that once "clamored" to see her in *Mean Girls* and that's about it. Even Lacey Chabert wasn't clinging to that shit with half as much rigidity for Chrissakes.

I can still see the glint in her drug-addled eye as the police apprehended me in the midst of trying to talk to her about the pain she'd caused me, the detriment to the once great prestige of celebrity itself. She knew exactly who I was. I could see the look of recognition. When asked by the police, she said without pause, "I've never met or seen this person before in my life."

"But you stole *my life*, don't you see?!" I screamed back at her. It didn't do much to help me seem not "deranged." Yet it's true. *Lindsay Lohan stole my life, and no one seems to care or believe me*, I told the other prison inmates day after day during my first year there (that is, when someone wasn't raping or ravaging my body). But since there's no tabloid record linking us together in any way other than my sudden appearance outside the Playhouse Theater as she delivered yet another shitty *Speed-the-Plow* performance that really dishonored Madonna, why would they believe me? The proof is in the ink. No ink, no evidence. But now, all the ink is here. Contained within the pages of a chronicle that should give you, at the very least, some idea of how much better it used to be (forgive the grandma vibes, but I am thirty-six, after all). Of how the mid-00s were even more mythic than these retarded little Instagram and TikTok accounts run by Gen Zers pretending to comprehend.

It was a time when celebrity *meant something*. When it wasn't so completely crude and graceless. In my estimation, the complete shift toward crass over class reached an apex when Kim, in 2014, appeared on the cover of a formerly reputable magazine called *PAPER* (the very one Lindsay would take sloppy seconds on in 2018 with the same "Break the Internet" headline that felt ultra-flaccid when taking into account that she dressed in the garb of Disney princesses that no studio would ever hire her to play in a live action remake). Undoubtedly you know the image. The one that features Kim's huge ass on full display, each cheek looking like a giant glazed donut you could bite into and watch jelly spew everywhere. For the most part, it was deemed "sex positive" or whatever. "Delightfully scandalous." But then there were the few people who tried to intellectualize it and found that they couldn't. One dweebo white guy writer for *TIME* in particular *ass*essed, "Kim Kardashian's butt is the biological equivalent of click-bait. We can't help but pay attention to it, but we're always upset by the lack of substance. We want there to be something more, some reason or context, some great explanation that tells us what it is like to live in this very day and age, but there is not. Kim Kardashian's ass is nothing but an empty promise."

And so is whatever is left of the once great construct of what it meant to be a celebutante. It is, to this day, my (non-legal) conviction that Lindsay was the one who first upset the balance and caused this unalterable shift toward the Dash Dynasty.

Epilogue: Razr's Edge

*F*or those of you who have been super concerned about my well-being in the face of conditions that don't exactly scream "self-care," first of all, fuck you, you're a fucking fake, but also don't worry. I know how to take care of myself. Or rather, I know how to take care of myself somewhat better than before, when I was reliant upon being able to pay for people to do that for me. I think that serving out my time here has made me a bolder, wiser person. Certainly a more physically unattractive one. It takes me back to the early aughts (ugh, that damned word) once more, when white girls actually went to jail. Maybe if more white twig bitches still did now, we wouldn't be suffering from such banality in our culture. I don't need to reiterate to you that there is absolutely nothing going on worth paying attention to, but: there is absolutely nothing going on worth paying attention to.

You can try to tell yourself that there is, but then, why does everyone—even Gen fucking Z with only their prized Billie Eilish to cling to—have such nostalgia for this period of time? Arguably more than the 90s because it wasn't as democratizing about fame, even if the existence of Hootie and the Blowfish might have inferred otherwise. Yes, that's what it was about the 00s that made it more, I don't know, special or something… Not to mention the internet's existence being more viable than in the 90s but also not totally pervasive to the point of turning everyone into having the same glazed-over expression as Kanye when he fucks Kim. I guess what I'm trying to say is that this decade offered me (and everyone else despite any claims to the contrary) the perfect Goldilocks balance. I'm not going to talk about porridge or what have you—not even if it's to mention Genesis P-Orridge is in the cellblock next to mine—I'm merely stating that the 00s offered just the right amount of "easy to become 'viral'" ingredients with just enough quality control (I mean, come on, compared to what there is now) interspersed to make the product output more, let's call it, "consumable" for a mind that was, if not exactly sophisticated, then at least not totally void altogether.

Whether it was David on *The Real World: New Orleans* "crooning" "Come On Be My Baby Tonight" and thinking it was fire or William Hung (side note: he was not hung at all) truly believing he was going to win *American Idol* with his "gift" (for destroying a Ricky Martin song), it was the genuine belief in one's talent in the face of not having any that separates the 00s from now. A time in which people not only feel it's their God-given right to be famous, but that they don't even need to bother with subscribing to the notion (they're already subscribing to enough YouTube and TikTok channels anyway) that they should at least pretend to have *some kind* of talent to achieve that fame. No, it's all about gimmicks and "aesthetics" and ripping off everyone who has ever come before them, knowing full well that no one will question any of it because everyone is too fucking lazy to research or fact check. Well check this: I don't want to live in a world where no one has taste. It's just so fucking bleak. Particularly since I have no money now to distract from that bleakness.

So I've made a decision. Either I'm going to cut myself tonight with shards from the Razrs I got 'lando to furnish me with (no questions asked) as a poetic show of my devotion to that brief blip in the twenty-first century when there was still hope for our pop cultural future or…institute the plan I've been hatching these past few years to seduce Elon Musk into letting me take a ride on more than just his anatomical spaceship. Because if I can get on one of his actual spaceships and enter a new planet, maybe I can start fresh again where 1) no one knows me and 2) I can teach aliens what right proper glamor is (I've already tried, with no success, to do that for other types of aliens, if you catch my meaning), which would automatically make me their top star. And, duh, I would ban any playing of Katy Scary's "E.T." after body snatching 'lando. It's only his body I'm interested in anyway.

Oh but, fuck. I keep forgetting I'm not under thirty-five anymore and it's so challenging to allure the way I used to. And what with missing my regularly scheduled face and body injections, I do my best to ignore the sight of myself in the mirror. Hence, my superhuman ability to always see myself as I was. But you know what? I'm still more famous than Lindsay ever was or will be. I think I'll secure that much by the time I get out of here, one way or the other…

<u>Acknowledgements</u>

I'd like to acknowledge myself for being the only quality person in the universe of modern socialites and for having the emotional stamina to retell this harrowing narrative, which, unlike Taylor, I have never wanted anything more than to be a part of.

www.ingramcontent.com/pod-product-compliance
Lightning Source LLC
LaVergne TN
LVHW031322190726
843493LV00013B/3009